Children are not the church of tomorrow. They are the church of today! We need to capture the hearts of this generation and transform them into powerful disciples of the Lord Jesus Christ. Written by Ron Luce, the manual you hold in your hands contains proven strategies that have generated amazing results in hundreds of churches all over the country. We've seen youth groups using these principles experience explosive growth in a short amount of time. It's not just about the number of kids you're serving but how you're serving them, and this book will equip your youth leaders to train bold, dynamic, and powerful influencers for the kingdom of God.

Ted Haggard, President
National Association of Evangelicals

Ron Luce has produced an easy-to-read "how-to" manual for growing a youth ministry. Moreover, it is written in an encouraging and nurturing style that can help jump-start your youth ministry.

Joseph Tkach, D. Min, President
Worldwide Church of God

As a denominational official, I can't wait to get *Revolution YM* in the hands of our regional, district, and local youth leaders. It is purpose-driven, passionate, and practical. Whether a veteran or novice in the high call to rescue a lost generation of kids—this "Complete Guide for High-Impact Ministry" will answer critical questions, give clear direction, and dress theory in denim. Ron has hit it out-of-the-park and over-the-wall.

Jeff Farmer, President
Open Bible Churches

Revolution YM is a great and necessary tool for youth workers. It is an on-the-edge approach to youth ministry that can indeed revolutionize your group.

Dr. Jack Hayford

The opportunities of these times call for dedicated youth leaders who will mobilize youth for meaningful ministry over a lifetime. We need youth leaders to move beyond social club ministry to equipping leaders for God's Kingdom. Ron provides effective strategies and essential advice for youth leaders who want to see God transform lives.

G. Craig Williford, Ph.D, President
Denver Seminary

Ron Luce and the team of Teen Mania are addressing one of the major issues of concern facing the church in the twenty-first century – bringing teenagers to Christ and engagement in his church. This manual reflects the best of church growth practice and wisdom gleaned from experience, sociology, business and the insight of Scripture. I strongly recommend its use.

Berten A. Waggoner, National Director
Vineyard Churches USA

A new generation of men and women are waiting to be inspired to something so large that they can't get their teeth around it. And just like the needle of a compass that is drawn toward true north, Ron Luce's book provides substance that will inspire the youth of today's generation to be pointed directly toward God. If it matters to you that your life and those whom you lead are headed in the right direction, then Ron Luce's book is a must read.

John E. Zuch, Executive Director for Church Ministries
The Christian and Missionary Alliance

WOW, Ron Luce hits a home run with this one! From rethinking as a youth volunteer or pastor to seeing one's self as a Youth Specialist; becoming a leader who has vision, a dream, and casting that vision before his/her people; having a plan and working the plan and actually working the plan into a reality—this is a must read for all those in leadership who work with youth.

Pete White, Student Ministries Coordinator
General Baptist Ministries

It is practical and principle-laden. This is not another "cookie-cutter" youth ministry manual. The principles shared will dramatically assist someone who is just starting in youth ministry while it helps the seasoned youth ministers to rekindle their passion for their purpose and fine tune their ministry.

Steve Ely, National Youth Director
International Pentecostal Holiness Church

Ron Luce has done an excellent job of not only identifying a major problem facing the world today, but has laid out a plan to deal with this crisis. A must read.

Thomas J. Usher, CEO
U.S. Steel Corp

Revolution YM

RON LUCE

AUTHOR OF *BATTLE CRY FOR A GENERATION*

Building the New Generation of Believers

COOK COMMUNICATIONS MINISTRIES
Colorado Springs, Colorado • Paris, Ontario
KINGSWAY COMMUNICATIONS LTD
Eastbourne, England

NexGen® is an imprint of
Cook Communications Ministries, Colorado Springs, CO 80918
Cook Communications, Paris, Ontario
Kingsway Communications, Eastbourne, England

REVOLUTION YM

First printing 2006
Printed in the United States of America
                  1 2 3 4 5 6 7 8 9 10 Printing/Year 11 10 09 08 07 06

Cover Design: BMB Design

Ron Luce is the founder and president of Teen Mania Ministries.

Library of Congress Control Number: 2005938075

ISBN: 0-78144-302-4

DEDICATION

This book is dedicated to those who have
poured their guts out for this generation.

ACKNOWLEDGMENTS

Revolution YM is the effort of many people's time and energy. I would like to acknowledge a few of those individuals.

I would like to thank Janet Lee, Doug Mauss, and the whole team at Cook Communications. You all put so much effort into making everything look and sound polished. Thank you for your mercy in working with me on this book.

Thank you to my Executive Team, Beth Powell, Rebekah Morris, Emily Johnson, Heidi Abigt, Laurie Fields, and LauRen Spillers. Thank you for all the work you do to keep things flowing and for all the hours that you put into making this book possible.

This book would be meaningless without all the Youth Pastors and Youth Workers in the world. If you are a Youth Pastor or Youth Worker, I want to thank you for the time, blood, sweat, tears, and pizza you have gone through to reach this generation.

I have to acknowledge my amazing children Hannah, Charity, and Cameron. My wife of over 20 years, Katie, you are a wonderful wife, mother, and best friend.

Finally, John 15:5 says, "I am the vine, you are the branches... without Me you can do nothing" (NKJV). My life is nothing without the Lord. There aren't enough words in all the books in all the world to express how thankful I am to You.

Part One: Developing Your Battle Plan

CONTENTS

Letter to You From Ron Luce 15

Introduction 17

Chapter 1 *Raising the Standard in Youth Ministry* 21

Chapter 2 *The 10 "Must-Haves" of a Youth Specialist* 37

Chapter 3 *Beginning the Leadership Journey* 57

PART A: DREAM IT! *(The Imagination of a Leader)*

Chapter 4 *I Have a Dream* 77

Chapter 5 *The Foundation of the Dream* 93

Chapter 6 *Essentials of the Dream* 111

Chapter 7 *Bold Pursuit of the Dream* 139

PART B: PLAN IT! *(The Work of a Leader)*

Chapter 8 *Plan to Turn Your Dreams into Reality* 153

Chapter 9 *BHAGs: Defining Them and Going for It* 167

Chapter 10 *Organizing and Managing the Plan* 185

Chapter 11 *Inventing the Future* 199

Chapter 12 *Funding Your Plan* 215

PART C: BUILD IT! *(The Sweat of a Leader)*

Chapter 13 *Building Your Dream Team* 237

Chapter 14 *Leading Your Dream Team* 259

Chapter 15 *Preparing for the Rollout* 273

Chapter 16 *The Ongoing Role of the Youth Specialist* 289

Chapter 17 *Preempting Problems as You Grow* 301

Part Two: The Personal Life of a General

CONTENTS

Chapter 18 *Keeping Your Spiritual Edge* 317

Chapter 19 *Watch Out for the Residue!* 337

Chapter 20 *Living a Life of Honor: The Tough Questions* . . 351

Chapter 21 *Living a Life of Honor: How Can You Tell* . . . 365

Chapter 22 *Mandate for the Family Man in Ministry* 377

Chapter 23 *God's Call for the Family Woman* 397

Chapter 24 *Avoiding the Ragged Edge* 413

Chapter 25 *Stay Saturated!* 421

Chapter 26 *The Message of the Youth Specialist* 433

Appendix: *Great Commission Competition* 447

Scripture Index 457

Subject Index 459

Battle Cry for a Generation Sample 463

Dear Youth Leader,

We are in the middle of a battle for the hearts of a whole generation. If you are like most youth leaders in America, you are in the trenches every day. You're wearing yourself out trying to do whatever you can to love kids, lead them to Christ, and help them grow. Even with all that's done in the name of youth ministry, we are still losing a generation. It seems like the media and the enemy have been working harder than we have. They are destroying a generation at a faster rate than we are rescuing it. At current rates of evangelism, only four percent of this generation will be Bible-believing Christian adults. If we continue doing youth ministry the way we have been, we will end up with an America unlike any we have ever known. Something has to change!

What you have in your hands is more than a book. This is a manual to provoke a revolution in communities, churches, and youth ministries across America. If we want to capture the heart of this generation before it's too late, we need thousands of youth ministries and groups to double and disciple every year. *Revolution YM* will help you to build a thriving, solid youth ministry that continues to flourish and grow *without* burning you out.

This book and its accompanying CD-ROM are embedded with proven strategies and principles for building a thriving youth ministry. Already, thousands of youth pastors across the country are seeing God work powerfully through these new paradigms!

I encourage you to begin to dream God's dream for you in youth ministry. Could you be one of the 100,000 youth groups needed to capture the hearts of this generation? I believe if we all throw our hearts into this, work hard, work smart, and ask the Holy Spirit to guide us, we can win this war! We need to have drastic change . . . it has to start now . . . it has to start with us.

I look forward to laboring with you and thousands of other youth pastors of every denomination and background. I believe we will see a miracle in the hearts of this generation!

Consumed by the Call,

Ron Luce

President and Founder
Teen Mania Ministries

INTRODUCTION

You have in your hands a document of war—a blueprint for strategic thinking about your local youth ministry. It is meant to help you launch a local offensive in your region to rescue teens caught in the middle of the current war for their hearts and minds. It is meant to provoke a revolution in youth ministry.

We must come to grips with the fact that—in spite of all of our best efforts to minister to young people—we are on the brink of losing a generation! The world and the enemy have been working harder, investing millions, and gaining more ground than we have. We cannot simply do more of the same old things and hope to turn this generation around. We must change what we are doing. We must change how we think about youth ministry before it is too late.

What do I mean by too late? First, consider the numbers: the millennial generation is the largest and richest generation in American history. Every year, 4.5 million

American teenagers turn 20, and research shows that the odds against someone turning to Christ after reaching this milestone are significant. (We know that 77 percent of people who receive Christ do so before they are 21 years old). At the present rate of evangelism, only four percent of this generation will be Bible-believing—so we must act NOW to prevent them from going into their adult years as unbelievers.[1] Our passion is fueled by the fact that in five to seven years MOST of this generation will be in their 20s. NOW is the time to capture their hearts.

With the urgency of the moment fresh in our minds, let us approach youth ministry with a new perspective. It is time to shift our focus off of maintaining ministry the way it's always been done—the weekly meetings, our regular programs, ski trips and bake sales. What will capture the critical mass of the youth in any region is a vision-driven, not program-driven, local youth ministry. And that is where you come in!

Those of us engaged in youth ministry need to redefine our job descriptions. In this war for today's generation, we are the generals. Wars are won by the generals in the field, and those generals must have a plan to win each battle. That is what this book is all about—a new paradigm that leads to a different kind of planning and a new way of executing local youth ministry

Don't be intimidated by the size of this book, or get weary in the planning process. You are invited to use the text of this guide with the included CD-ROM as a tool for the battle-planning process. These steps are the work of generals that are determined to win. Let us all commit ourselves to becoming generals.

1. The Barna Group, "Research Shows that Spiritual Maturity Process Should Start at a Young Age," (November 17, 2003) http://www.barna.org/FlexPage.aspx?Page=BarnaUpdate&BarnaUpdateID=153

PART I

Developing Your Battle Plan

CHAPTER ONE

Raising the Standard in Youth Ministry

OUR IDENTITY

> "What do you do?"
> *"I am a minister."*
> "Oh, you're a pastor!"
> *"Well, I'm just a youth pastor."*

This is where our problem starts.
Too many individuals involved in youth ministry today trivialize the role God has given them. Some youth leaders can barely look you in the eye when they tell you what they do. What their embarrassment communicates is, "I don't work with real people, I work with teenagers." Okay, some of you might argue that you've got teens in your group

God is trusting you with the
next generation of Christians.

who fit in the "not fully human yet" category; nevertheless, do not underestimate the role God has for you in His strategy to reach today's young generation.

"Don't let anyone look down on you because you are young, but set an example for the believers in speech, in life, in love, in faith and in purity" (1 Tim. 4:12). Ever preach that passage to your students? Paul exhorts Timothy not to let anyone look down on his youthfulness, so why let people look down on those who work with youth? Youth work is not a second-class calling—it's not a holding pattern until you become a "real" pastor. This is where the action is! This is the final frontier of the future church.

Think about it! God is trusting you with the next generation of Christians. If you don't do your job, in a few years your pastor won't have a job because the number of teens entering adulthood and joining the ranks of the unchurched will continue to escalate. Whenever a friend of mine leaves youth ministry to become a "senior pastor," I always tell them how sad I am for their demotion; they are walking away from where the action is.

So I propose we redefine what it is we do. The next time someone asks you, "What do you do?" answer, "I am a Youth Specialist." When they ask what that is, confidently tell them that you "specialize in reaching people that no one else knows how to reach and many have given up on."

Youth Specialists. The title comes with some expectations. Youth Specialists are skilled practitioners in youth work. They are professionals who are committed to doing their work faithfully and with excellence. Youth Specialists are leaders with a specific area of expertise that is of value to others. Youth Specialists are trained to do what no one else can do.

HOW WE GOT HERE

Many of us got into youth ministry when we heard our pastor say, "Brother Dave, could you help out for a little while with the young people? We're between youth pastors, and we need a volunteer for just a month or two, until we get back on our feet."

Five years later, you're frantically filling balloons with whipped cream in preparation for another meeting, and you're running late. You still have to hop in the church van to pick up the "outlying" members. But first . . . mop up the soda spill from last week . . . arrange those chairs . . . and . . .

I honor you. You saw the need; you chose to act.

Now you've been working with kids for years. You love it but you still feel less than qualified. True, there's a noble, positive side to this scenario. Thank God you are using your time and energy to touch lives. And God, by His marvelous grace, definitely uses the willing, whether you're qualified or not: "For the foolishness of God is wiser than man's wisdom, and the weakness of God is stronger than man's strength" (1 Cor. 1:25).

If you are called to youth ministry, you are called to something that's worth doing right.

You may also be thinking, "Well, I know this ministry isn't all that great or organized but it's better than what the kids had before. The guy they had before just left them. It's way better than nothing." Or, "C'mon, I'm only a volunteer. What do you expect?"

Here's my point: Whether you are a volunteer, a paid staffer, or a regular helper, if you are called to youth ministry, you are called to something that's worth doing right. For too long youth ministry has been languishing at the bottom of the totem pole. As a result, our image and performance have suffered. Since others don't treat us as if we are important, we begin to believe that we're not very important. Then we don't treat the students as if they are very important. Yet, how important is our Boss? Doesn't He deserve better?

GOD IS WORTHY OF...WHAT?

Maybe we need to back up a bit and ask ourselves: Why is the world doing things in a world-class way, while God's people are always playing catch-up? God's model for doing things—from Creation to Incarnation to Resurrection—is extraordinary, yet we settle for average. Christians need to realize that we ought to be setting the pace and defining excellence for the world instead of letting the world set the standard. Listen to the Lord Himself for a moment:

> "A son honors his father, and a servant his master. If I am a father, where is the honor due me? If I am a master, where is the respect due me?" says the LORD Almighty. "It is you, O priests, who show contempt for my name.
>
> "But you ask, 'How have we shown contempt for your name?'
>
> "You place defiled food on my altar.

"But you ask, 'How have we defiled you?'

"By saying that the LORD's table is contemptible. When you bring blind animals for sacrifice, is that not wrong? When you sacrifice crippled or diseased animals, is that not wrong? Try offering them to your governor! Would he be pleased with you? Would he accept you?" says the LORD Almighty.

"Now implore God to be gracious to us. With such offerings from your hands, will he accept you?"—says the LORD Almighty.

—Malachi 1:6–9

In Malachi's day, the law required people to bring the very best to God, the firstfruits, the thing without blemish. What has changed? Surely the basic principle remains: our God is worthy of the best.

He doesn't want our scraps.

He doesn't appreciate our odds and ends.

He isn't seeking "pretty good."

He won't be satisfied with "just okay."

No, here in the Scripture He wonders, "How dare you bring your junk to me?" Yet, in youth ministry, we become quite comfortable with not having our messages prepared before the kids come. We're okay with our youth room not being put together and our Xerox copies being hard to read. We excuse away lots of little things—lots of little blemishes—things that God notices. But if we keep letting

No more thinking, "It's just youth ministry. We don't have a budget for it, and it's better than what the last guy did."

a few blemishes slip by, we'll soon be letting the whole infected hippo waddle in.

No more thinking, "It's just youth ministry. We don't have a budget for it, and it's better than what the last guy did. I'm just trying to help these kids!" Yes, we need to do all that and help the young people. But if it is worth doing for God, it is worth doing well.

> *"And you say, 'What a burden!' and you sniff at it contemptuously," says the* LORD *Almighty.*
>
> *"When you bring injured, crippled or diseased animals and offer them as sacrifices, should I accept them from your hands?" says the* LORD.
>
> —Malachi 1:13

Like the people of old, we're tempted to moan, "It's just too hard!" And it is hard, because . . .

> *we don't have money;*
> *we don't have a budget;*
> *we don't have the time;*
> *we don't have a staff;*
> *we don't have a secretary;*
> *we don't have a salary;*
> *we don't have the parents;*
> *we don't have the kids.*

So much we don't have. All we have is the Almighty.

I recently visited Disney World with my family, and I noticed how it resonates with excellence. Everywhere you go, everywhere you look—you can feel it. I thought of Dr. David Yonggi Cho, the great Korean pastor, and his Disney experience. As he walked down Main Street with his American hosts, he began weeping uncontrollably. Someone asked, "Dr. Cho, why are you crying? Most people come to Disney World and get happy."

"Why does the world emphasize excellence so much?" he replied. "Yet we Christians just give God our leftovers."

For the sake of money—for a dream, for a wildly imaginative piece of fantasy—people will work hard to create a work of excellence, with not a gum wrapper lying on the ground.

Full-time or paid staffer or volunteer. If we are called to do youth ministry, it is worth doing with excellence. Excellence is important because:

Excellence melts young hearts. At an event with 60,000 kids in the Pontiac Silverdome, I was speaking with an 18-year-old young lady who was a believer but had backslidden. Before the program even started, her heart was turned. How? Walking into an awesome, perfectly excellent stadium, "I felt so loved and cared for," she said. "Just to think that there are adults who would care about me and my generation so much—to provide all of this!"

Tears streamed down her face.

She hadn't even heard a preacher yet.

There is profound, persuasive power in anything that's excellent. Maybe it's because when we pursue excellence, we are tapping into the transcendent, which ultimately finds its source in God.

Look again at your calling to youth ministry. Were you called to provide a bunch of clean activities for kids? Were you called to be a Christian babysitter, to merely make sure the teens don't get into trouble, don't get pregnant, don't do drugs before they graduate?

I think not. You are called to capture young hearts for the kingdom.

Were you called to be a Christian babysitter, to merely make sure the teens don't get into trouble, don't get pregnant, don't do drugs before they graduate? I think not. You are called to capture young hearts for the kingdom.

Excellence makes everybody feel important. Think about it. In the midst of excellence, don't you feel kind of, well, excellent? At the end of that event in Pontiac, the man who oversees all Silverdome operations called our chief sound-and-light manager into his office. This top-flight executive sat our manager down and showed him dozens of pictures of our event.

Every aspect of our program, day by day, was there in full color for our manager to see. As our guy sat wondering what was coming, this Silverdome head honcho said, "In all the years I've been running this venue, I've never seen a production this excellent. We've had every rock-and-roll group you can imagine, every kind of production with sound and light. But I've never seen anything like this. Would you be willing to let us rent your equipment and your people? Could you come in and run other productions for us in this building?"

Isn't that the way it should be? I know, it's an amazing reversal, but isn't it time that the world looked at the church and said, "I want what you've got!"?

Excellence makes victory plausible. One of the most pressing reasons for demanding excellence of ourselves is that we are right in the middle of an explosion of teenagers.

Here's what I mean. Right now about 33 million teenagers live in the U.S., up from about 27 million just a few years ago. In the next few years, the number will swell to 35 million.[1] The world is ready for this explosion. They are marketing potato chips, shoes, video games, cars, clothes—everything you can imagine—directly to these kids because they know "if we can get them to buy when they're young, they'll buy for the rest of their lives." We're talking a hundred billion dollars a year spent by teenagers.[2] Product marketers know they have to do whatever they can to snag these spenders and hold on tight.

The implications for the church? If we remember that about 77 percent of those who come to Christ do so before the age of 21, we'll recognize the critical importance of our job.[3] The world is going after them for rap music and low-riding jeans. Are we seeking them just as passionately for the Lord?

ARE YOU READY FOR THE EXPLOSION?

Ready or not, the explosion is happening. So, the question is, "Are you ready for this explosion?" You'll need to prepare in at least three major ways:

1. Make a crucial change—from minding to multiplying. We need to change our mind-set. Many of us entered youth ministry when the pastor called us up: "Our congregation is full of adults and these adults have kids. Could you do something to help keep the youth busy?" Sound familiar?

Isn't it time that the world looked at the church and said, "I want what you've got!"?

Maybe this was just God's way of getting your attention. What He really wants is someone to love all the teens in your region, so He used your pastor and the need in your church to get you started. God wants to reach kids through you, and not just the kids of your church's pew-dwellers, but all of the teens in your community! Now is the time to step into all that He had in mind when you got that first phone call.

God is trusting you with an unprecedented explosion of young people. So say farewell to the old way of thinking and tear down your boxes. You need to double and disciple for the next five years.

If your youth group has 30 teens today, next year it needs to have 60. Just think, in five years you will be impacting 480 young people on a weekly basis! And beyond just showing up on Wednesday night, each of these young people will be growing into true disciples.

Think kingdom big! It is not our job merely to mind the store.

2. Set a lofty goal—from local to global. We know we're called to reach a generation in a world-class way, a generation that is now united around the globe by a common youth culture. Demographic researchers have discovered that the bedrooms of teenagers around the world look virtually the same. Posters of the same rock-and-roll and sports stars, the same computer games, and the same MP3 downloads. Yes, MTV and its counterparts have created a global youth culture. While this is scary, it's got a powerful upside. We have a ready-made superhighway for taking the Gospel throughout the world. Cultural barriers that once posed massive communication problems are now less daunting. We're not limited by the walls of our church or even the borders of our nation. We can think globally from day one in our youth ministry.

3. Redefine a job description—from meeting-making to people-making. Now is the time to decide what's driving us. Have we set out to produce programs or disciples? Do we ask ourselves, "What are we going to do this week?" Or do we frequently stop and think, "What do we want the product of this ministry to be?"

I believe our job description is to equip teens to be like the biblical David. When he was a teenager, he killed a bear, killed a lion, and—at 17 years old—he killed the biggest (literally) enemy of his people. Our job is not just to keep people in church or to decide what games to play during Friday night's lock-in. Our job is to train up more Davids.

Our job is to encourage teens like John Mark, the teenage missionary companion to both Paul and Barnabas. He, too, was a young guy about 14 years old when he heard a knock on the door while meeting with other Christ-followers. It was Peter standing on the front porch, recently escaped from jail. A few months later, John Mark went on a mission trip with Paul and Barnabas, and later we see him hanging out with Paul. What happened to this young man as a result of constant interaction with these adult mentors? He wrote a Gospel book for our Bible! It all started while he was a teenager. Our job is to mentor teens like John Mark.

Or to build up more Timothys. The apostle Paul's young protégé was probably about 19 years old when he became a bishop, an overseer of many different churches.

Now is the time to decide what's driving us. Have we set out to produce programs or disciples?

Are we just going to produce meetings and a fun time, or are we going to impact young men and women to be world-changers?

He discipled pastors. (Paul wrote 1 and 2 Timothy to encourage him.) Our job is to raise up more modern-day Timothys.

Are we just going to produce meetings and a fun time, or are we going to impact young men and women to be world-changers?

IT'S TIME TO STEP
INTO YOUR NEW ROLE

If there's a title out there for what you do, you've heard it: youth pastor, youth guy, youth leader, youth minister, youth guide—any way you cut it, the reaction is likely the same. "Oh . . . so you're not the real pastor. You're just that guy who makes announcements on Sunday mornings."

It's time to redefine who we are and what we do. We are Youth Specialists. We are people who dedicate ourselves to reaching those nobody else knows how to reach, the ones whom even the psychologists have given up on. We know that those are our kids.

The newspapers proclaim how messed up kids are, and the 10 o'clock news stresses how much trouble they make. But you, the Youth Specialist, think . . . those are my kids. You drive by a football stadium full of kids on Friday night . . . those are my kids. You see them hanging out at the mall Saturday afternoon . . . those are my kids. They don't know it yet, but they're mine!

Why are they mine? Because they are breathing, because they're in my town, and because God gave them to me. I am claiming them! I'm going to win them into the kingdom!

Now, you have to watch out if you call yourself a Youth Specialist because it is going to demand something from you.

You have to view yourself differently and behave accordingly. Why? Because there is a big difference between a "youth guy" and a Youth Specialist. Notice the contrasts . . .

- **A "youth guy"** looks and acts like an overgrown teenager who's delaying his adolescence into his 30s and 40s.

- **A "youth guy"** is just kind of there. She's the young lady who's just having fun with the kids, playing Christian pin-the-tail-on-the-donkey. She's keeping the kids occupied in a clean way.

- **A "youth guy"** uses the least amount of effort to get the job done—just to keep the pastor and parents happy.

- **The Youth Specialist** concentrates on reaching young people no one else knows how to reach. It might involve a clean and fun activity, but it will definitely have a clearly defined purpose.

We are Youth Specialists. We are people who dedicate ourselves to reaching those nobody else knows how to reach.

There is a big difference between a "youth guy" and a Youth Specialist.

I specialize in touching the lives and the hearts of young people. I am a Youth Specialist.

- **The Youth Specialist** knows the kids in her community, knows what they need, and knows exactly what she's going to do to meet those needs.

- **The Youth Specialist** faces a divine demand; he lives with his destiny. He lives with this imperative: "I absolutely must do something that impacts the young people here in a huge way. While I have breath in me, I will breathe some life into them."

When someone inquires about what you do, you know exactly how to answer: "I'm glad you asked. God has given me a vision for the young people in our city. We are building an outreach center. We're buying some buses, and we believe that by the end of the year we're going to have 500 kids with us. We are helping the kids who are _____ (name your vision). And did you know we have five girls right now in our local high school who are pregnant and don't know what they are going to do—adopt or abort? That's not all. __ percent of the teens in our high school have parents who have divorced in the past three years."

"How do you know that?" they ask.

And you say, "What do you mean, 'How do I know that'? I get paid (or don't get paid, as the case may be) to know this stuff. I have got to know this stuff! It's my calling; it's my life. I live it; I breathe it. It's beating within me."

You pause then, letting the eye contact linger for a moment. "Maybe there's something you need to remember about me, whenever you see me around here. It's this: I specialize in touching the lives and the hearts of young people. I am a Youth Specialist."

1. US Census Bureau
2. Zollo, Peter, "The Cosmetics Category: Talking to Teens," American Demographics, November 1995, http://www.ecrm-epps.com/Expose/V3_3/V3_3_A8.asp (accessed October 25, 2005).
3. The Barna Group, "Research Shows that Spiritual Maturity Process Should Start at a Young Age," (November 17, 2003) http://www.barna.org/FlexPage.aspx?Page=BarnaUpdate&BarnaUpdateID=153

Notes

CHAPTER TWO

The 10 "Must-Haves" of a Youth Specialist

Not just anyone can call him or herself a Youth Specialist! There are some requirements to become a general in this battle for a generation. You don't have to be perfect, and you don't have to be the king of cool. But there are some imperatives.

Of course, any "youth guy" can grab a ton of resources and get by. You can go to youth leader workshops and find all kinds of curriculum, tools, magazines, videos, planning guides, and every other teen-oriented doodad imaginable. You can go to a youth pastor conference with inspiring speakers and come home fired up, but what does it change?

We end up with lots of good intentions but not a lot

We have so many ideas, but without a clear philosophy of ministry to guide us, it is unclear how to apply them all.

of results. We have so many ideas, but without a clear philosophy of ministry to guide us, it is unclear how to apply them all.

Stepping into your role as a Youth Specialist is a radical mind-shift; it's a new philosophy that will dramatically impact teens in your region. But you must realize that it demands we do many things differently.

So, of all the things you could do, what are the 10 things you must do (or be)? As we explore these Youth Specialist essentials, I will ask a pointed application question with each of them. I hope you'll write your answers in the boxes provided and mull them over during the weeks and months ahead.

A YOUTH SPECIALIST . . .

. . . must have fire. Have you ever found yourself living from revival to revival, rather than living day by day with glowing coals inside? That's how our hearts ought to be— constantly glowing with the awareness of Christ's presence. We need to keep feeding that awareness so that it flames into gratitude and compassion, power and zeal.

I am not just asking if you have the fire. Notice that I'm asking, "Are you feeding it?" Look at the apostle Paul's words to young Timothy:

I constantly remember you in my prayers. Recalling your tears, I long to see you, so that I may be filled with joy. I have been reminded of your sincere faith, which first lived in your grandmother Lois and in your mother Eunice and, I am persuaded, now lives in you also. For this reason **I remind you to fan into flame the gift of God,** *which is in you through the laying on of my hands.*

—2 Timothy 1:3–6 *(emphasis added)*

Now think about this for a moment. Paul is writing to Timothy, who is a leader, right? Paul had laid his hands on Timothy, and this young man spent time with Paul, listened to his sermons, and watched the miracles flow late into the nights. And even he—with all his awesome advantages—must keep fanning the flames?

Was Paul thinking, "Timothy, for some reason, I sense your fire waning a little bit"? It can happen. Even if you are a Timothy, you have to keep throwing logs on the flames of your spiritual passion. In fact, I encourage you to quit looking like a summer barbecue pit that's gone cold.

Begin by asking yourself some tough questions:

Do I use clichés without substance?

It is easy to do. You can disguise the fact that you don't have fire if you use clichés like, "Well, let's all praise the Lord! Say this with me . . ."

Do I only remember the days when I was really fired up—in the past?

You have to keep throwing logs on the flames of your spiritual passion.

But what am I like right now? So many people talk about being on fire for God, but they are referring to yesterday rather than to what happened in their quiet time this morning.

How is my quiet time with the Lord?

Are you fully opening your heart to Him, dealing with the flesh, including all the areas that are kind of out of whack?

Do I tolerate compromise in my life?

Think about the times you used to say, "I would never do that!" What is excusing it now?

How can I tell if there's a fire burning inside me?

The kids can tell; they see through fake spirituality in a second. You can have great sermons and programs, but if you have no fire, you have nothing. You can only pass on what you are; your sheep will never have real spiritual fire if yours is not alive and raging out of control. A Youth Specialist MUST HAVE FIRE.

Question: *What am I doing to keep my own spiritual life burning brightly?*

. . . ***must have honor.*** Paul writes in Ephesians 4:1, "As a prisoner for the Lord, then, I urge you to live a life worthy of the calling you have received." To have this worthiness, we must live with honor. And honor calls us to look within and ask: Do I find myself excusing or justifying small compromises? Elsewhere, the Bible says we are to avoid even the appearance of evil.

We're not just talking about the words we use when kids aren't around or the movies we rent on our day off. Honor is so much more. We cannot compartmentalize it. Honor should color our entire lives, characterizing who we are rather than just what we do.

This book will deal with honor extensively, so let me start here with just one example. Let's talk about the youth minister who comes into a group and says, "I know you have had five youth pastors in the past four years. But I want you to know that I am here to stay. I am going to be here with you guys, no matter what. I am here to plant my heart with you, and you can trust me." Six months later, he receives a job offer from someone who is actually going to . . . pay with money! So, at the next meeting, the kids hear, "I feel the Lord leading me over here to this other job."

See what he's doing? He may claim, "I never told them I was going to be there for two years!" But didn't he imply it? He put it out there because he wanted them to trust him. Later, he walked away saying, "Well, I can't help it. God led me. I guess I was supposed to be over there the whole time."

This is not honorable. Worse, will these kids want to trust another leader in their lives?

Honor should color our entire lives, characterizing who we are rather than just what we do.

Do I demand more from others than I'm willing to do myself?

Sadly, we all have the tendency to woo people into following us. Then we stomp on their hearts, and it's "out of sight, out of mind."

So when striving to live honorably, always ask, do I demand more from others than I'm willing to do myself? Am I just taking the easy road this time because the right road is harder? Remember, the easy road is always . . . easier; but it often leaves honor behind.

> **Question:** *Am I living with any gray areas in my life?*

. . . *must have a strong family life.* It's easy to get so wrapped up in ministry that our families are lost amid our hectic activity, and their spiritual growth gets shifted to a back burner. When we realize this, we are jolted into focusing on them for a while; but before you know it, we're sucked back into the ministry again. And again and again.

Paul was very clear about the priority of families when he instructed young Timothy:

Now the overseer must . . . manage his own family well and see that his children obey him with proper respect. (If anyone does not know how to manage his own family, how can he take care of God's church?)

—1 Timothy 3:2, 4–5

In attempting to "manage" my own family, I've found it helps to ask myself frequently: Do I know where my kids are right now . . . spiritually?

Recently the Luce household took an eagerly anticipated vacation in Florida. We decided to begin our first day the same as we start every other day: with our quiet times.

Cameron—five years old and the proud owner of Buzz Lightyear and Woody toys—was up early that day, looking at the pictures in his Bible. "Cameron," I asked, "did you help Woody and Buzz have their quiet times this morning?"

"No, they didn't want to have one," he answered, already feeling the pull of the Magic Kingdom.

"Maybe they need to give their hearts to the Lord, huh? Here they are, sitting right here. Want to see if they'd like to give their hearts to Jesus?"

So Cameron started into his little "altar call," saying, "Do you want to give your heart to the Lord?"—and boom, Woody's hand went up, and Buzz's hand went up too.

"Tell them what to do," I said.

"Okay, c'mon down here and kneel, Buzz and Woody."

Do I know where my kids are right now . . . spiritually?

We may live in the same house with our families, eat the same food, look out the same windows, and drive in the same car—but do we know their hearts?

So I helped walk the toys down to the "front," and set them on their knees.

"Can you lead them in a prayer, Cameron?"

He led them right through a prayer, and they gave their colorful, plastic lives to the Lord. And from that day on, I noticed that Cameron and his two converts often had their quiet times together, with him telling the action heroes his favorite Bible stories.

Here's the thing: I felt that I'd touched base with Cameron on a spiritual level—on his level—about our life with God. It wasn't formal and it didn't take a lot of time, but we connected. Remember: we may live in the same house with our families, eat the same food, look out the same windows, and drive in the same car—but do we know their hearts?

Question: *Do I know where my children are spiritually?*

. . . must make good use of time. Wouldn't you agree that time management is a huge issue for people in youth ministry? Most of us feel stretched to the breaking point by the sheer number of things—good things—we have to do in a day. But think about it: the president of General Motors has 24 hours in a day just as you do, and he manages thousands and thousands of employees. The problem is not that we don't have enough time; it's how we use the time we have.

For example, do you "leverage" your time? That is, do you choose to do only the things that will have the greatest impact (though there are many other things you could do)? It may not sound very spiritual on the surface, but Youth Specialists must get the "biggest bang for the buck" with their time.

These first four "Must Haves" relate to the heart and life of a Youth Specialist. Now let's look at six which deal with leadership qualities which will propel your ministry forward.

Question*: How effectively am I using my hours today?*

Others won't believe in your plan—no matter how great—if they don't believe in you.

Let God begin to spark your heart with His dream!

. . . must carry oneself with dignity. Many times the way we carry ourselves gives people a false idea of who we are. If we dress like a teenager, talk like a teenager, and swagger like, well, a teenager, others will continue to see us as "just the youth guy." Instead of getting rid of this negative stigma, we've now perpetuated it. Ask, "How do I carry myself?" The answer will reveal your true identity as a leader.

The things we do, the things we say, certain habits that show through—any of these things can give us dignity and draw people toward us . . . or cause disrespect and push people away. If you find yourself constantly wondering, *why don't these parents just support me?* check your Dignity Quotient. If you're acting like a kid, they'll treat you like a kid. Or if you feel like a second-class citizen, they'll treat you like . . . you get the picture, right?

How you carry yourself will determine how much credibility you have. You may think, "But I'm in youth ministry, I don't care what adults think of me." You should care. You need the older body of Christ to stand with you in reaching the younger generation. The great thing is that if they believe in you, then they'll believe in your vision. If they believe in your vision, they'll fund your vision.

It's all about credibility. Others won't believe in your plan—no matter how great—if they don't believe in you.

. . . must dream big. God wants to give you a dream. Why? Because if you can't dream it, it won't happen. God honored Joseph because he dared to dream. In the same way, God is excited to hear you say, "Wow, look at this amazing thing—it's grown! It's doubled every year for the last three years! Just like I imagined." He wants you to tune out the noise long enough to hear His voice and dream His dream.

A lot of people live empty lives, even in the ministry, because they refuse to dream. They go to this meeting and that meeting, and they wear themselves out. They care about kids, but they are not fulfilled. There's something about dreaming that fuels your fire and ignites fulfillment.

There are no limitations to dreaming. You might think, "I'm just a youth pastor at this church. How does this apply to me?" I'm simply saying that the size of your church should have absolutely nothing to do with the size of your youth ministry. According to the national average,

There's something about dreaming that fuels your fire and ignites fulfillment.

10 percent of the church is youth. If you have less than 10 percent, you don't even have all the kids who come to your church! If you are doing more than that, you are beating the odds.

I think all of us should beat the odds. Why? Because it is up to us to populate the next generation for Christianity. Sadly, some big churches have four or five thousand members but only about two hundred kids in the youth group. They don't even have all the kids who come to the church.

As you can tell, I am less impressed with numbers than ratios here. God's perspective requires dreaming big to outpace the averages. If you have 100 people in your church and 10 kids in your youth group, that's great. But don't stop there! You could have 100 kids—or more! In fact, I know of churches that have to swap room assignments on Wednesday nights. The adults meet in the youth room so the overwhelming numbers of teens can use the main sanctuary for a youth service.

Could you dream something like that? Let God begin to spark your heart with His dream!

Question: *If Jesus Christ came back and was the youth pastor at my church for a year, what would it look like?*

. . . must be a planner. I admit it. I was intimidated for a long time by this whole idea of planning. It seemed tedious and boring. I used to tell my staff, "God wants us to do this and this and this . . . Now go make it happen, and God bless you as you do it." Their favorite line was, "Ron dreams, and we sweat." I didn't want to plan everything out and think about money and people and programs; that stuff bored me.

Think about this for a moment: our God is a planner. Here's what He told Jeremiah about the time before there even was a Jeremiah: "Before I formed you in the womb I knew you, before you were born I set you apart; I appointed you as a prophet to the nations" (Jer. 1:5).

Now that's planning ahead!

On the other hand, I hear some youth pastors say, "I don't want to put God in a box. I want to be free, to move with the Spirit." Those are good Christian sentiments, but they can be used to cover a subtle form of laziness. Isn't it true that sometimes we just don't want to pay the price in terms of desk time and sweating through the details? Or maybe we don't know how.

It's true I haven't always been a planner, and for a long time I just wanted to stick with "preach and pray." In fact, I did everything in the world to avoid planning. You could always find me mowing the lawn, doing stuff around the facilities, or fiddling with projects around my house. Why? Because dreaming is one thing; planning to make that

Your firm recognition of a heavenly calling doesn't mean it will always be easy.

dream a reality is another. Be encouraged. One of the most exciting eras of my ministry kicked in after I learned how to plan.

> **Question:** *Can I discipline myself to slow down and think through the whole process—regularly?*

. . . *must be a builder.* The apostle Paul was a builder—one who devised a plan and strategically pursued it with a final, lasting structure in mind. At first glance, his journeys to visit the early churches might appear to be random ministry, with six months here, nine months there, and a year and a half somewhere else—a sort of early house-to-house visitation. Not so! Look again at how he revisited those converts for follow-up and never failed to write them letters—even from prison! Paul was conscious of building something significant.

Remember the parable of the sower? How many times have we haphazardly "spread our seeds" without thinking about where they would land? But if you could choose to use your energy to plant seeds that went only into good ground, why would you also drop them onto rocks? Few people use their energy strategically.

What does it mean if a youth guy says: "Yes, I was at First Church, but then I felt led by the Lord to go over to

Second Church"? I'll tell you what it means to me: this person probably wasn't in the middle of building something at First Church! When you are invested in building a house, you don't just walk away from it. Neither would you casually leave a youth ministry made effective by the certainty that you are laboring together with God to build something significant, something eternal.

Unless you like walking around in circles.

Unless you like the ministry merry-go-round.

Wouldn't you rather stay and build something that will last and become a legacy?

Question: *How am I using my personal energy?*

. . . must grow as a leader. If you find that you and your ministry helpers are simply "doing what you've always done," then you are probably leading by default. It's easy to slide into this pattern even with the best of intentions. But if you'll learn how to lead with purpose, the results in changed lives will be multiplied. Sure, the status quo is always much more comfortable than taking up the task of figuring out how to most effectively transform the present situation for the kingdom. When you learn how to be the leader God wants you to be, your dreams will become a reality, and your job will be a lot more fun.

Consider what I call the leadership cup theory. (I'll explain this more fully in Chapter 3.) Every one of you has a leadership cup that can hold a certain number of youth. Your youth group can grow only as large as the capacity of your cup. We all get frustrated in ministry when we try to grow our group without growing our leadership cup. It is critical to recognize that we must first widen our cups to catch more of the fruit we are harvesting. Thus, growing as a leader means widening your cup.

I once asked Dr. Bill Bright, founder of Campus Crusade, what he had done to develop himself as a leader over the years. He said, "I'm just a voracious reader." He reads constantly—the Bible, of course, but also every form of leadership material he can get his hands on. He is a great example to follow.

Question: *Am I leading only by default these days?*

. . . must have formidable faith. What does it mean for you to have a deep faith in God? I can only tell you how it plays out in my life. Nineteen years ago when Katie and I started Teen Mania Ministries, we sent out support letters to everyone we knew—just 120 people. Every day, we'd run

to the mailbox to see whether anyone had sent us some support money. After about three weeks, we had a grand total of three checks. That was all the money ever to come from those 120 letters.

"Katie," I said, "we've got to do this ministry. I don't know if people understand what we are doing, but we have to do it anyway." So we took the first shaky step of faith.

I remember being on the road, calling any place in the world just to get the name of a church. If I had a friend in a particular city, I'd ask him, "Could you mail me a phone book from your town?" Then I'd look in the Yellow Pages for churches in the area.

I finally pulled together a little itinerary and we left home in October for six weeks on the road. We traveled all through the South and held rallies at night with massive crowds of 10 and 20 people at a time.

We packed out living rooms all across America!

We would do about two or three meetings a week, take offerings, and live on whatever was graciously placed into "the hat." (Do you know what it's like to live off teenage offerings? That takes some faith.)

In those early days there were countless last-minute cancellations. We didn't have an office yet and packed everything in our little car. We'd arrive two or three days before a service with all our gear in tow and stay in a host

It is critical to recognize that we must first widen our cups to catch more of the fruit we are harvesting.

The momentum that drives a youth ministry forward is nothing other than a firm conviction of God's call and bold faith.

home until it was time to leave for the next church. So when someone called to cancel, that would mean no place for Ron and Katie to stay for a couple of days. Since we seldom had more than $200 in the bank at any given time, shelling out money for lodging or unexpected car repairs was a continual opportunity to practice our faith!

I can just hear the violins playing in the background, but let me say from experience: faith sustains us through everything. Katie and I knew one thing: God called us to a task, and we had to do it. It didn't matter if no one believed in us, everything worked against us, and we had no money—because our calling was so real. It was from God and depended upon God. We had to act in faithful obedience.

It takes boldness and faith like that to be a Youth Specialist. Without it, you can pack up, go home, and pull out the classifieds. There are easier ways to make a living, but is there a more fulfilling, rewarding life?

Your firm recognition of a heavenly calling doesn't mean it will always be easy. I know people walk into *Acquire the Fire* events each week, see auditoriums filled with five to ten thousand teens, and think, *Oh, look at all these kids. It must have been easy for him.* No, it wasn't. But we had a clear mission and an unshakable belief that God would accomplish His purposes. The momentum that drives a youth ministry forward is nothing other than a firm conviction of God's call and bold faith.

After all, God never called us to do something that was *possible*. If we think it's *possible*, we're not dreaming big enough.

> **Question:** *Do I have the boldness to go for it?*

Notes

CHAPTER THREE

Beginning the Leadership Journey

Leadership. It's very much a buzzword today. But what exactly is leadership, and how does it actually affect my youth ministry? The title above should give you a hint—that's what this chapter is about. Understanding godly leadership will be the framework for the rest of this book.

There's a big difference between growing as a leader and growing as a minister; there's also a big difference between growing as a leader and growing as a Christian. I always thought that the closer I got to Jesus, the better leader I would be. But the two don't necessarily go together. Just because you grow as a Christian doesn't necessarily mean you become a better leader. Just as you

Just as you need to be deliberate about growing in your relationship with Jesus Christ, you also need to be deliberate about developing your leadership skills.

need to be deliberate about growing in your relationship with Jesus Christ, you also need to be deliberate about developing your leadership skills.

Your passion for God and continual growth as a Christian is the foundation of godly leadership. Let your heart for the Lord grow and your love for Him explode! Never back down on meditating on the Word and letting Him increase your spiritual fire. This vibrant spiritual health is the cornerstone on which you build a model of Christlike leadership. Effective leadership requires us to exercise and develop *both* our relationship with God and our skills as a leader.

What does it look like if you are a well-developed minister and Christian, but not a developed leader?

Maybe you've seen a church or a ministry where the preacher is just incredible. I mean, fire from heaven is spilling from his lips and it just rips at your soul. His preaching gets you fired up, but you wonder why there are only 50 people to hear him? *This is so good there ought to be thousands here!* You scratch your head and wonder why it's such a small group. Perhaps it's because that preacher is very developed as a minister, but not very developed as a leader. Other times, you may see the ministry of a big church with lots of programs, small groups, and even a television ministry. But their preacher is nowhere near the same level as the other preacher you heard. That person is very developed as a leader but not as a minister. You don't have to choose between one and the other. There are many ministers who have developed as both a minister and a leader.

It is essential for a Youth Specialist to develop both dimensions. When you have a small youth group, the pastor says, "You need to be faithful with the few." But if, after 20 years of ministry there are still only 10 or 20 youth, and the ministry is not growing or flourishing as it should be—it's time to take a closer look. It all rests on leadership development. If you don't grow as a leader, your group will not grow either.

On the other hand, you may hold an outreach event, get a ton of kids there, and see 50 of them get saved! But two weeks later you'll still have the same 10 kids you started out with, even after you had this incredible outreach. How could that happen? It's not that you need more activities. What you need to do is learn how to catch a lot of fish and *keep them* once they've been caught.

When you grow as a leader you begin to discover how to keep them in the boat. Part of that hinges on understanding the leadership cup theory. It goes like this:

Each one of us has a cup—our leadership cup. One person's cup is 10 people big; another's is 20 people big. Some might hold 50 or 100. Whatever the size your cup is, that is the number of people your leadership skills have equipped you to lead. You can do every outreach and

If you don't grow as a leader, your group will not grow either.

evangelism project you can think of, but if you have a 10-person cup, that will be the limit of your group. That's all you're capable of leading. Your group will never grow.

You could try another outreach, do more activities—work yourself to death—but your group would still be limited to the same number of people that fit in your cup. However big your cup, that's how big your group stays. The extra ones won't fit in there and will just spill over the top.

This is where some "youth guys" will quit. They start believing that God only wants 10 in their group, since no matter what they do the group doesn't increase. We need to be careful here—don't let your experience dictate your theology. Maybe you don't have more youth because you haven't grown your leadership cup before you tried to grow your group.

The good news is that you can expand your cup. That's what growing as a leader is all about: learning how to expand your leadership cup. This is what will catch the fish and keep them in the boat.

Maybe you still don't see a reason why you should grow as a leader. I understand. For a long time, I felt the same way.

10 REASONS WHY
I NEVER GREW AS A LEADER

1. I didn't know that I should be growing as a leader. I thought just growing as a Christian was enough. It's like being lost. If you're lost, and you know it, then you can look at a map and get direction. But if you're lost, and you don't know it, then you'll just keep doing the same things and never think of trying to find a way out.

I didn't know that I should be growing as a leader. I

thought I was fine, since I was on fire for God. What else did I need? I thought leadership training was only for people that were going to be the presidents of corporations or nations. Presidents need to learn about leadership, but ministers, like myself, need to learn about ministry.

That was just ignorant and no one ever told me anything different. Well, now I'm telling you. You can and must grow as a leader.

2. I didn't know how to grow. It's easy to say that you should grow as a leader. But how? Where do you start? Wouldn't it be great if there were just a leadership pill? You could just take the pill—bam! You are now a robust leader. I haven't found that yet. If you find it, please let me know.

I'd love to take that pill. In the meantime, I'll give you tips on how to grow as a leader. Continue to educate yourself. There are plenty of other resources out there that focus exclusively on leadership; I'll be focusing more on how it applies to being a Youth Specialist.

3. I didn't know where to start. Once I realized how lost I was and how ignorant I was, I got really frustrated. When we first started the ministry, my leadership was more like a bull in a china shop. My leadership "horns" were knocking everything over, breaking things, but I didn't notice because I was "so on fire for God."

I was running over my staff and making their lives miserable. I was dreaming big and all my staff were just

If you don't grow as a leader, you won't influence a many people.

getting worn out. "More vision" to them only meant that they had to pedal faster. I had no idea where to begin to fix things. Finally, I realized I needed to change myself.

But where to begin? The list of all the things I was doing wrong as a leader was so long, I didn't even know where to start. It's pretty embarrassing, but it's true.

4. I couldn't find any leadership direction in the Bible. I'd been reading through the Bible, and I couldn't find any chapter where it said, "A good leader does _____." I would read and read, and ask, "Where's the leadership chapter?"

Of course, 1 Timothy talks about the qualifications of a leader—his life and character—but it doesn't give the "10 Action Steps to Be a Wise Leader." I discovered if you're not used to looking for leadership principles, you won't see them in the Word.

I had to start somewhere, so I started reading leadership books, listening to tapes, and going to seminars where they laid leadership principles out for me. Then, like a bloodhound, I caught the scent of leadership. I knew what it smelled like, and suddenly I could see it all through the Bible. Now I can look through the Word and leadership principles leap out at me. Once I was trained to recognize what to look for I could see it; before that I was blind to it.

5. I didn't think it really mattered. I thought as long as I was passionate about the vision, passionate about God, that was all I needed. Yes, that was sufficient for my own personal relationship with Him. But what about sharing His grace with others?

If you don't grow as a leader, you won't influence

many people. You'll have great times alone with God, but you'll be alone in your ministry, because people don't want to come to watch you and God be alone.

You can only run on passion for so long. Running on passion burns other people out. When you're passionate, you drive yourself hard and you drive others hard too. When my people burned out, I dismissed it. "They just weren't committed enough." I was wrong. I finally realized I had to develop something besides passion.

6. I thought leaders were born, not made. Have you ever felt that way? You see people who make awe-inspiring leadership decisions, and you think, "Man, how *do* they do that?"

These people used to make me mad. I remember growing up jealous of the "natural leaders" at my schools. I figured they were born with their ability, and because I didn't have any, I gave up. Some of you may think, "I just don't have the gift." This is not true. As you look around, people may look like they're born leaders, but there are often other circumstances you don't see. Perhaps there were other leaders in the family who modeled those skills for them—an older brother, for example, who was the captain of the ball team. Maybe there were parents who coached or ran a store and exhibited leadership traits.

No matter what your age, you can surround yourself with good quality leadership material, whether it's

You can only run on passion for so long. Running on passion burns other people out.

After the altar call is when evangelism ends and leadership begins.

reading, listening to tapes, or finding mentor leaders in your life. Surround yourself with those influences because it's never too late to acquire leadership skills.

I was not a natural leader—in fact the only thing I was good at naturally was being obnoxious (and I was really good at that). As a result, I was the last person you would ever want to follow. I've had to work hard to develop leadership ability.

7. I couldn't see how growing as a leader applied to ministry. I always thought leadership applied to business, politics, and government, but how does it apply to ministry? I thought if someone gave a great altar call, that made him a great leader (I was wrong—that makes him a great evangelist). After the altar call is when evangelism ends and leadership begins.

The lack of leadership training is a huge problem in the church today. I went to college, studied the Bible, and learned about ministry, but I never learned a single thing about leadership. I never learned about management or delegation or finances. Part of every ministry—no matter how small—is its leadership/business side.

That's right, there's a business side to ministry. If you develop only the spiritual side and ignore the business/leadership side, you just won't grow. Most of the churches in the United States are for sale. Do you know why? They're run by people who hold master's degrees—

sometimes PhD's—in theology, but who don't know anything about leadership. They were never trained in management or finances and drifted into the red financially. No amount of pleading for more offerings or loans of money can pay for the building and the church goes up for auction.

Church splits are another result of poor leadership. Church splits occur when weak leadership at the top doesn't keep people focused on the vision and moving in that direction. Some churches will never split because there is strong, sound biblical leadership in place. I can go into a church anywhere and tell just by the flavor and the style of leadership whether or not that church is in danger of a split.

8. I didn't realize that by not choosing a leadership style I was choosing. What do I mean by that? When I first started learning a little bit about leadership, I saw that there were different models and styles. No single style grabbed me. I thought, "I don't really want to be completely like that, and I don't really want to be like that. I won't be a pigeonholed leader. I'm just going to keep learning and stay neutral."

RUNNING ON PASSION

Before, we were running on pure passion, but after using the [principles in this book], I was amazed at . . . how our youth ministry became well-rounded, and we grew spiritually, not just numerically. I found out you can't run a youth ministry based on passion alone.

—Brandon, Youth Specialist

If God has called you to lead a ministry, youth ministry, youth group, church, then He has made you smart enough to lead it!

I didn't realize that by not choosing I was really abdicating my role. My style of leadership was haphazard. No one really knew what he could expect from me: sometimes one thing would happen, sometimes another. I was unpredictable. Unpredictable leadership destroys confidence. People wonder if they'll have a job next week; they don't know what behavior you expect from them.

Eventually, I realized that when I refused to choose a style of leadership it cost me staff. I figured out that choosing a style and committing to it was better than not choosing anything. Even a bad philosophy of leadership is better than no philosophy of leadership.

At least if you choose a philosophy, you have something to work with. If you realize part of it is bad, then you can tweak that part. But if you just fly by the seat of your pants, you don't really know what to adjust. You are swayed by whatever comes your way.

9. I didn't think I was smart enough. I'll be honest with you; I didn't think I was smart enough to be a world-class leader. I saw really smart people leading awesome ministries, and I thought, "Who am I?" I knew I was smart enough to love God. I was smart enough to stay close to God, have good quiet times, and give a good sermon every now and then. But I didn't think I was really smart enough to be a leader. There was so much to learn and do, and I was just . . . well, me. I lacked confidence.

The breakthrough for me came when I gave my life to Christ and learned that my value and worth are found in Him. Here's what I learned: people are just people. Any of us can develop our potential to learn and grow. Geniuses aren't the only ones allowed to be great leaders; the rest of us can be too.

If God has called you to lead a ministry, youth ministry, youth group, church, then He has made you smart enough to lead it!

10. I didn't understand that ministry, leadership, and management all work together. I thought I could just pray and preach and let other people build the organization. But ministry, leadership, and management all work together. You can have a great ministry vision, but if you can't lead people, you'll be working alone; and if you can't manage the ministry, it will fall apart.

The most successful ministries integrate all three things. If you're lacking one of them, you're trying to operate a tripod ministry on only two legs. A dream won't motivate people by itself; they have to see leadership that's dedicated to accomplishing it. As coach Tom Landry said, "Leadership is getting someone to do what they don't want

If you don't grow as a leader, you may rob people of their chance to be saved. Youth who could be affected by your ministry won't be.

When you don't grow as a leader, you run over people in the name of passion for the Lord.

to do, to achieve what they want to achieve." People want to achieve ministry, but it takes a leader to get them there.

WHY SHOULD YOU GROW AS A LEADER?

So you won't rob people of their chance to hear the Gospel. Up to this point, you may still believe that growth as a leader is an option. Listen carefully: If you don't grow as a leader, you may rob people of their chance to be saved. Youth who could be affected by your ministry won't be. Kids who could grow in the Lord won't grow.

What if honing your leadership skills means that your youth group will grow from its current 10 or 20 or 30 kids, to 300 in a year . . . wouldn't it be worth it? Think, too, about all those kids who wouldn't be in your group a year from now if you didn't grow as a leader—you'd be robbing them of their chance to be impacted by the Word of God through you. When you grow as a leader, you grow your leadership cup, and the number of people you can minister to grows. It's not an exact science. You just start to think differently: deliberately and strategically. Your ability to lead grows.

So you can treat those who work with you respectfully. When you have vision and passion for your youth ministry, but don't grow as a leader, you disrespect the people who have volunteered to help you.

I used to think that the only people who were really committed were the ones on my staff who worked hours of overtime like I did. I believed they were the best workers. I was glad they were as committed as I was . . . until their wives began to complain that they never saw their husbands and their kids wondered where their daddy was. Even then, I didn't think it was a serious problem—after all, they were impacting youth for God's kingdom.

I started to dream bigger, and told them I needed more effort even though they were working 20 hours a day. I wasn't a good enough leader to recognize that they needed balance in their lives.

When you don't grow as a leader, you run over people in the name of passion for the Lord. All you care about is the vision. Your ministry may be growing, but your people aren't. Leadership means taking care of your staff and your youth so that they can take care of the vision.

So you can better serve those you lead. We do our teens a disservice by not growing as leaders because we can't serve them as well. In the early days, I thought that the leader was the guy who told everybody else what to do. Once you become a leader you find out the leader is the one who serves others.

Many of you have discovered that being a leader is a lot more work than what you first thought it was. It's not just holding the microphone.

You must train yourself to think like a leader, like a wise general. We are in a battle for the souls of a whole generation.

Many of you have discovered that being a leader is a lot more work than what you first thought it was. It's not just holding the microphone.

You need to learn best how to serve your teens. How can you help them have better quiet times? How can you help them grow? How can they have a better worship time? If you don't develop yourself as a leader, you won't serve them well.

Before I started to grow as a leader, I read motivational books about leadership, but I didn't take them seriously. I thought, "It's not like there's a test on this material." But *there is* a test on it. The test is life. The test is every Wednesday and every Sunday. The test is meeting with your leaders. The test is how you carry yourself. Life is your test, and if you fail, you've just failed all the kids in your group and all the kids who could have been in your group.

You need to decide right now. Are you committed to growing as a leader, so that you can better evangelize and equip your teens?

HOW DO YOU ACTUALLY GROW AS A LEADER?

Transform your mind. This is what I do. I take four or five main points from a book, type them out, put them in bullet points on a piece of paper, and carry it around with me. Then I use it in my quiet time and pray those leadership principles into my life. The Bible tells us in Romans 12:2 that we are transformed by the renewing of our minds. So I would renew my mind with leadership principles. Since I was *not* a natural leader, I had to train my mind to go in that direction.

I had to learn how to think, talk, and act as a leader. I would drill in those four or five points, and then I'd read another book and add four or five more points. Read another book, add four or five more points. Pretty soon I'd internalized a lot of information. Part of my quiet time was spent praying; part was in the Word; but I also always meditated over leadership principles because I wanted to grow as a leader.

I encourage you to do this as you begin your quest to become a better leader. I listen to tapes all the time and take notes—you can too. Once you start to recognize leadership principles, you'll be able to listen to preaching tapes that aren't necessarily about leadership, and "sniff them out" there, too.

Eventually I got to the point where I could listen to a pastor telling an anecdote and tell what style of leadership he uses by the way he interacts with his staff in the story. It's really not the point of his sermon, but I can understand

We all know youth ministry is hard work. So if we are going to work hard, we might as well do the right work — the work of a leader — so we can have maximum impact on lives.

how he acts as a leader. You too can recognize leadership principles everywhere.

Ask questions. Don't be afraid to ask questions. I ask questions wherever I go. If I'm at a rental car counter, for example, and I see an employee who has a badge that says "12 years of service," then I stop and talk to her. I'll ask, "What has made you want to stay here for 12 years?" What I want to learn is who led her to a place where she would commit 12 years of her life to rent cars to people. I would like workers who are that loyal. So what does a rental car company do that I'm not doing? I'm willing to learn from Avis. I might ask a pastor, "What do you do for your staff meetings? What makes people want to be here?" You can learn from anybody.

You must train yourself to think like a leader, like a wise general. We are in a battle for the souls of a whole generation. We'd better begin to think like generals and leaders. Yes, we need to grow as Christians and ministers, but we can't stop there. We must grow as leaders in order to reach this generation.

As you begin to do these things and meditate on the leadership principles, you'll find your leadership cup will grow a little bit without your realizing it. Pretty soon you'll be thinking differently, managing differently, and there'll be 20 kids in your group. And it will grow from there.

Wouldn't it be great if there were hundreds of ministries in your region with a hundred or more kids in each youth group? Wouldn't it be fantastic to see youth ministries all over the place with a thousand kids coming every week? Shouldn't there be? Doesn't it make you mad that the devil's youth group is bigger than ours? The world knows how to organize and lead and plan, and so must we if we want to influence a lot of people.

The rest of this book will give you practical tools to develop your youth ministry and yourself as a leader. You will learn the imperative, behind-the-scenes work of a leader. You will learn time-tested principles that work for our ministry and for thousands of youth ministries around the country. But it *is* work. Be ready to read and work in each chapter.

The good news is that the frustration of not knowing what to do is about to end. You will have a very clear picture of what to do. We all know youth ministry is hard work. So if we are going to work hard, we might as well do the right work—the work of a leader—so we can have maximum impact on lives.

Take some time and ask God to open up your heart to the leadership potential He has for you. Then keep reading.

Notes

PART A

Dream It!

CHAPTER FOUR

I Have a Dream

Martin Luther King was not the only one to proclaim this statement with great boldness. These are the words of every great leader.

Moses had a dream of going to the promised land. Abraham had a dream of going into another land. Joseph dreamed about being a great leader. This is God's model of leadership in the Bible. He chooses a person, gives him or her a dream, and gathers others around to help accomplish that dream together.

Every great work for the Lord starts with a dream. Every great leader has a dream, a glimpse down the path of spiritual transformation where you will lead others. You

Every great work for the Lord starts with a dream.

may not have contacts, money, helpers, or facilities, but if you have a dream you have the most important ingredient!

When I speak of a dream I am talking about vision—opening your eyes to see what God sees, and to feel His heartbeat for teens in your town.

> *Where there is no revelation [or prophetic vision], the people cast off restraint.*
>
> —Proverbs 29:18 (NKJV)

In these few words is a powerful truth. Without a vision or dream, people have no restraint, no way to harness their energy for productive use. Vision is the bridle that couples energy with purpose, and generates the power of horses pulling a huge stagecoach! Today, we have a generation without a vision—they use their energy for this and that, with no direction or restraint. The end result? We have a lot of kids in church who are fooling around, getting into trouble, and living compromised Christian lives because there is nothing harnessing their energy to use for God.

Whether or not to have big dreams isn't an option. It is mandatory! A sports coach recognizes this and sets a vision for his team: "This is where we are going to go; this is what we can become!" His vision inspires them to run and sweat and work hard. It focuses their passion and energy.

Sadly, our youth groups suffer because we don't dare to dream. We wonder why our students haven't gotten fired up, done something for God, risen up to take their school back—much less take America back. Yet, we are the ones who must paint the picture for them. We have to dream it first and show them where they fit into our vision. Don't expect them to figure it out themselves. We must compel them with our vision to go for it!

When we talk about dreams and visions, let's dream big. If we are going to see something huge happen here in North America for the cause of Christ for young people, it has to be about more than just filling arenas and stadiums. Don't get me wrong; God has a use for arenas and stadiums. I'm just glad that someone else built them for us! (They think that they built them for basketball teams and football teams and rock concerts. But they really built them for the kingdom of God.) The fact is, if God is the foundation of our dreams, we won't be limited to just filled arenas and stadiums. We ought to see youth ministries that go from 10 to 50 and then from 50 to 100 and then from 100 to 200 and then from 200 to 500 and then 500 to 1,000. All over America, there ought to be thousands and thousands of youth ministries that have a thousand or two thousand or three thousand teens.

Some time ago, I heard about a youth group down in Bogotá, Colombia, that draws 40,000 teens every week. Forty thousand! I had to see it for myself. When I walked into the arena, I saw 20,000 teens—and they fill it twice each Saturday! Each week, 2,500 teens give their lives to Jesus, and all the youth are involved in 13,000 cell groups. See what can happen with a vision!

So, yes, I am all for dreaming big. I just don't think you can outdream God. He "is able to do exceedingly

I just don't think you can outdream God.

abundantly above all that we ask or think" (Eph. 3:20 NKJV). If we can think it, He can do far more. So we are the only ones limiting God when we think tiny or dream small.

When you dream big, you must consider not just the size, but the nature of the group. Will they be soul winners, passionate for God? Will they be hungry Christians? What does it matter if you have the biggest group in the city if they're all lukewarm? Mere size is not the issue; size is only important because it means that you are reaching more people. You must still make sure that you are really reaching them. Part of your vision has to include how you are reaching them and how you are truly discipling them. Are they really growing strong? Are they in the Word? Dreaming big is the key.

LET'S TALK ABOUT WHY WE DON'T DREAM

"Having a small group keeps me humble." *"Well, God wants to keep me humble, and I just want to be a humble servant of the Lord."* This one really grates on me. I have heard leaders excuse themselves: "If God has called you to be the youth pastor of 10 kids your entire life, then you ought to be content with that." What? God is a God of destiny! He is a God of potential! Where you are now is never where He wants you to remain. "Potential" means those things that you haven't done yet. If you've already done something, it is no longer potential. Our God is a God who sees the very best and raises people up and breathes life and dreams into them. Besides, small does not necessarily mean humble. You can be small in size, but still haughty and arrogant in your attitude.

"Having a small group keeps my pride in check." "I might get prideful if my group gets big, so God is keeping it small." This is simply another twist on the last point. So instead of dealing with your own sin issues, you will just let the kids you haven't yet reached go to hell? No, this is just an excuse to keep from following God's bigger plan: God's plan is always for us to share His Good News with more people.

"I don't think I can do it." "I can't do it anyway, so why dream it?" This is an unholy inferiority complex. It's another twist on the first two excuses because it is, ultimately, a form of pride. "I'm too proud to trust the Almighty with my inability." The truth is, we don't have to do anything. But through God, we can change the world. If your dream is only as big as your own capacity, then it is not big enough. There isn't room for God in small dreams.

"I've failed in the past." "I've dreamed big and fallen flat on my face. How long can I keep doing that?" Most of us have tried things that failed. We've been mocked or ridiculed for past screw-ups. If you've given up on dreams, or given up on trying to do something great, or given up on functioning outside of your comfort zone or box—it is time to dream again. Some of you are still letting people beat you up for what you did two or three years ago, and it is handcuffing you from fulfilling your potential. Shake them off. Joseph—the Bible's best dreamer—had to fall flat several times before his big dreams were realized.

There isn't room for God in small dreams.

It is okay to dream big; just be careful when and where you share your dreams.

"People might scoff at my dreams." "When I tell people my vision, they tell me to be realistic." The world—even when speaking in the voice of our pastors—can be devastating to our God-given dreams. People throw cold water on your bold imagination and audacious faith. It is time to forgive those—deacons, pastors, leaders—who have mocked your dream or put you down. Don't you dare let their past infringements on your dream harness your future potential.

I can't begin to tell you how many times I have had people laugh at me when I shared what God was calling us to do. My own board of directors used to laugh at me. Our first summer in ministry, we had 30 young people on the mission field. When we came back the board asked me, "Ron, what are your goals for the next year?"

"Next summer, I want to take 200 young people on the mission field!"

They laughed out loud! Literally! Because we had seen others try to get more young people on the mission field, and the most anyone could get was 30. So they laughed, "Come on, get real! Come back down to earth. How many do you want?"

I said, "Two hundred. I want to take 200 kids to Guatemala."

The next summer came around and we took 260 kids, some to Costa Rica, some to Guatemala. After the second year they said, "Great! What an awesome summer! What an awesome year! Now, where do you want the ministry to be in five years?"

I said, "You know what? When we are celebrating our five-year anniversary, I want to be taking 1,000 kids every year to the mission field."

They laughed out loud again. But the fifth year came and we had 1,057 on the mission field, and they quit laughing.

It is okay to dream big; just be careful when and where you share your dreams. Don't be like Joseph—who told his brothers before they were ready to hear it—or you may end up in a ditch like he did. Sometimes even the people you think you can trust the most won't be able to handle your dreams.

When we first started Teen Mania there were some things in my heart that I never told anybody except Katie. I never shared them because sometimes when you dream big, people think you are arrogant, just like Joseph's brothers. But there's a difference between arrogance and faith in God's big dreams. I can remember when we first got the idea for Teen Mania; we were in Indonesia getting ready to go into India. We had a heart for the unreached people groups of the world, but the Lord was speaking to us so clearly about reaching young people in America.

I said, "Forget about those American teenagers. There are many people who can reach them. What about all the Muslims and Hindus and Buddhists here? They've never even had a chance!"

Dreaming is the real work of a leader.

The Lord spoke to my heart again: "What about the young people in America?" And something flashed into my mind, which for years I kept to myself. I saw myself speaking in front of an arena filled with thousands of teenagers. It wasn't a stadium—it was an arena, and it was suddenly there and then gone again. It wasn't like I got caught up in a heavenly vision or anything; I just saw it in my mind.

I thought, "There's no reason anyone would ever come to hear me." I had no idea what that vision was all about, because I still had a heart for the nations. But I never told anybody that I was going to be speaking in front of thousands. Some things you just shouldn't say until the time is right. Until then, cherish them between you and God.

"Dreaming big is hard work." "I don't have the time or energy to do more than I'm already doing." I know you already work very hard, for such long hours, and you just don't feel like you have any more time to do anything else. It sounds like dreaming big means even more time away from the family, right? Not necessarily. Many times the problem isn't how much work you're doing; it's that your work lacks focus and isn't harnessed to your vision. As a result, you spend a lot of energy doing a variety of activities, none of which brings about a big, bold dream.

Dreaming is the real work of a leader. People think the real work is getting up in front of crowds, speaking, and preaching, but they're wrong. Dreaming is what happens before anyone ever sees you preach to an audience. Before he ever sees a big crowd, the Youth Specialist is on his knees crying out, "God, I have to dream! I have to hear what Your dream is for me and my youth ministry."

Do you know what is the great thing about dreaming God's dream? Our distinctiveness gives us each a slightly different dream. God delights in these differences and uses them to reach very diverse groups of teens. If we will just walk in the fullness of the vision God has given us, we will awaken in this generation a new determination to live for Him.

Don't fall into the trap of comparing the size or population of your youth group with the megachurch down the road. If we are in competition, we are in competition with the enemy. Remember that the devil's youth group is bigger than all of ours combined. We need to rescue the souls in his grip, and not worry about counting the ones in other churches. The devil is selling out secular concerts; rappers are dictating morals to this generation. There is a lot of work to do, and worrying about another church's numbers doesn't accomplish anything.

I hate it when the world dreams bigger than we do. I hate it when idolatrous people pack our teens into stadiums and fill them up with garbage. If they can dream about infecting a generation with garbage for profit, can't we dream about infecting them with truth for the Lord?

Remember that the devil's youth group is bigger than all of ours combined. We need to rescue the souls in his grip, and not worry about counting the ones in other churches.

What are some of the things that have held you back from having a great dream? Now is a good time to turn to your computer and open your CD-ROM to the file titled "Dreaming Big." Think about the reasons you haven't dared to dream big and record these reasons on the first page. You can either fill this page

out on the computer or print out the Dream Questions and do it by hand. Then come back to the book and read on.

SO, WHY SHOULD WE DREAM?

You dream to fulfill your potential. You were born with an ability to do incredible things. In fact, you were made in the image of God (Gen 1:27). We, of all His creation, were made to be fellow creators. When you begin to dream, you tap into the creative nature that God breathed into you, and all of a sudden you begin to really live—food tastes better, the air smells fresher, and even the kids look pretty terrific!

Too many people never tap into their creative potential; they just punch a time card and go home. These people miss connecting with an incredible source of power and life! The truth is, you actually become more alive when you begin to dream and utilize some of the potential you were born with. The Holy Spirit dwells in us and wants nothing more than to empower us for great things. Don't die with unexploited potential.

You honor God when you dream big. God is the biggest dreamer ever. He imagined the world, the stars, and the galaxies into being. He thought up molecules and atoms. He is infinitely creative. So when you dream big, you take after your Father. You embrace being a daughter or son of the Most High by becoming more and more like Him. Look at one example of honoring God by dreaming big:

> At Gibeon the LORD appeared to Solomon during the night in a dream, and God said, "Ask for whatever you want me to give you."
>
> Solomon answered, "You have shown great kindness to your servant, my father David, because he was faithful to you and righteous and upright in heart. You have continued this great kindness to him and have given him a son to sit on his throne this very day.
>
> "Now, O LORD my God, you have made your servant king in place of my father David. But I am only a little child and do not know how to carry out my duties. Your servant is here among the people you have chosen, a great people, too numerous to count or number. So give your servant a discerning heart to govern your people and to distinguish between right and wrong. For who is able to govern this great people of yours?"
>
> The LORD was pleased that Solomon had asked for this. So God said to him, "Since you have asked for this and not for long life or wealth for yourself, nor have asked for the death of your enemies but for discernment in administering

God is the biggest dreamer ever.

Are we being humble at the expense of other people's eternity?

justice, I will do what you have asked. I will give you a wise and discerning heart, so that there will never have been any-one like you, nor will there ever be. Moreover, I will give you what you have not asked for—both riches and honor—so that in your lifetime you will have no equal among kings."

—1 Kings 3:5–13

Solomon honored God by dreaming bigger than short-term, personal gain. And God responded by going above and beyond Solomon's hopes and expectations.

There are people at the other end of your dream. If we don't dream, there are people who will never be touched by the Word. We like to say, "Well, I am just being humble," but are we being humble at the expense of other people's eternity? God wants us to have an impact on those unbelievers.

When I say to the wicked, "O wicked man, you will surely die," and you do not speak out to dissuade him from his ways, that wicked man will die for his sin, and I will hold you accountable for his blood. But if you do warn the wicked man to turn from his ways and he does not do so, he will die for his sin, but you will have saved yourself.

—Ezekiel 33:8–9

God holds us accountable to witness to the people He places in our lives. Ephesians 2:10 tells us that

God has planned out works for us to do. Do not let those opportunities pass you by.

You dream to make the most of your efforts. If you don't harness your work to your dream, your energy goes unrestrained and undirected. It requires a lot of work to be a youth pastor. A Youth Specialist focuses the energy he already expends toward the dream. You are doing so much anyway; you might as well make it count to the max.

> *Moses took his seat to serve as judge for the people, and they stood around him from morning till evening. When his father-in-law saw all that Moses was doing for the people, he said, "What is this you are doing for the people? Why do you alone sit as judge, while all these people stand around you from morning till evening?"*
>
> *Moses answered him, "Because the people come to me to seek God's will. Whenever they have a dispute, it is brought to me, and I decide between the parties and inform them of God's decrees and laws."*
>
> *Moses' father-in-law replied, "What you are doing is not good. You and these people who come to you will only wear yourselves out. The work is too heavy for you; you cannot handle it alone."*
>
> —Exodus 18:15–18

A Youth Specialist focuses the energy he already expends toward the dream.

We challenge and push ourselves to the outer limits of our capabilities, and in doing so, we ask God to step in.

Moses was a godly man who was working too hard. More specifically, he was doing work that did not move his vision for the people forward. Others had to tell him to delegate so that he could focus on the parts of his ministry that advanced God's plans. A similar situation confronted the apostles. As the church grew, so did the daily ministry needs:

> *So the Twelve gathered all the disciples together and said, "It would not be right for us to neglect the ministry of the word of God in order to wait on tables."*
>
> —Acts 6:2

We have servant hearts, so we're tempted to do everything that needs to be done. But God calls us to use discernment and work in a way that moves ministry forward but doesn't burn us out. This means doing the work that pursues His vision, and not simply doing a ski trip because the youth group always goes on a ski trip.

Dreaming is fun, daring, exciting, and challenging. It is very easy for us to get trapped in the comfortable routines and patterns of our lives. We know how to prepare a sermon, lead a Wednesday night study, and hang out with the kids. But our competence in those things can actually keep God from showing up with His full power.

> *But he said to me, "My grace is sufficient for you, for my power is made perfect in weakness." Therefore I will*

boast all the more gladly about my weaknesses, so that Christ's power may rest on me. That is why, for Christ's sake, I delight in weaknesses, in insults, in hardships, in persecutions, in difficulties. For when I am weak, then I am strong.

—2 Corinthians 12:9–10

When we dare to dream, we push outside the boundaries of what we can do in our own strength. We challenge and push ourselves to the outer limits of our capabilities, and in doing so, we ask God to step in.

Please return to the CD-ROM file titled "Dreaming Big" and begin to dream. As before, you can either fill out page 2 on the computer or print out the Dream Questions and do it by hand.

This is the first step in launching the assault and building the ministry God has for you. Remember, there are souls on the other side of your dream.

Notes

CHAPTER FIVE

The Foundation of the Dream

BEGIN WITH THE END IN MIND

No one constructs a building without first deciding how tall it should be and planning for an appropriate foundation. The foundation is the support and anchor that makes the rest of the building possible. Similarly, youth ministry demands that we think deeply about what we are building so we can lay a strong foundation.

> Youth ministry demands that we think deeply about what we are building so we can lay a strong foundation.

WHAT ARE WE BUILDING?

Then Jesus came to them and said, "All authority in heaven and on earth has been given to me. Therefore go and make disciples of all nations, baptizing them in the name of the Father and of the Son and of the Holy Spirit, and teaching them to obey everything I have commanded you. And surely I am with you always, to the very end of the age."

—Matthew 28:18–20

Matthew 28:18–20 is known as the Great Commission. Many teens don't even know what it is, and judging by how well most Christians obey what Jesus said in this passage, the "Great Suggestion" might be a better term. Yet, the foundation for youth ministry can only be this: *a vision for the whole world.*

WHY THE GREAT COMMISSION AS A FOUNDATION?

It's the most important order Jesus gave us. How important is the Great Commission? Think about it. After three years of teaching and performing miracles, Jesus died and rose from the dead. These words—the last desires He expressed to His closest friends—were their final "marching orders" before He ascended to heaven. The words emphasized what He had taught them so many times before: *reaching the world.*

This has been God's heart from the very beginning, and He wants His people to have the same driving passion.

Look at Matthew 24:14. "And this gospel of the kingdom will be preached in the whole world as a testimony to all nations, and then the end will come." The end hasn't come because the job is not yet done! This must be the foundation of our dream. Our vision must be to train up a generation of young people crafted for this specific purpose and excited to get the job done. This is the kind of Christian that we want to pump out. Youth ministry has to get away from the attitude of simply begging kids to come to church, to read their Bibles, and to stay committed to God. This self-centered focus is not what Christ called us to do.

Revelation 7:9 tells us that, one day, every tribe, every tongue, every nation, and every language will gather at the throne of grace. Every group will have a representative around the throne, and then Jesus is going to return. Today there are still 10,000 different people groups without a church.[1] If God is reserving His Son's return until this happens, we'd better make sure the dream of our youth ministry is in line with His purpose.

Jesus sent His disciples out. Think about Jesus and His disciples. He sent them out for two weeks, brought them back, and talked about the world. Then He sent out 72 more for two weeks, brought them back, and talked about the world. Jesus started with a vision for Judea and Jerusalem and expanded it to the *ends of the earth.* When we confine our thinking to our own Jerusalem, our purpose becomes too small. Yes, it is good to reach our own city, but clearly God doesn't intend for us to stop there. What then

The end hasn't come because the job is not yet done!

is the point of reaching teens in our town? Is it just to build a big youth group? What is God's perspective on blessing a youth group and making it large? He is looking for an army with a passion to influence the people He loves and gave His life for.

It answers the "why?" question. Why get strong in the Lord? Why be discipled? Why live a holy life? Why have quiet times? Why go to church? Why read the Bible? Why live in purity? Why stay away from drugs and alcohol?

Of course the typical answer given is "because the Bible says so." But *why* does the Bible say to live this way? The answer lies in God's character: our God is a holy God. He calls us to live this way because He needs an army that is disciplined and prepared to represent Him well. When we represent Him well, *that's* when and how we'll reach the world!

God's heart is for people. Moses was the youth pastor of three million people. I call him a youth pastor because the people he led were all about 40 years younger than he was. His ministry started with an encounter with God. He saw the fire and the burning bush and knew he had met with God. We as leaders need to make sure that we also have a personal *encounter* with God—what else do we have to give our kids? I'm not talking about simply praying to the Lord. I am talking about baring your soul before God, getting real with Him, and worshiping Him like the angels do. We need to get personal and real with no distractions.

Moses started with just such a personal interaction. As a result, when he spoke to the kids (the children of Israel), he spoke with authority: "I talked to I AM and HE sent me with a message. I am not fooling around here and I am not doing this because I have nothing else better to do. I can't do anything else; I've been given a message."

That message is revealed in Exodus 3:7: "I have indeed seen the misery of my people." When you get close to God's heart, you will hear Him talk about His people around the world. So many times, all we think about are the people who speak English or the people we see at the ball games. While the people around us are important and need to be incorporated into our dream, we also need to see the big picture—people around the world. Most of the people in your own town have been exposed to the Gospel, but billions around the world have *never had a chance* to hear of Jesus.

Let's look at the statistics: Out of six billion people in the world, two billion are Christians; that leaves four billion left to reach. Of those four billion, about two billion *have never had a chance to hear* the Good News (about 10,000 language groups make up those two billion people.)[2]

God says, "People are in misery. I have heard them crying out because of their slave drivers." Sin is that slave driver to the people of the world who have never had a chance to hear the Word of God. We need to listen to God and hear His heart for the people of the world, realizing that whatever we do to lead these people out of Egypt (each teen has his own Egypt) we lead them out *for a purpose.*

Why did Moses persevere even when the people did not want to follow him? He knew he had a mandate from heaven. He had heard from the burning bush, and he

The point is we must raise up a generation that cares about the world.

knew God's heart for His people. God's leader must keep the vision alive and real in front of the people regardless of whether those people agree or not.

We as leaders must resolve to build a youth ministry with God's heart for the world at the center. Our focus should be: "In some way, my kids are going to impact the four billion." You may not reach all four billion, but you might reach 400 or 4,000 or a million of them over the next 10 years as you send some of your youth out on missions trips, some into full-time outreach, and some to become evangelists. The point is we must raise up a generation that cares about the world. Even if teens are not involved in full time ministry for the rest of their lives, they need to have the lost world beating so strongly in their hearts that they continually live to find a way to impact the nations.

If we don't have money or parental support, it doesn't matter. We will help parents and leaders to understand that their children are meant to be *world changers*. If you have no pastoral support, that's okay. Convince your pastor of the biblical foundation behind your dream, and you'll get it. Don't let obstacles discourage you. Let God's vision for the nations be the foundation of your big dream. There is no bigger dream than to reach the world.

WHAT DOES "HAVING AN IDENTITY" MEAN TO MY GROUP?

Missions is our DNA. A young person gains a deep sense of Christian identity when he or she makes an impact on someone who otherwise wouldn't have had a chance to hear the Gospel. All of a sudden, it becomes much bigger than *me, my* town, where *my* eyes can see, where *I* have been, where *I* have driven before.

> The LORD had said to Abram, "Leave your country, your people and your father's household and go to the land I will show you. I will make you into a great nation and I will bless you; I will make your name great, and you will be a blessing. I will bless those who bless you, and whoever curses you I will curse; and all peoples on earth will be blessed through you."
>
> So Abram left, as the LORD had told him.
>
> —Genesis 12:1–4a

In the days of Abraham, God set a people aside because He wanted to bless "all peoples on earth." Today, God is still in the business of blessing the peoples on the

ALL OVER THE WORLD!

I started off with no experience, and the group had no sense of direction of purpose. Now, three years later, we have grown tremendously, and there is a sense of purpose. . . We have sent countless students and adults all over the world!

—Youth Specialist

Our job is to help people understand that this is not only about you or your town—it's about the world.

earth through those who are faithful to Him. Every church and every youth group should be urged to ask: "How can we affect the whole world?" We are here for a purpose larger than ourselves and need to find our connecting point with Abraham and his purpose: "How can I be a blessing to others on this earth?"

We can never afford—as a church—to merely talk about our blessings and once in a while listen to a visiting missionary. Like Abraham, we have a mandate from God: to be a blessing to the world. What does this mean? Does it mean that everything in our whole youth ministry should revolve around missions? Well, if we see students impacting the world as the basis of our dream, then . . . yes. That perspective will color everything else that we do. We won't do anything for the sake of doing it. We will purposefully cultivate in our teens a view to bless the world.

As stated previously, we want kids to be like young David, who, as a youth, killed a bear, a lion, and a giant. He made an impact for the Lord in Saul's court and everywhere else he went. The whole world was amazed as he represented a living God. Let's train up young men and women who will have that kind of impact!

Look also at John Mark. He met Paul at his mother's house after Peter escaped from prison, and was only 14 when he went on his first mission trip with Paul and Barnabas. Later, John Mark was with Paul in prison and helped him to write letters. Later still, John Mark wrote one of the four Gospels. Traveling with the "missions team" didn't get missions *out* of his system; it got missions *into* his system!

Our job is to help people understand that this is not only about you or your town—it's about the world. We must hear the call of the Great Commission as more than just a cultural metaphor in the Bible. It is the *foundation* of the Bible. The whole Bible describes God's mission heart. He is intervening in human history and He wants us to partner with Him.

Acquire the Fire and Teen Mania sponsor a lot of mission trips, but not because missions is a fun teen thing. Missions is *THE thing*. Missions—being a blessing to all nations—is the heartbeat of purpose in the church. There is a world yet to be reached, and we aim to be a part of finishing the task. Every dream with a solid foundation will have this same conviction.

We are a part of something BIG. Each of us will have a different expression of God's dream. Your dream will be different from everyone else's and that is great. We all must aim at something big. And the world is a pretty big thing to aim at.

If our purpose is smaller than *reaching the world*, then our kids will find a bigger purpose that will demand more of them. If we don't give them something huge to be a part of, then they will find it elsewhere. We will hear them say, "*My youth group is fine, but my soccer team is going to the national championship.*" Or, "*My choir is going to sing before the president.*" And, "*Our band will be in this year's Rose Parade.*"

If you don't share God's big purpose with them—to reach the world—they will find something bigger than your youth group. They'll go to some world-famous,

As a result they will find their identity in the counterfeit things of the world rather than in the authentic things of God.

secular concert with 20,000 other kids and feel like they are a part of something momentous. As a result they will find their identity in the counterfeit things of the world rather than in the authentic things of God.

We need to help them develop a mentality that says, *"We are all about rocking the world! We might be from a small town or a small youth group, but we are going to have an impact on this world."*

When we set a vision like this for our local youth ministries, our kids can be part of something significant when they become a part of our youth ministry. A vision this big requires their all, and *teens are willing to give it.* People think that youth are self-centered and lazy, but that's only because they don't have a vision to rally behind. Teens will spend hours a day working hard for a sports team or drama practice. They'll do the same if the church gives them something important to work for. But if you ask for their all, and don't have a vision that is worthy of their efforts, then you'll find yourself begging them to come back. They may come back, but their identity will be somewhere else. You will get commitment from your teens by giving them a vision that demands their all.

You know how desperately kids want to belong to something? When we ask them, "Why didn't you come to youth group?" the most common answer is, "I had practice (or some other group activity)." If that's where they've found their group identity, we'll be left like a cowboy with a whip trying to round up the cattle (by asking them to come back with bribes or guilt trips). On the other hand, a shepherd simply walks out in front and the sheep follow. We have to be like shepherds and give them such a great vision—a great opportunity—that they beg to come! They'll want to know what else they can do to be involved. They'll find their identity . . . something worthy of giving their all.

Set up a vision for your youth ministry that is an expression of God's dream for the world. When you challenge your youth to change the world for Christ, they will identify with a purpose that is bigger and more compelling than any school, ball team, or club. And it is something that is worthy of their involvement for the rest of their lives.

This is a good place to stop reading and think about your purpose for your youth ministry. Go to the computer now and open the CD-ROM file titled "Foundation." You can print out these two pages and record your

When you challenge your youth to change the world for Christ, they will identify with a purpose that is bigger and more compelling than any school, ball team, or club.

God is counting on this generation to make a difference in the world. There are people waiting to be rescued by them!

thoughts on paper, or you can fill them out on the computer. These questions will help you zero in on how your dream fits in with God's purpose.

Everyone can make a difference. I remember the story of a man and his little boy who would go to the beach together every morning. They were looking for starfish washed up on shore, and, once found, they would throw the helpless creatures back into the surf. One day a huge storm hit, washing millions of starfish onto the beach. The father and son desperately tried to throw all the starfish back before they died.

Another man approached the two and asked what they were doing. "We're just trying to do some good here," they said.

"But you'll never make a difference! All these starfish are dying by the thousands!" said the onlooker.

The little boy stopped and looked at him. Picking up a starfish, he threw it to the waves and said, "I made a difference for *that* one." He picked up another and said, "I made a difference for *that* one . . . and for *that* one . . . and for *that* one . . ." and on and on he went, throwing starfish into the sea, one at a time.

Not only can everyone make a difference, lives are at stake if we don't. God is counting on this generation to make a difference in the world. There are people waiting to be rescued by them!

Teaching teens to live and to give. Here in America, we live in one of the richest nations in the world, and it is easy to become a self-centered Christian. We pray for our family, our church, our town, our country, and ourselves. Many people who call themselves Christians are just as selfish as non-Christians. They go to church on Sunday, but are absorbed and preoccupied with the American dream. Ultimately, living to get more "stuff" becomes their priority.

If we will show our teens God's heart for the world, we can teach them a different purpose for living in this prosperous nation. When God calls some to go live overseas and minister full time, others must stay behind and funnel some of the wealth from this great American system into the kingdom of God. It's critical that we do everything we can so that those who are called can get to the nations of the earth.

> *"I am never going to get sucked into the American dream and live and pay tithes and die. No! I am going to capitalize on the American system and seize its resources for God's kingdom."*

The world has never seen the impact of a whole generation of Christians focused on God's heart for His world.

Start with the end in mind—the purpose—and let that dictate everything else you do.

This should be the passion for those called to live here in the States. The Mormons seem more committed to spreading their message than many Christians are in spreading the Truth. May such a thing never be said of the young people who come through your youth ministry.

Instilling in teens a passion for the world teaches them "to live and to give." God wants more than a tithe; He wants tithes, offerings, and the hearts of young people. These teens who stay in the USA may very well get rich, but they will live to give. They are here to start companies and dot-coms and become wealthy so that they can channel money toward the fulfillment of God's vision for the world. Their passion will be: "I have to make an impact on two billion people that have never had a chance!" If we can crank out a generation of people like that, watch out! The world has never seen the impact of a whole generation of Christians focused on God's heart for His world.

The beginning and the end of the foundation. In light of this mandate, what does God want you to do? This is where our plans must begin. We can't begin to dream about the future until we look at the foundation, the bedrock. We must contemplate how we are going to instill kids with this mandate for the rest of their lives. I'm not just saying this because I want people to come on Teen Mania Global Expedition trips. Use any missions group you want. But don't just use them for a summer or short-term trip and be done. Show teens that they can make a difference in the world for the rest of their lives! We want to instill in them a conviction that says:

"I have to do something for the world! I need to pray and give like crazy. I have to keep going to the poor and unreached! When I see missionaries come to my church, I am going to bless them like crazy."

So the whole purpose for teen Christianity will not be to just stay saved until they die; it will be to make an impact on the world. In light of this mandate, how do we proceed?

Start with the end in mind—the purpose—and let that dictate everything else you do. Again, each of our dreams in ministry will be a little different; but if we all begin to build on this foundation, we will finish with the same goal and direction. When we develop a vision that expresses this mandate, our focus will not be to have the biggest youth group in town or to please the pastor and the parents. We will keep the bigger picture in mind: to nurture a generation of passionate Christ-followers who are committed to blessing the world.

An imperative part of your dream must be to make teens into world changers.

The vision of the Youth Specialist must be to confront every student with a question that demands a response: "How is your life going to count for the sake of the Great Commission?"

WHAT A GREAT COMMISSION FOUNDATION CAN LOOK LIKE

Even though I love reaching the world and leading a missions organization, I have to keep my missions heart fresh. For that reason, I read missions articles, look at missions videos, and remind myself that there is a world out there.

I remember when I first got turned onto the Lord. I wouldn't even have thought about being a preacher. I thought, "What does God need another preacher for? There are lots of them already." And missionaries—there are lots of them to go around, right? The fact is, *about five percent of all the missionaries in the world work with those two billion who have never had a chance.* This is a tragedy of the highest magnitude.

Our dream for our youth groups is not just to create fun for the sake of activities. We don't want to double our attendance every year to impress. But there is a big world out there that needs to be reached. We need to take kids who are broken and hurting, and put them back together for a purpose—so that they can share their testimonies with the world!

How's this for a testimony? "We had kids on drugs,

their families were broken, but now God has restored them. Their families are back together, and God is using these teens to win hundreds or thousands to the Lord." We want to have a small army of young people with testimonies: "I am making a difference in this nation," or "I helped to reach this village that never heard of Christ before," and "I helped to get Bibles into this nation that never had them before."

I believe that God wants leaders who are overcome by His big picture. An imperative part of your dream must be to make teens into world-changers. Ted Haggard, President of the National Association of Evangelicals, began his youth ministry with this Great Commission focus. Rather than setting out simply to build a big youth group, he focused on "raising up young people to take the Bible where people don't have one." Everything in his ministry revolved around this. It affected how they organized, planned, and recruited. It's what they told parents and teens. And, sure enough, it's what they did—they raised up kids to be Bible smugglers, and they took Bible-smuggling trips on a regular basis.

With this Great Commission foundation, Ted's youth ministry became the largest in Louisiana with over 1,000 kids. What's the bottom line? They were focused on giving their lives away and changing the world!

Now is the time to think about a people group you would like to reach. Maybe your church has been focusing on a certain nation, or perhpas you're passionate about reaching Muslims, Buddhists, or Hindu people. It's time to make this mission the focus of your youth ministry.

As Youth Specialists, your goal is to get youth seriously plugged into either going or sending for the rest of their lives—not just for a summer. Your training and mentoring before and after short-term summer trips is the glue that makes the lesson stick. You want your teens constantly talking about what happened last summer or what is about to happen this summer. You want them involved all year with the nations by supporting missionaries and raising money for them or maybe supporting some needy children in another nation. They might raise money to help build an orphanage or help buy a four-wheeler for a missionary who couldn't before find a way to reach a middle-of-nowhere mountain tribe. You want to build into your students lifelong habits of thinking past themselves to the needs of the world outside their door.

The bedrock purpose of our youth ministries is to make an impact on the world, to reach the world. As a result, the vision of the Youth Specialist must be to confront every student with a question that demands a response: *"How is your life going to count for the sake of the Great Commission?"*

1. Global Prayer Digest for August 28, 2005, http://www.global-prayer-digest.org/ (accessed October 25, 2005).

2. Larry Caldwell, "Reaching the Really Unreached." BGC World (March, 2002), http://www.bgcworld.org/newstand/standard/stnd0302/10,11.pdf (accessed October 25, 2005).

CHAPTER SIX

Essentials of the Dream

Now that you have begun to dream about all your ministry could and should become, I hope you are filled with a contagious excitement. You are on your way to making a massive impact on this generation! Like the apostle Paul, you're on a path of no regrets that will end someday with the words, "I have finished my course." Each of us longs to hear "well done!" not "well . . . done?" when we meet God face to face. But first, we dream of reaching all those we are supposed to reach!

No one can tell you what *your* dream should be, but there are some core ingredients that all high-impact youth ministries must contain. *(Notice I call them "youth ministries," and not "youth groups." The word "group" sounds exclusive, rather than a growing and thriving youth ministry!)* To discover these essentials, the simpleminded youth leader may call out, "Lord, just tell me what you want me to do. Just write

We can't get them all single-handedly. So which ones are you going to reach?

it in the sky or on a tablet." The serious Youth Specialist, on the other hand, asks deep questions that demand answers. God has already deposited within you many aspects of your vision. Now it's time to ask the right questions, questions that will reveal the core ingredients of your ministry.

Getting a clear vision of God's dream is like painting a picture. Remember those paint-by-numbers you did when you were young? At first you had no idea what the picture would look like. But slowly, as you filled in the numbers, the images got clearer. Each one of these questions is like a number in one of those paintings. When you answer the question, the vision will become clearer. Take time to pray over each question as you read on and continue dreaming.

WHO AM I GOING TO REACH?

"Duh . . . I'm going to reach kids!"

Seems at first like a pretty easy question to answer, but take a second look and you'll find that it's a lot more complicated. Before hitting the streets with "reaching young people" as your vague objective, you need to decide *which* ones you are going to pursue. Which type? Most likely, you are excited to reach kids, but if you try to reach them all, you will probably end up reaching very few. None of us can reach them all on our own. I can't reach them all, you can't reach them all, and not a single ministry can reach them all. So we each must define which kids we're going after.

At the *Acquire the Fire* events I host, we often have guest speakers. Most of the time, we invite speakers who are *not* very much like me. I can reach and touch and minister to certain kids, but I can't get them all. So we invite someone of a different ethnicity or with a different story to share. We can't get them all single-handedly. So which ones are you going to reach?

Reach those who are ready. When deciding whom you are going to reach, follow Jesus' lead. He shared His message first within the church. But when they rejected His teaching, He turned to the broken outside the church; He shared His love with those who realized they needed Him.

What's the lesson in this? *Quit trying to chase the ones that don't want to get caught.* These are often the kids whose parents go to church. You jump through every hoop and do every kind of song, dance, and activity to attract them. In the meantime, there are a lot of hurting kids walking the hallways at school every week, just waiting for someone to show they care.

Don't just reach the ones like you. When thinking about those you are trying to reach, consider the ones who are *not* like you. If you are a clean-cut middle-class adult, you

There are a lot of hurting kids walking the hallways at school every week, just waiting for someone to show they care.

HUNDREDS HAVE COME!

We bring in about 600-800 youth each [outdoor music] festival. It's a ministry to skater and at-risk teens. A youth church has been started as a result that meets on Sunday nights. Hundreds have come to the Lord! Praise God!

—Neelka, Youth Specialist

will naturally attract clean-cut middle-class kids. If you are a surfer-type, then you will probably attract other surfer-types. So if you don't intentionally go after kids who are not like you, you probably won't reach them.

Think about the students in your town. Are they just one big clump of similar people? Of course not! Adults tend to think that all 13–16 year olds are about the same because they are all the same age. But this is a huge mistake! It's like thinking that everyone from a specific country is alike—they all speak the same language, so if we know one of them, we pretty much know them all. What a vast misconception! In reality, every large group of people can be subdivided into smaller groups.

Your teens can help you figure out what these subcultures are. Ask them, "How is your school divided into groups and cliques?" You need to know what they are so you can decide which to address. Which group should you go after?

Marketing groups never go after *everybody*—they know they cannot. So you will see the same potato chip advertised *this* way for one group and *that* way for another group. This is called niche marketing. It's a good model for us to follow because it recognizes a truth—it takes different methods to get different groups to buy the same thing.

So pick your target audience. If you are called to reach the party animals—that's the burden inside of you—then make that group your priority. Designate a large place in your dream for the party animals. Or maybe you realize you must reach girls who are pregnant and unmarried. Whatever your deepest burden, address it in your dream. This is part of what the dreaming process is all about—thinking about which groups are burning in your heart.

HOW DO I REACH MY TARGET AUDIENCE?

After you have decided whom to reach, the next question is obvious: how do I reach this group? This question leads to others (remember at this point to concentrate on the practical):

- *What issues are the kids in this group dealing with?*
- *What interests them?*
- *How can I fill a need in their lives?*
- *What kind of outreach activities do I need to do?*
- *What gifted individuals would I need working beside me in order to effectively reach these kids?*

For example, if your burden is for drug-addicted teens, you will need to recruit leaders who are specially trained to counsel in this area. Maybe you are not an ex-druggie, but you have someone on your team who is, and she is totally on fire for God. Perhaps she would be a great person to help reach a small group or lead an outreach to minister to certain teens.

As you decide how to reach your audience, always work to maximize the leaders that you already have on board.

HOW AM I GOING TO KEEP THEM?

You now know who you are going to reach and how you are going to reach them . . . now you need to ask, "How am I going to keep them?" Perhaps you've figured out what outreach you will do, what type of band you will have, what kind of kids will come in, and how they will all get saved. But if you haven't put any energy into keeping them—in the kingdom and in your youth ministry—you will lose kids. You'll end up wondering why kids keep getting saved but the group doesn't grow. Remember, kids won't stay accidentally—they have to make an intentional choice.

Several subquestions fit here. The simpleminded youth leader would only ask, "How am I going to keep them?" The Youth Specialist asks,

> *Why do I want to keep them? (So they will grow in faith . . . not just so I have a lot of attendees.)*
> *What do I want them to become?*
> *What is my goal for them once they give their lives to Jesus? Is it just to be good church-going folk the rest of their lives?*
> *Where do I want to take them in their walk with God?*
> *How do I want them to grow once they are committed to Him?*

Pizza parties and lock-ins won't keep them coming, but the answers to these questions will.

HOW MANY COULD WE REALLY REACH?

As a Youth Specialist, you need to dream about how big this thing could really get. When you talk about numbers, it's because you're thinking about the *kids* you want to reach. After all, each number represents a living soul—we're not in the math business; we're in the soul business! When people say, "You're only in this for numbers," don't worry—you know that numbers equal people.

Have the courage to dream a little bit about numbers! Your energy will skyrocket when you start thinking, "Wow! We really *could* have 100 or 200 or even 300 kids in our group! It has never been done in the history of our town, but we could do this!"

One of the first-ever Teen Mania rallies was in Erie, Kansas. I hadn't intended Teen Mania to become a whole ministry; it was just something I was doing while in college. I couldn't stand just going to class—I wanted to reach out and see people get saved. So we did an outreach for some young people. We planned on going into a little town and thought the name "Teen Mania" might just create enough curiosity to get young people to come. One month in advance, we put big banners across the street all over this two-horse town. The banners read, "Teen Mania is coming! Get ready!" We hung up posters and passed out bumper stickers to all the high school kids. Curiosity grew.

As a Youth Specialist, you need to dream about how big this thing could really get.

Dare to step out and do something that has never been done in your town before. This is how revolutions are started!

When the day of the event came, we had *more kids at the event than the entire population of the town of Erie.* Teens flooded us from outlying towns. They were listening to the bands and getting saved!

When you think big, there is a tangible excitement that fuels your heart. People will catch your enthusiasm when you dream bigger than they've ever imagined. Think about how big it could get by the end of one year or two years. Dare to step out and do something that has never been done in your town before. This is how revolutions are started!

WHAT ARE THE REAL NEEDS OF THE TEENS I WANT TO REACH?

What needs are not being fulfilled for youth today? Many statistics and surveys show that kids in our society are very relationship-driven right now. Maybe it is the vacuum caused by their moms and dads working all the time. Maybe it's the hole created by divorce. Maybe it's addictive Internet use. Statistics show that there is a direct correlation between the amount of time kids spend on the Internet and the degree of loneliness they feel. Imagine what will happen as Internet use increases more and more. Forty-eight percent of kids already use the Internet on a regular basis, and the numbers continue to rise.[1]

Some needs are felt needs, meaning kids know they need help in a certain area (for example, they are lonely or depressed or pregnant). Other needs are real issues that they don't even know they need help with. Kids with these unfelt needs are like children who need vitamins and don't know it, so their parents have to find a clever way to get them to take the pills. We must consider how we are going to address those needs, whether felt or unfelt. We need to show youth that the Bible is the answer to those needs, and not just a "spiritual, but irrelevant document."

A huge need for this generation is the need for a father. You will have teens who don't know their dads or have divorced parents. You must understand that we can't just be big brothers or happy-go-lucky youth guys. These kids need a godly authority figure in their lives. That goes for both guys and girls. We know what happens to a girl who doesn't get enough attention from her father: she tries to get attention from guys in other ways. So if you give her fatherly, godly attention, suddenly she realizes she doesn't need the false attention of boyfriends. By understanding the needs of those you intend to reach and how you will meet those needs with the ministry team you assemble, you will begin to attract those very students to your ministry.

By understanding the needs of those you intend to reach and how you will meet those needs with the ministry team you assemble, you will begin to attract those very students to your ministry.

WHAT IS THE NATURE AND CHARACTER
OF THE GROUP THAT I AM TO LEAD?

The size of your group in the future is only part of the dream. There are many groups that grow in numbers but never become anything more than a fun "Jesus rally" with no solid disciples. You need to decide what is to be the nature of your group. You may think, "Well, the group's nature will be determined by the dynamic and personality of the kids who form the group." Not so. It will be determined by whatever you allow or train them to be.

Ask yourself, what kind of Christians do I want these kids to become? Let's say you want the personality of your group to be distinguished by the fact that these students really love to worship God with all their hearts. Start to imagine what your Wednesday night meeting should look and feel like in order to grow an army of worshipers. What would have to be there in order to inspire them to worship like that? A band? PA system? Lights? A real worship team? If they are the best worshipers in the whole church, then everyone else in the church will realize that these kids really love God.

What other words would you want to use to describe your youth ministry? Do you want them to be soul winners? Then the question, "How do I turn these kids into a group that will bring people to the Lord?" ought to plague you until it is answered. Set a goal to instill in them a passion to reach out to others as a natural part of their lives and they won't be ashamed or afraid to win people for the Lord. Remember, this means more than just a once-a-year sermon on how they need to win souls and then hoping they do it. This could mean that in addition to training, you take them with you to go out and win souls. If you want to turn them into "soul winners," you need to *define what that is in your mind and determine how you will accomplish it.*

The important thing to remember here is that you, as leader, need to develop a clear picture of what you want the personality of the group to be, and then you must engineer your group to become that. We must help them develop into people who have: *respect, self-control, honor for their parents, love for purity, hate for sin, discernment about the lies of the world. They must become disciples and disciple others.* These are just a few of the essentials.

HOW WILL I MEASURE THEIR SPIRITUAL GROWTH?

I would encourage you to think about how you can measure the growth in your teens' spirituality. This is not done very often. Many Christians don't know that they are supposed to grow, or in what areas they should grow. Research shows that most Christians feel they stop growing after their first two years in the church.

So many times we just tell our groups to keep reading their Bibles, praying, and coming to youth group, but we

WHAT ALL THE BUZZ IS

[I had] eight to ten kids, mostly skeptics and "fringe players." Only about two of them were really committed Christians. Now I have 20 very energetic young Christian teens, and they are constantly bringing in new kids to see what all the buzz is about.

—Denny, Youth Specialist

Whether it is sending some kids or supporting other missionaries, reaching the world must be a priority of every Youth Specialist.

fail to intentionally disciple them. If you have some serious God-followers, they are going to want spiritual food so they can grow. If we don't do that, they will starve to death under your supervision! No wonder your teens get bored and walk away from their commitment to Christ.

There ought to be some benchmarks of growth in your church. Benchmarks might include: how much time they are spending with God, how much of the Bible they are reading each year, character traits that they are really developing, sin that they are overcoming, how many books that they have read about walking closer to the Lord or devotional types of books, etc. Think about how you will chart the growth of these God-followers and how you are going to be able to tell they are growing. This is imperative for a Youth Specialist. Teens need to see they are on track as soon as they commit to the Lord.

It is like joining the military. Everyone knows that if you enlist as a private, there are a lot of ranks you can progress to. It is inherent to the process. NO one wants to stay at a private E1 status. In fact, if after 20 years in the army you were still an E1 you would be a laughingstock! Yet it seems we have plenty of E1 Christians in our pews today.

So as part of your dream, think of how you will track teen growth and what track you're going to give them to run on so that *they can see* that they have grown in Christ.

HOW WILL I POINT THEM TOWARD THE GREAT COMMISSION?

As we discussed in the last chapter, I am quite confident that any wise leader's dream is going to include missions because that is the most important thing on God's heart. Are we raising up a generation so that they can do something to dramatically affect this world? What does that look like? Well, it could mean having a youth group missions trip every year, *and* sending two or three kids from your group on a longer trip every year as well. Truthfully, I am not trying to advertise Teen Mania's Global Expeditions. This is about raising up kids that care about the world because it is so easy to be an American and be self-centered and only think about your youth group and your town and your country.

God needs the whole Body of Christ to be thinking about the rest of the world. And as we talked about earlier, we get the chance to set the pace for the next generation of Christians. So whatever we breathe into them as imperative, is what they will think is most important. So, how do missions connect to your youth ministry? Whether it is sending some kids or supporting other missionaries, reaching the world must be a priority of every Youth Specialist.

Our problem has been that we beg teens to come each week, but don't give them the substance needed to really belong.

WHAT IS THE IDENTITY OF YOUR GROUP?

Ask any teen, "What are you into?" and they will tell you about the activities in their lives that they feel are most important. Whatever they say to you is where they find their identity. Some will say, "I'm into sports, or a certain band, or friends, or school." Realize that their first comments are what they feel "a part of." Even Christian teens—when you ask them that question—will say "drama, school, sports, or choir." They come to church, but their identity and center of their lives are found elsewhere.

One of the reasons that youth have a hard time coming to youth group each week or to your special events is because they feel more a part of something else than your youth ministry. For example, when you tell them your group is doing something exciting, they are noncommittal until they figure out if they have a ball game or other activity *more important to them.*

I dream of the day that a coach says to his team at school they have practices and games, but the student says, "Well, I need to check my youth ministry calendar to make sure I can fit in my practices!" Kids are so committed to these other things because it's where they find their identity. They *go* to church and they *go* to youth group, but their *identity* is with their ball team.

So one of the most important reasons to dream is to figure out what the vision is and where the group is going so that kids understand *this is who we are and this is what we are about.* When teens understand that, then they can decide if they want to be a part of it. Our problem has been that we beg teens to come each week, but don't give them the substance needed to really belong. Teens don't want to just come to a meeting, *they want to belong to a vision!*

Here are some practical elements of teen ministry that will help clarify the identity of your group.

Identity requires a name. Part of a team's identity is a name and mascot. I would encourage you to have a name for your youth group or ministry. Don't just call yourself "the youth group of whatever church" because that is just an add-on. School sports don't just call themselves the "football team at Hennery High," they call themselves by name, the name of the mascot. The name, like *180* or *Crossfire*, can be something unique that you invent, or you can vote on it. (I don't normally encourage voting on many things, but a name is an okay thing to vote on.) You could have a contest and the one who thinks of the name that YOU choose wins something great.

Identity is easier with a symbol. Another thing to consider when creating identity is a symbol or logo. Even the early Christians had a logo. They drew a fish to represent their leader, Jesus Christ. Think about artwork for a few minutes. We live in a society that likes flashy things, which is why advertising works. Our product is a billion times better than anything the world can offer, but if we never get the kids' attention, they will never know about the product. Kids are used to seeing things and receiving information through a cool brochure or video clip, and we need to communicate our vision in a way that is clear to

Teens don't want to just come to a meeting, they want to belong to a vision.

them. Sure, we can sit back, leave it boring, and hope they will come, but the fact is, *if you don't use the right bait, you won't catch the fish.*

So what kind of artwork do you need? Maybe some type of brochure or flyer that talks about your ministry. It should appeal to both Christian and non-Christian. Another piece, or even the same piece, could appeal to adults inside and outside of the church, explaining what you are doing to help teens. What would that look like? This is not the kind of flier that you need really quick, so you run something off the Xerox machine, and it's crooked. Design something exciting, attractive, and time-less that you can use for the next year for both kids and adults. You don't want to have to print a new concept every time you need something. I know some youth groups have printed small, four-color invitations that fold out. Kids take them to school and pass them out to all of their friends, and they use them all year long. Even dreaming big we should still be wise stewards with our resources. A lot of the cost of printing is the setup of the press. To run 1,000 extra copies is really cheap. It's doing the artwork setup that's expensive. And there are many teens who can do artwork on their computers for you; ask them to help and to give ideas that THEY think are cool.

Identity requires a place. Part of the identity of your group will come from a name and a symbol, and part will come from a youth facility. If you do not have a youth room or a youth facility, I would encourage you to find a way to pray one in. Part of dreaming is to forget what money is needed and not let it harness your vision. Teens need to walk in and *like* to be there—not be embarrassed to bring their friends. Where teens hang out is part of their identity. We want them to feel like part of a team, its dream, and its place.

If you don't know how to decorate, ask someone. You could decorate your space like a bedroom (without all the clothes on the floor). Create a place where they'll feel comfortable and want to be. Marketers have done research and found that there is a globalized youth culture now. The bedrooms of teenagers all around the world look the same: same posters, same heroes, music, sports; all are almost identical. So it shouldn't be too hard to figure out how to decorate. It should make your teens feel comfortable. In your youth facility, you are going to want to think about:

- *How big should the space be, and what color?*
- *Should it have lights?*
- *What functions does it need to fill?*
- *Should it have video screens?*

Forget about the money, and think about the dream. If Jesus were the youth pastor trying to reach these kids, what would the room look like? What would it be? What *could* it be?

Identity requires a specific service. Part of the identity of your group is the kind of service you have. Imagine holding the most amazing, Spirit-filled, saving-people-in-masses service; what would that look like?

If you don't make room for teen leaders, they will never rise up.

- *What would the worship be like?*
- *What would the preaching be like?*
- *Would there be altar calls?*
- *What would object lessons be like?*
- *Could kids be leading others to get saved during the service?*
- *Could young people be hanging out in the back so struggling teens would have peers to talk to?*
- *Could young people be a part of actually presenting and doing dramas up front to go along with your message?*
- *Would you have handouts that go with your sermon for kids to take notes on?*
- *What about teenage leaders?*

HOW WILL I RAISE UP TEEN LEADERS?

Every highly productive youth ministry will raise up teen leaders. What are you going to do to develop those leaders? The fact is, you already have too much to do, especially as you start to dream bigger. You can't do it all yourself. If you could do it by yourself, then you wouldn't be dreaming big enough. So how will you recruit them, how will you develop them, what jobs will you give them? Make room in your system for teen leaders. If you don't make room for teen leaders, they will never rise up.

HOW WILL I ENGAGE ADULT VOLUNTEERS?

Another essential of any world-class dream is adult volunteers. More than just parents helping out on a weekend, these adults are committed to moving your vision forward. What specific role do adult volunteers play? How many will you need? Your dream is going to require many of them. How will you get the ideal people? How do you make sure the adults who come are the right ones?

We'll address this issue of raising up teen and adult leaders more fully in a later chapter.

HOW WILL I USE NEW MEDIA?

Since we live in the new millennium, you need to be thinking about where TV, radio, and the Internet will play a part in your vision. Instead of just meeting every Wednesday, how can you connect with youth every day? This is a media-driven generation. Studies show that on average, people see 30,000 messages each day coaxing them to buy this, try this, do this, etc. If we are only there for kids once a week on Wednesday nights, we will be irrelevant to their lives and will not connect with them. Jesus connected with people. He used object lessons out of everyday life to connect. He pointed to lilies as an example of God's provision for clothes. He looked at the birds of the air and used them to teach God's loving provision for all of our needs. To fishermen He talked about fishing, to farmers He talked about a sower and the seed. He

Find out how God wants to use the media in your dream.

If we are only there for kids once a week on Wednesday nights, we will be irrelevant to their lives.

helped people understand spiritual truths using things they were familiar with. We need to do the same thing.

As we talk about the Internet, TV, radio, and other media, we need to think about how to make it work for us in the 21st century to communicate truth to kids. Maybe you've never thought about having a weekly television program on a local TV station, but you need to. You need to dream about it. I know that there are many Youth Specialists reading this right now who could have a weekly television program, reaching out to people in the area and almost for free. You can't even imagine now how to get it, but you *could*. Think about how you could "expand your tent pegs."

Using the Internet, local radio, and other forms of media or what is called now the "new media" is a way to be where the teens are living. I know some youth pastors who run quick, thought-provoking, one-minute ads on the local secular stations. I remember when I first had an opportunity to do TV programs for teens, I thought it was crazy. I had never seen myself as a televangelist and I wanted nothing to do with TV. I was offered a regular national TV program for free and even then I was not sure I was interested. The Lord dealt with my heart about dreaming a little bigger. How are we going to reach all the young people that must be touched if we do not use the airwaves? If we don't seize the airwaves and Internet, we are letting the enemy grab all the teens' attention. It was over 10 years ago that I started using TV, and I cannot tell you how many lives have been changed! I have heard stories of teens who were ready to commit suicide, but saw the program and stopped, gave their lives to Jesus, and are now making a huge difference for God! Find out how God wants to use the media in your dream (even if it is as simple as a Web page for your youth ministry so your kids can stay updated).

HOW WILL I INVOLVE THE PARENTS OF MY TEENS?

Your dream needs to include how you are going to engage the parents of your teens. You need to make them feel a part of what you are doing with their kids. Pull them into the vision. Meet with them regularly. Give them the notes on your sermon topic for next month. Give them tools to hold their kids accountable. Give them tips for parenting. Give your parents' group a name if you want . . . for example, a youth ministry I know calls themselves "Warriors." The parents are called "Parents of Warriors," or "POW." Whatever you do, don't overlook your parents.

How are we going to reach all the young people that might be touched if we do not use the airwaves?

HOW WILL I CAPTURE THE HEART OF MY PASTOR AND LAYPEOPLE?

Part of your dream should cover how you are going to keep your pastor and laypeople engaged. You don't want to be doing this vision in another time warp. You need your pastor to be your biggest cheerleader. You need all the laypeople praying for you, giving large offerings to all the initiatives you are dreaming of, and volunteering to help. You must think of all the ways you will keep them informed of what's going on. You want to give them more than just information, you want to make part of your mission *to get them to love teens just as much as you do.* This is not one sermon, or one video clip. This is regular face time with them in front of the church, handouts, and finding ways for the group of teens to regularly serve the laypeople. You want to be very visible.

One practical thing you can do is to have the adults in your church go through the *Battle Cry for a Generation* book and study guide. (Go to **www.battlecry.com** to order the book.) This will shock them and open their hearts for the battle for a young generation. It will help them to see how they can be part of the answer. The study guide encourages accountability and can be a strategic tool to get the whole congregation on your side. Make it an aim to get 10 percent, then 20 percent, then 50 percent of your church to go through it, so you will have an army of church members who are fully engaged in helping you to rescue a generation and find a way to plug into your vision.

AT THE END OF MY LIFE, WHAT WOULD I FEEL TERRIBLE ABOUT LEAVING UNDONE?

This is a little broader question. When you consider your dream, what is the one thing—if I never do it—that will make me feel like I totally blew it. One of the ways that God speaks to us is through convictions. He puts a conviction inside of you that you have to reach a certain group of kids, and if you don't live up to that thing you will feel like you have failed. Identify some of those convictions. For example, it might be "If I don't start an outreach for the down-and-out kids, whatever it may be, I'll feel terrible." Identify what are some of the convictions by asking yourself, *if I don't do them, how will I feel at the end of my life?* Terrible? Then you better do that thing.

There is a difference between *good ideas* and *"must-haves."* In your dream you will have a lot of great ideas; you will also have some you know you *must* do. Make a list and ask the Lord to help you define how much of it is *must-do* and which part of it is *a pretty good idea*. Which is good, and which is God?

When Katie and I started we felt a conviction to reach out to young people but I also felt a conviction to reach the people of the world through missions. I was frustrated because I didn't know how it could all happen. Sometimes you have to wrestle with God like Jacob did. Too many of us spend a total of five minutes daydreaming, asking God to handle it, and then we can't figure out why it doesn't

Just because God's behind a vision doesn't mean He doesn't want you to do the grunt work.

happen. Instead, you need to wrestle and pray and wrestle and pray for an understanding for priorities. We are talking about your destiny here, the reason you were born. We are talking about reaching a generation here. Surely it is worth wrestling over for a season!

I remember talking to Rich Mullins about his song "Awesome God." I asked him how he wrote that song. I assumed he had a great quiet time and there he was with God and his Bible and he was in worship, maybe with a piano, and God just spoke and glory filled the room and it was awesome. I wanted to know what happened and how God spoke to him. After thinking he said, "It was just a lot of hard work." At the time, I thought that was kind of unspiritual, but it isn't. Isn't it interesting that *something that takes a lot of hard work ends up being incredibly anointed?* So it will be with your dream. Just because you are working hard on it, does not mean you are trying to do it in the flesh. Now a whole generation has sung Rich's song in worship and it's become a classic.

Just because God's behind a vision doesn't mean He doesn't want you to do the grunt work. God wants to *know how bad you want it,* how hard you are willing to work, how hungry you are, etc. Will you pray and stay on your face?

Before we started Teen Mania, I had to wrestle with God about young people, missions, and how the two could possibly be connected. Finally I told Him I would get on the floor right there in my little loft area on my knees and I was not moving until I heard from Him. I decided that I was not going to go through my whole life wishing I had done something else. I could not figure out how these two could go together. I didn't want to go get another "job"—

tread water for a while—then hope to do the dream He'd called me to later. And there is something about that level of seriousness that lets God say, "Okay, now you are ready to hear." That is when He breathed into me the dream of Teen Mania. It had never occurred to me before, but He wanted us to *raise up an army of young people to love God like crazy and give them a chance to go and change the world.*

I think we need a generation of leaders who are dreamers that won't be stopped, no matter what. If we don't dream it first, there is no way we will do it. What a tragedy for us to hold God's hand back from what He wants to do with young people all because we dare not dream big enough.

I would encourage you to do what Mary did in Luke 2:19 when the angel Gabriel told her she would be pregnant: Mary cherished these things and treasured them up in her heart.

Some of the things that God wishes for you, you are just going to have to cherish them between you and God. Keep reminding Him that you know it's in there and that He spoke it to you. Other people may still not understand, but you and God cherish your dreams together. Don't start proclaiming parts of your dream from the mountaintops yet. As your dream matures, there is a very clear and diplomatic and well-thought-through way to introduce your dream to people that will make them want to participate.

If we don't dream it first, there is no way we will do it.

God will breathe His dreams into your heart and then you will go and walk those things out; this is the adventurous life of a Youth Specialist!

Later, we'll spend time developing and refining and putting some teeth to your dream.

I encourage you to start the dreaming process. Write down everything that comes to your mind, crossing out things that do not really matter, things that are nice to have but are not imperative. Begin to do this and you are on your way to stepping into a whole new realm of life. God will breathe His dreams into your heart and then you will go and walk those things out; this is the adventurous life of a Youth Specialist!

I want to encourage you to build some time into your schedule to look at your dream again and begin to refine it. Go back to your computer now and open the CD-ROM file titled "Find Your Dream." Take all the time you need to build your vision here. This is important; don't let anything interrupt you. We cannot continue doing the same thing we have always done. We cannot get consumed with lots of "youth ministry activities" that have no purpose.

God's way of advancing His kingdom is putting a dream in the heart of His leaders, and bringing people alongside to help implement that dream. Now go be that leader!

1. Daniel L. Weiss, "The Online Life of Teenagers," Citizen Link, Focus on Social Issues (August 11, 2005), http://www.family.org/cforum/fosi/pornography/facts/a0026839.cfm (accessed October 26, 2005).

Notes

CHAPTER SEVEN

Bold Pursuit
of the Dream

The sad fact is that too many youth pastors (and pastors, for that matter) do not have a dream. They plod on day after day struggling to stay a step ahead of what they will preach next week. Dreaming is work and quickly makes us weary. Yet without one, we find ourselves pedaling faster and faster just to keep up. In time, we burn out (maybe this is a reason for so much turnover among youth workers). Then we either get out of the ministry or we complain, "Man, that pastor worked me too hard!"

Since you are still reading this, I am confident that this doesn't describe you and, hopefully, you're doing the dreaming exercises. Now that you have tapped into God's big vision for your life and youth ministry, what comes next? Well, prepare yourself for some opposition. Once a

Prepare yourself for some opposition.

Youth Specialist starts seeking God's *big, far-reaching, and amazing* vision, the devil lines up troops for battle. Why? He has had a stronghold on this generation for a long time and suddenly you have drawn them to the kingdom of God. Now you're treading in his territory. Do you think the devil will take this lying down?

Look at the example of Daniel's story. He set out to follow God more closely, and an angel explained to him exactly what happened when he set this godly course:

> *"Do not be afraid, Daniel. Since the first day that you set your mind to gain understanding and to humble yourself before your God, your words were heard, and I have come in response to them. But the prince of the Persian kingdom resisted me twenty-one days. Then Michael, one of the chief princes, came to help me, because I was detained there with the king of Persia."*
>
> —Daniel 10:12–13

When one of you steps up to be a general in this battle for our youth, your resolve is known immediately in heaven. And just as quickly, the devil responds by sending his generals to oppose you on the spiritual front.

Opposition may also come from within—people may dismiss you as just a dreamer. I often heard that in the early days of Teen Mania, and I still hear it in some circles today. People refuse to believe how many kids are willing to take their faith seriously and how many kids we can attract to conventions or send on missions.

Whether from the enemy without or doubters within, *do* expect opposition. *Don't* expect it will be a walk in the park. How, then, do you boldly overcome opposition? Let's look at Joshua's example of leadership.

JOSHUA'S BOLDNESS

Boldness comes from a gut-level conviction that your dream is a mandate from God. It's not just a whim or man-made hope. When you encounter opposition you need to be certain that *this is from the heart of God, this is right, this is real, and this is where we are supposed to go.*

You will recall that Moses too had a dream from God which he shared with the Israelites—the promised land. He sent 12 men to spy out the land and 10 of them ridiculed the dream: it was too dangerous—after all, there were giants! As a result of their lack of faith and boldness, not one of those guys entered the promised land. After Moses' death, Joshua took over the leadership of Israel. You could call him the next youth minister! He did not shrink from fearlessly leading his group to possess the land.

When one of you steps up to be a general in this battle for our youth, your resolve is known immediately in heaven. And just as quickly, the devil responds by sending his generals to oppose you on the spiritual front.

Just because you have a huge dream doesn't mean that you don't have a reason to be terrified!

Wherever you step out. What was the dream? Joshua was only promised the land that he stepped on. He had to go forward in faith.

> *I will give you every place where you set your foot, as I promised Moses. Your territory will extend from the desert to Lebanon, and from the great river, the Euphrates—all the Hittite country—to the Great Sea on the west. No one will be able to stand up against you all the days of your life. As I was with Moses, so I will be with you; I will never leave you nor forsake you.*
>
> —Joshua 1:3–5

The proper frame of mind. In verse 6, God tells Joshua, "Be strong and courageous." In verse 7, He says, "Be strong and very courageous." Verse 9: "Be strong and courageous. Do not be terrified; do not be discouraged, for the LORD your God will be with you wherever you go."

Are you starting to see a pattern? *Be strong and courageous.* It is one thing for God to repeat Himself once, but three or four times? Obviously, it was important to reassure Joshua. Did Joshua have a reason to be terrified? Of course he did. This was a land of giants!

Just because you have a huge dream doesn't mean that you don't have a reason to be terrified! Huge dreams are formidable. You want four-color brochures instead of

Xerox copies; that's huge! You want buses and vans, video projectors, and your own local television program on every night of the week! All this looks as daunting as a whole tribe of giants!

I want you to pay attention to something here. God wasn't merely comforting Joshua. He wasn't saying, "Oh, Joshua, I just want to encourage you; you can do it!" No, He said, "Be strong, I am commanding you!" This was not an option; it was a *choice God expected Joshua to make.* In other words, even when you don't feel like it, you'd better be strong, and you'd better be courageous! Why? "Because I am counting on you, Joshua. These people are counting on you. There is a dream and a vision and unless you are bold and courageous, it will not happen." God was counting on His man to be bold so the dream could be fulfilled.

A giant step of faith and boldness. Nine years ago when Teen Mania first moved to Texas, we had been at our headquarters in Tulsa for 10 years renting different offices. When we outgrew one, we would rent another. We owned a couple of vans, but never anything of great value. I would look at churches with big buildings and marvel at the cost and fundraising involved.

Then God put the idea of a permanent headquarters into my heart. I realized we were wasting a lot of money renting things. This was most obvious at a hotel in Miami. Every year we'd pay them a lot of money to stay with them, and then the next year we'd come back and they had renovated their lobby. We began to think that we had a ministry of renovating hotel lobbies all over Miami. I knew it would be much better stewardship to build a place for the kingdom of God where kids could get trained. So we

The tragedy is that too many look at the giants and miss God standing big behind them.

began to search the country and finally found a suitable place in Garden Valley, Texas. But it cost over a million dollars! How do you raise a million dollars in youth ministry? It was overwhelming.

The tragedy is that too many look at the giants and miss God standing big behind them. The truth is, *if there are no giants in your dream, your dream is not big enough.* God has never called us to do something that is *possible.* God wants to do it, not you. Know your dream and be courageous about it. Don't let the giants intimidate you!

Put your foot in the water! Joshua had an unshakable conviction—"If God is for us, who can be against us?" Imagine Joshua that day they marched in to take possession of the promised land. He ordered the priests with the ark of the covenant to march to the edge of the river and *put their feet in the water.* They didn't yell to God, "Roll back the river first! Then we will walk through!" They put their feet in the water first, *and then* the river rolled back. Do you have that kind of faith? Be daring enough to say that you're going to double or triple the size of your youth group and change the world! If you don't have the faith to step out into the water, it will never roll back.

Roll up your sleeves and get busy. Here is the other side of that coin. Many people, once they conceive their dream, sit back and wait for the Lord to make it happen. They're so convinced He'll step in that they take no action themselves. Well, maybe He's waiting for you!

God's plan is to partner with mankind. He is the source of all power, but *He does it with us,* not without us. Your job is not to sit idly by and wait for God to do something great while your dreams flounder and go unrealized. It's to roll up your sleeves, pick up the task, and labor alongside God to bring those dreams to fruition. Get your hands dirty!

Too many people simply talk about the great plans they have for the future. These people will likely fail to touch the people they were meant to reach. Do you know why? Because they were not willing to sweat.

> *Remember the command that Moses the servant of the Lord gave you: "The Lord your God is giving you rest and has granted you this land. Your wives, your children and your livestock may stay in the land that Moses gave you east of the Jordan, but all your fighting men, fully armed, must cross over ahead of your brothers. You are to help your brothers until the Lord gives them rest, as he has done for you, and until they too have taken possession of the land that the Lord your God is giving them."*
>
> —Joshua 1:13–15

The divine partnership. Isn't that interesting? Scripture says, "Until they too have taken possession of the land that the LORD your God is giving them." It sounds like an

God's plan is to partner with mankind.

Partnership with God means accepting the dream He gives you, and going after it with all your strength.

oxymoron. They are *taking possession* but *God is giving it to them.* In other words, they didn't just walk in and the armies fell down; they had to fight and take it.

Roll up your sleeves! If you want your dream, you'd better be willing to fight for it. Get ready to sweat! You may even bleed a little bit. You're not involved with youth ministry because you want a vacation. I know that most of you are already sweating and caring and staying up late nights with kids. You're willing to work.

So get ready to work. Don't sit around waiting for God to make a miracle. Partnership with God means accepting the dream He gives you, and going after it with all your strength.

Jesus displayed the same picture of partnership. This partnership can be seen in Jesus' ministry as well. When Jesus fed the crowd of 5,000, He made His disciples do all the footwork. Jesus told them to seat the crowd in groups of 50 (I'm sure they felt very honored to get that job), and He told them to distribute loaves and fish to everyone.

After the picnic, Jesus told them to clean up the leftovers as well. That's when they realized they had played a part in Jesus' miracle.

Here's the point. Couldn't Jesus just have rained fish and loaves right down into the crowd's hands? He is, after all, the Son of God. He could have saved the disciples a lot of work. Instead He chose to use *their sweat and labor to accomplish the miracle.* God doesn't want to do the work alone; He wants to partner with us.

Little by little. Moses described to the Israelites what would happen when they went into the promised land:

> When the LORD your God brings you into the land you are entering to possess and drives out before you many nations—the Hittites, Girgashites, Amorites, Canaanites, Perizzites, Hivites and Jebusites, seven nations larger and stronger than you—and when the LORD your God has delivered them over to you and you have defeated them, then you must destroy them totally.
>
> —Deuteronomy 7:1–2

Here's that same paradox again: the *Lord* will *deliver them to you* but *you still have to defeat them.* He is delivering, but we are defeating. It's still a partnership thing.

Look at another truth that comes out a few verses later:

> The Lord your God will drive out those nations before you, little by little. You will not be allowed to eliminate them all at once, or the wild animals will multiply around you. But the Lord your God will deliver them over to you, throwing them into great confusion until they are destroyed.
>
> —Deuteronomy 7:22–23

> If a dream is really from God, we need to set our faces like flint and realize that we are going to have to knock down doors, endure some discomfort, and persevere until the job is done!

He is speaking of *persistence*. Notice it says "little by little." The Israelites were very excited about the dream of entering the promised land—they had been waiting for 40 years! But here God warns them it isn't going to happen overnight. How often do we receive a vision, work hard at it for three weeks, then decide that it wasn't God after all and give up? Then a month later we get excited about something else only to abandon that dream when it doesn't come to pass right away.

If a dream is really from God, we need to set our faces like flint and realize that we are going to have to knock down doors, endure some discomfort, and persevere until the job is done! Resist the feeling of frustration when you don't accomplish your goals at once! God knows what He is doing. If you went in and took the whole land at once, unseen wild animals may gather round and devour you and your flock. God's timing is perfect.

If God withholds part of our dream, we can trust that it is for our own good. I remember many times when, if we could have seen the entire scope of His plan, we would have been too intimidated to take a step forward! Our decision to move ahead with the purchase of the property for a big campus was one of those times.

The property needed some work—it didn't have enough buildings, the dorm was barely big enough for the interns, and the office needed to be gutted. It wasn't everything we thought we needed, but it was enough. So, in faith, we made a down payment on the $1 million and moved in. Quickly, we began to raise money to develop and expand the facilities. Once again, God showed up and did more than anything we could have imagined in "our plan." Now, nine years later, we have put nearly $30 million into the grounds.

The point of this story is that if God had revealed all the details of His plan for our headquarters right at the start, it would have been too overwhelming. We would have said no way and headed in a different direction. But when God fills in His vision little by little, it "chases out the wild animals" and makes it less intimidating. (Actually, we had to literally drive out wild animals too! There were red ants everywhere!) So, be willing to let your dream fill in little by little. Make the most strategic use of each step of the way.

That is exactly what the next section of this book will help you accomplish. It's time to plan!

Notes

Plan It!

CHAPTER EIGHT

Plan to Turn Your Dreams into Reality

I haven't always been the kind of planner that I am now. In the early days of ministry, I was much more focused on the end result (seeing people's lives transformed by the power of God) than on how to get there. Does that ring true for you too? I know we all want to be flexible, creative, and open to the leading of the Holy Spirit. But can't the Spirit just as easily lead you in advance so that you can better plan how it should be done? Of course! There are many good reasons to plan.

WHY PLAN?

God is a planner. Do you think God created the universe without thinking it through first? Do you think He

You may dream big, but you'll never *do* something big unless you have a plan to get there.

creates any one of us on a spur-of-the-moment whim? Somehow, I never really thought that God planned ahead. He does, in fact. We saw in Chapter 2 that God planned Jeremiah's ministry before he was even born (Jer. 1:5). Revelation 13:8 says that before the foundation of the world, Jesus Christ was crucified. *Now that is planning in advance!* Let's give up excuses about our lack of planning and take a giant step toward becoming more like God. God is a planner.

You'll never do something big without a plan. You may dream big, but you'll never *do* something big unless you have a plan to get there. Too many people never realize their big dreams because they never make a big plan. Their unrealized dreams are a source of never-ending frustration.

God has blessed us here at Teen Mania. We just had our first teen stadium event with 73,000 people. We've expanded the number of buildings on our campus. Our intern program and global missions have grown. This is absolutely a sign of God's grace, but a lot of people also worked, sweated, and planned those things for years to make them happen.

Again, we see the synergy of God's favor and your labor (in this case, planning labor). Few youth pastors are lazy. You're willing to work hard—but are you willing to do the right kind of work? Are you willing to plan when no one is cheering you on? This is the work of a leader.

It turns your dreams into reality. As great as dreams are, it's even greater to see them turned into reality. Dreams that stay dreams soon become regrets. God has sparked huge ideas in your heart! Plan them into reality.

It makes your dream seem possible and believable. When you plan, dreams become realistic. Planning shows what steps you have to take for the dream to become reality. Some of you may argue that you already have it laid out in your head. That's not enough! Not only do *you* need to know your plan, your people need to see how your dream may be possible. The plan—the vision—is for your kids, the people in your church, your pastor, and your adult volunteers. They need to know that you are not just carried along by a pie-in-the-sky whim. They need to think your dream is doable, and a step-by-step process shows them that. As you plan with them, talk through the process you've envisioned. Suddenly, they will begin to say, "You know what? We really can do this!" *As you plan, it makes the dream believable.*

I am not really a natural planner or a natural leader. But I learned that planning is the work of a leader. It won't bring you glory and most people will never see it, but that is what a leader does. Planning is how a leader becomes productive. One day, people will look at you and say,

Dreams that stay dreams soon become regrets.

DOUBLED IN SIZE

Our youth group exploded! We doubled in size in one year by following the teachings in [*Revolution YM*].

—John, Youth Specialist

"Wow! You are reaching a lot of kids," and they'll think you're a really terrific leader because of what they see. You'll know it was the planning in advance that made it possible to reach all those students, not what happened up on stage. Don't feel bad if you are not a natural leader or planner. I learned it and so can you!

HOW TO PLAN

Step 1: The Mission Statement

What is it and why do I need one? Every world-class organization has a mission statement. A mission statement is a one- or two-sentence synopsis of your goals. It clarifies your dream and focuses people on the real aim of your ministry. Here are some characteristics of a good mission statement:

- **It's short.** Take your dream and turn it into a two-sentence piece of fire. It is a high-impact synopsis of what is burning within you.

- **It's fun to say.** Make sure your mission statement rolls off the tongue. The result is that every time anyone says it, they get fired up about your dream. It should make you feel exhilarated: "Yahoo! I am glad I am doing this!"

- **It's specific.** It should be unique to your vision. It's too general to say, "We want to reach teens." It should say something about what kids you want to reach, how you want to reach them, and what you want to *see them become.*

Assemble the thoughts you want to include in your mission statement, then refine them to include only the most important ones. Wordsmith those ideas so they're concise and meaningful. You're building your whole plan on this statement; it's worth getting it right. Take your dream, boil it down, and then boil it down again to a few potent words.

Involve your pastor in the process to make sure your mission statement is in line with the mission statement of the church (or at least doesn't contradict). Some may say that you should ask your kids what the mission statement should be. No! That is why *you* are the leader. The leader goes to God and says, "God, what is your vision?" Then the leader brings it to his kids, saying, "This is what God has called us to." Moses didn't ask for the Israelites' input on the Ten Commandments or whether they should really head for the promised land.

Too many youth ministries have been run that way. Does that mean you should never seek input from

Take your dream, boil it down, and then boil it down again to a few potent words.

students? No. You frequently seek their input, but you *don't let them drive who you are, your mission, or your purpose!* You can get input from them later in the planning process on *how* to do certain parts of the vision, but *what* the vision is must come from you the leader, as God lays it on your heart.

How do you use your mission statement?

Put it everywhere. Since this statement describes your heart and ministry you will want to put it on everything. Put it on your business cards (if you don't have cards you should make some). Put it on the banner behind your stage in the youth room. Put it on T-shirts, so everybody understands who you are and what you're all about. Use it every chance you get.

Clarify identity. Why is a mission statement so important? The group gains its identity from a mission statement. They already know the group name; the statement tells what the name represents. For example, if your name is *Wildfire,* and everywhere they see the logo for *Wildfire* they see the mission statement, there is an instant burst of understanding. When they read, "*Wildfire* stands for _____!" they'll instantly be reminded of who they are.

Line everything up with it. Now use your mission statement to evaluate everything you do in your youth ministry. Anything you do must line up with your mission statement. After all, this is the pulse of what is beating inside of you. You must not waste your efforts on any activity, retreat, conference, concert, or camp that comes outside the span of this mission statement. Harness all your efforts to it.

One of the reasons you are so busy is that *you do so*

many things that have nothing to do with your purpose. Yes, they are good activities, but if they don't move your purpose forward, they need to be stopped (at least some of them). Otherwise, they'll distract you from doing God's specific work. A mission statement should become the litmus test for all your youth ministry plans. Everything you do must pass or it shouldn't become part of your youth program.

Bring purpose to every worker. Every teen who attends your group should know your mission statement. They should be able to see *how every activity fits into the mission.* At Teen Mania, everybody knows the mission statement:

> *Our Heartbeat is . . . to provoke a young generation to passionately pursue Jesus Christ and to take His life-giving message to the ends of the earth!*

Every intern and staff member here is a part of this—if you ever come here, stop and ask any one of them. Each person understands how his or her job is connected to the mission. The guy mowing the lawn is more than just mowing the lawn—he's providing an environment of first-class excellence to help bring the life-giving message of Jesus to the ends of the earth.

If people don't feel part of something big, or see how their job fits into the mission statement, then they have very low motivation. At Teen Mania, kids don't just lick stamps. They realize they are helping to reach every kid in the country, so they get excited about their part of

A mission statement should become the litmus test for all your youth ministry plans.

Kids want to belong to something, and a mission statement helps them to belong to the ministry God has given you.

the outreach! The mission statement fuels them. It brings them identity! Kids want to belong to something, and a mission statement helps them to belong to the ministry God has given you.

Just about every secular company has some type of mission or vision statement:

- The goal of Robert Woodruff, President of Coca-Cola, is to have "every person in the world taste Coca-Cola."
- Wal-Mart wants "to give ordinary folk the chance to buy the same things as rich people."[1]
- 3M aims "to solve unsolved problems innovatively."[2]
- In the early 1900s, the Ford Motor Company set out to "democratize the automobile."[3]

The challenge for Christians is to meet or surpass their vision and purpose.

Your mission statement needs to be narrow enough to define who you are, but broad enough not to limit you. A mission statement should define exactly who you are. For example, Disney's mission statement doesn't say, "We want to make great cartoons." It says they want to "make people happy" through "creativity, dreams, and imagination."[4] They started with cartoons, but then expanded into Disneyland, Disney World, and other media which provide entertainment.

Let me give you some examples from a few youth ministries:

- *3-D Ministry in Norman, Oklahoma:*
  "We exist to direct young people of the Norman area to discover their identity in Christ Jesus, to develop a life-changing relationship with Him, and to demonstrate a life of integrity to others."
- *Upper Room Fellowship in Maryland:*
  "Our youth ministry department exists to glorify God through worship, serve Him through ministry, serve His world through evangelism, and strengthen others in Christ through fellowship and developing our faith in Christ through discipleship."
- *North Bay Christian Center in Mobile, Alabama:*
  "Somewhere to go, someone to know, something to do."

Stop now and go to the CD-ROM file titled "Why Plan" and start writing and refining your own mission statement. Teen Mania's mission statement is given as an example to help you. This is the beginning of the planning stage. It is the foundation for everything else.

Your mission statement needs to be narrow enough to define who you are, but broad enough not to limit you.

Core values steer your culture. When you don't develop your own core values, you have a culture that is made up of values from somewhere else.

Step 2: Core Values

The personality of your ministry. Your mission statement and core values are the two pillars that you build your ministry upon. They work in tandem. The mission statement declares *what* you are going to do, while your core values decide *how* you are going to do it. How you are going to carry yourself as you do those things? The core values are your ministry's character.

But what does that have to do with youth groups? Because you have a distinct culture in your youth group. In other words, what is the normal way that your kids act with each other? That is your *corporate culture,* or your youth group culture.

Core values steer your culture. When you don't develop your own core values, you have a culture that is made up of values from somewhere else. You get it by default. Core values describe how you act.

Why is this so important? Let me tell you why by using the example of Teen Mania. Teen Mania used to be a place where people didn't like to work (including me). Our corporate culture was terrible. I couldn't figure out how to make it better, but I knew we needed to do something. So we identified five core values: Faith, Relationships, Vision, Excellence, and Integrity. We wanted these words—and the actions associated with them—to describe our every action. You might point out that the Bible sums up your group's core values. Yes, but the danger there is that the Bible is so full of truth that without a specific focus you may end up doing none of it. With core values, we were saying that *in our ministry we choose to place value on these five things* (or eight, six, three, in your case). We want to emphasize *these* traits.

How to use core values. Once you have developed your mission statement, you will rally your leaders and your group to that cause and pursue it resolutely. Your core values will dictate how you accomplish your mission, steering you and all the others within your ministry. Core values say, "We value this behavior so much that we will abide by these things, no matter what."

How to create core values. You may wonder how to create core values for your group. I would look to the group itself and discern some of the biggest challenges that you have. Are your kids always putting down one another? Then maybe a core value needs to be, "We will encourage and lift each other up." Adopt this as a core value and have

Your core values will dictate how you accomplish your mission.

Planning is the work of a leader; it's your desk time that makes what is up front valid and credible.

the members of your group sign an agreement to abide by this value. Another challenge might be your teens' disobedience and not respecting leadership. So a core value could be, "We will honor our leaders." If you value honesty, you may create a core value that says, "We will act with integrity." Define the nature and the character of your group through the values you declare important.

Distribute them. Once you've adopted your core values, print and distribute them. Put them on mouse pads, plaques, and shirts. Just like your mission statement, you want these to be at the front of everyone's consciousness.

The real power of core values. The real power begins when you plant these values into the hearts of your students. It will become an attitude. You probably don't even want to call them core values. You could call them something like: the "Five Fighting Points of a World Changer;" or if your group is called *Wildfire,* "Five Wild Points of Wildfire," etc. You are telling students: "This is our code; this is the way we live; this is our identity."

Core values create corporate culture. Ultimately, after you have talked about it many times, shown them examples, passed out the cards, and made up the shirts, this mentality *will* take hold. You make an agreement that if someone goes against your core values, anyone can call him or her on it. You should even give them permission to call you on it, if they think you're in violation. (I've done just that here at Teen Mania. Any intern can confront me, or any member of the staff, if they think we're not living up to the code.)

You must find creative ways to keep these core values visible. Remind students again and again. What will ultimately happen is this: when you are not around, your kids will enforce these values with *each other*. It will happen *without you because it has become a part of the culture*. You won't have to be the code enforcer because they will have taken ownership and grabbed hold of these values for themselves.

When you get that kind of pressure working for you, hallelujah! You are on the right path. You won't have to run the store all the time; the core values will set the atmosphere and direction of the group.

Start planning today. Planning takes patience and perseverance, and, quite truthfully, it isn't always very exciting. The fruit of planning, however, is awesome! Planning is the work of a leader; it's your desk time that makes what is up front valid and credible.

Read over the notes you made about your dreams for your group so that they are fresh in your mind. Then open the CD-ROM again to the "Why Plan" section and begin to work on your core values.

Pray for God's guidance as you develop these two pillars, your mission statement and core values, for your ministry. Start doing the silent work of a leader.

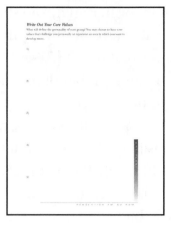

1. "Sample Mission Statements for Inspiration," Family Business Experts, http://www.family-business-experts.com/sample-mission-statements.html (accessed October 26, 2005).
2. Ibid.
3. Ibid.
4. Ibid.

CHAPTER NINE

BHAGs: Defining Them and Going for It!

There is a cancer in youth ministry that has plagued us for a long time. It's the idea of *feeling holy when you are faithful with a few*. What a tragedy to have the potential within us to do something that affects hundreds (or even thousands) for the Kingdom and not tap into it!

Our "holy, faithful" folks grieve me because everything I see in the Bible tells me this: when God's favor is upon a thing, it grows. If a ministry is alive with His Spirit, it thrives and flourishes. If we haven't figured out how to grow it, maybe it just means we haven't found the right nutrients. Certainly, it doesn't mean the ministry isn't *supposed* to grow.

When God's favor is upon a thing, it grows. If a ministry is alive with His Spirit, it thrives and flourishes.

It isn't a pride issue. It's just that God cares about kids—all kids. And when you start reaching a lot of them, they add up.

Some may say, "Well I have tried everything and I still have 10 students in my group, so God must not want me to grow." That person is in danger of *letting his experience dictate his theology, rather than God's Word.* Maybe he has just not tried the *right* things yet. Therefore, a part of your whole planning process is to attack the attitude that says you can't do it, that you aren't supposed to reach a lot of teens.

Once you've created your mission statement and determined your core values, the next step in the process is to develop some BHAGs, Big Holy Anointed Goals (or, as some like to say, Big Hairy Audacious Goals).

WHAT ARE BHAGS (PRONOUNCED BEEHAGS)?

A study was conducted of successful companies to identify a number of things that these companies had in common. One thing very clearly set them apart from all others: every single one of them had huge goals. They didn't settle for five or ten percent growth in a year. Instead, they set the bar much higher. As they planned and pursued that giant goal, they grew exponentially. What a shame that secular companies can dream more than many leaders in the Body of Christ.

Take NASA, for example. In 1960, John F. Kennedy announced his intention to put a man on the moon by the end of the decade. That goal seemed bigger than life. Not quite impossible, but stunning to think that maybe we could just do it! Money poured in. The nation rallied around its president and its rocket scientists—and the first rocket launched from the pad! Then another and another. Each one took on a bit more adventure, a bit more of the space between Earth and moon. Then, in 1969, Neil Armstrong finally took "one small step for man, one giant leap for mankind." President Kennedy was long buried, but he had given the nation a tangible dream. The nation responded with hard work and success.

BHAGs galvanize the dream. They are a statement of the faith of the leader. BHAGs don't seem possible in the natural, but they don't seem completely off the map either. They may not seem reasonable at first, but they are not irrational in scope. If President Kennedy had said, "Let's put a man on every planet in the solar system," people would not have supported that. But they could grasp the possibility of the moon. Tough to believe, but within the realm of possibility. So, your BHAG could not be "We'll have a million kids in this youth group by the end of the year." Okay, it *could* happen . . . but most people will think it's ludicrous. This doesn't mean, however, that you shouldn't have BHAGs that *seem impossible, but just might be attainable.*

BHAGs don't seem possible in the natural, but they don't seem completely off the map either.

Andy Grove, former CEO of Intel Corporation, had what some people thought was a "crazy" goal. He wanted to double the speed of the computer chip every 18 months. The company has done it, and they keep beating that 18-month time frame.[1] Most big companies like Intel have a few huge, looming goals that say: "Just take aim at this!" Those somewhat outrageous goals pull everybody together to focus on getting great things done.

STEP 1:
TIME TO DEVELOP YOUR BHAGS

Now is the time to take your dream and put some meat on the bones. It is time to start putting specific goals for the first year of ministry on the table. Where do you want to be in one year? Two years? Three years? Five years? Can you dare to dream as big as God dreams and set some real goals? Can you see your ministry doubling in size in the next 12 months? Can you imagine an amazingly cool youth room? A worship band? Can you imagine doubling again the next year, and again the next? Remember what it says in Ephesians 3:20: "[He] is able to do immeasurably more than all we ask or imagine, according to his power that is at work within us." That means if you can think it, He can do 100 times more than that.

Keep in mind the question we asked during the dreaming process: *If Jesus were the youth leader in my church, what would the group look like in a year? . . . in five years?*

Specifically, how many kids might be here? You dream and then bring that dream into *specific* focus. In other words, a BHAG gives you something concrete to step on as you walk toward your dream. And it is always bigger than what seems possible.

Setting some Big Holy Anointed Goals will crystallize your dream into a very concrete direction. It will show your group and leadership team that you are serious about taking this generation back!

There are three distinct advantages of having BHAGs:

1. BHAGs inspire faith and commitment. Unfortunately, big goals can often discourage people if they are not conveyed in the right ways. I used to announce, "I want three thousand kids on the mission field next year." At the time, we had 500. Naturally, my staff members were immediately discouraged, thinking they would be working 24/7 throughout the next year! If we don't introduce our BHAGs properly, they can be a heavy load to others and hardly inspiring.

Let it not be! BHAGs can inspire great faith, virtually *daring* your faithful workers to believe. And this is a good thing. After all, the kids themselves want to be part of something that's bigger than they are, bigger than life. We want them to say, "This is the most happening thing I have ever seen in my life, and I want to commit every spare minute of my time to it!" Why would a kid ever say that? Because he's identified with the mission statement and the BHAGs connected to it!

Now is the time to take
your dream and put
some meat on the bones.

We must give teens a vision that will capture their attention, their heart, and their energy—or the world will.

One thing to know about commitment: one reason a coach often enjoys more commitment than the "youth guy" is that he gives his players BHAGs from day one. "Guys, I really think we could go to state this year. If we do *this* kind of work, do *this* workout, and run plays like *this,* I really think we could do it." And his players, who hope against hope, begin to believe it too.

We must give teens a vision that will capture their attention, their hearts, and their energy—or the world will.

2. BHAGs define the dream. So you have your dream, and it's sort of "out there." You have all kinds of ideas scratched on paper, and you've refined them with your must-haves (and also a few "nice-to-haves"), but it's still kind of broad. Here's where BHAGs help you focus. They put *numbers* to your dream. Yes, you're going to make a big impact . . . but *how* big?

Here is an example:

1. By the end of this year, I would like to have X number of things happening, with X number of kids.
2. By the end of two years, I would like X kids doing these things.
3. By the end of five years, I would like X churches in our town working together on these X projects.

This gives you a way to evaluate your success. It's hard to know if you're doing things right if you only have a vague goal to grow. A BHAG lets you define what you're trying to accomplish, so you can know whether you're accomplishing it or not.

Just like President Kennedy's specific BHAG inspired a nation, an effective BHAG can make the hair stand up on the back of your neck. It inspires and pulls people together to go after your amazing goal.

3. BHAGs force you to take action. Lots of people find it fairly easy to sit and dream, never putting their names on the line. But is it really better to withhold your name just so no one will ever know whether you accomplished anything or not? Instead, BHAGs proclaim to the world, "This is what I am signing up for, planning for, and working for. This is where we are going."

They force you to get off the sidelines. You don't have to be pretentious about it. Just roll it out and tell folks that you believe with all your heart that this is the dream God has called you to.

If you make that goal—or 80 percent of it—praise God! Look at how much you have grown. If you shoot for the stars and make it to the moon, you did well. It's better than sitting down and just *looking* at the stars.

> An effective BHAG can make the hair stand up on the back of your neck. It inspires and pulls people together to go after your amazing goal.

For years at Teen Mania we've had awesome BHAGs, and we've typically accomplished them at a level of half or three-quarters of the way. But we made it a lot further than we would have had we settled for no big goals at all (or tiny, safe goals).

STEP 2:WHAT WILL IT TAKE?

Make a master list of everything you'll need. I know this doesn't sound like rocket science, but seriously, sit down and ask yourself, "What is it going to take to pull this off?" Then start writing. Once you have your BHAGs clearly laid out, then start writing down *everything* you'll need to accomplish these goals. Everything. Assume the sky's the limit, and money is no object. Your list might begin with things like . . . money. (Be careful here. Some "youth guys" assume that if they just get the money then they'll accomplish their BHAGs. It actually takes a lot more than money to do what you want to do. The best approach is to write down everything you need, and then write out next to each item how much it might cost, if money is a factor.)

- *money*
- *a place to meet*
- *adult volunteers*
- *teen leaders*
- *printed materials*
- *media equipment*
- *transportation plans, buses*
- *supplies of all kinds*
  and on . . . and on . . . and on . . .
     (make this a long list!)

You're putting some legs to your vision by asking yourself: What is every single thing I need, whether it's human or physical stuff, in order to get that BHAG accomplished? Now some of these things might seem completely unattainable, but it doesn't matter at this point; just write them down.

Of course, this list is more than a practical planning tool. It's also a big item on your daily prayer list. You have something to bring before the Lord with an aching heart, lifting your specific petitions to Him—because of the kids who must be reached. Will God fail to respond?

And don't forget: you'll find it much easier to get buy-in from others if you have a tangible need list. After all, you're not the only one who must believe in the dream and the BHAGs. You must have many other people with you to do this, right? So as you introduce your BHAGs and speak enthusiastically about them, be sure to have a thorough and specific answer to the question, "What, exactly, do you need to get this to happen?"

I would encourage you to build the list together with a team of your leaders (or people you would like to become your leaders). This way, *you* set the direction as the leader (with agreement from your pastor), but you get others to buy into the dream since they are a part of thinking through what it will take to get there. When you

You're putting some legs to your vision by asking yourself: What is every single thing I need, whether it's human or physical stuff, in order to get that BHAG accomplished?

tell your key leaders about your dream and its BHAGs, be careful how you word them. Here is something that works well:

"Let me ask you all something. I have been praying and thinking a lot lately, and I feel that God wants to do something HUGE here in our youth ministry. What if God wants us to grow to 200 by the end of the year and have _____(whatever your BHAGs are). What if this were God's plan? What would it take to get there? What would we need to do to be ready for it?"

> *"What if* this is God's plan?"
>
> "Just *what if* God really wants us to have 500 kids here?"
>
> "I'm not saying I heard directly from God. But . . . *what if?"*

Do you see what this little question does? It unlocks their imaginations. "If, just by chance, I actually *have* heard from God, then what do you folks think it would take to get there?" People naturally start brainstorming the possibilities:

"Well, just *if . . .* then we'd need to do *this* and *this* and *that."*

"Really?" you say. "So you think if we did *that* and *that* and *that,* we could attain this BHAG?"

"Yeah, we do."

"Well, then, what else would we need?"

"Maybe we'd need *this* and *this* and *this . . .*"

See how it goes? People start contributing, and they believe the possibilities. And you already have your list, so you can add your own ideas in the conversational gaps.

You're helping them see the believability of the BHAG while maintaining an exhaustive laundry list of everything you think it might take. "So you guys are telling me that if we did this and this and this, we could have 500 kids at the end of the year? Hallelujah! Let's start praying over these things."

You're simply being a wise leader. You don't go to them with all the things on your list and try forcing it through because "God told me." Oh, you'll share a few ideas, of course. But let the church leaders and members come up with their own lists so you can add to it as necessary. You're allowing them to participate in the building of this thing so they'll be there with you as it unfolds.

Go to your computer now and open the CD-ROM file titled "BHAGs," and begin to record some of your big ministry goals in the first section. As you develop those BHAGs (Big Holy Anointed Goals), think about everything it will take to implement those BHAGs and itemize them in the next section. It's very important to spend time with your team praying for these things that will make your ministry successful.

STEP 3: WHAT ARE THE BARRIERS?

You've got the list of what will it take. You've put monetary figures next to each item. Now you pull your team in and talk to them about the opposition.

Write the word BARRIERS at the top of a large sheet of newsprint. Then go for it! You're looking at your BHAGs and you're looking at the list of everything you need; now you write down the things that will try to stop you.

What are the hardest things on your list to acquire? Think long and hard about this together. Try to leave nothing out. Determine to be open, honest, and vulnerable with your team and/or the people working with you. List all the things that are screaming at you, saying, "There's *no* way!"

At first you'll hear only one response: money. Everybody thinks money is the most ferocious BHAG-eating monster. But no, there are a lot of other barriers, and many are much more terrifying than money.

Some more scary barriers: *we need the pastor to buy into youth ministry a lot more.* Or: *we need parents to help us.* And: *we don't even have our own youth facility.*

Write them all down.

Why? So you have something in writing—a "whine list"? No. We write down all the barriers *so we have a target for prayer.*

We can't pretend there are no barriers. We Youth Specialists are like Joshuas heading into the promised land. We know the giants wait there with spears and swords, ready to squash us. But we're going in anyway.

We're taking the land by the power of the Lord. But we won't be ignorant about it. We know what wants to stop us, and we plan accordingly.

Make a point of writing down the areas that you can see no possible way to get around. Once you have all the barriers listed you can ask your leaders, "So, if we can find a way through these barriers, we can accomplish these BHAGs?" Then when they give their agreement, it is time to attack!

You can prepare for this meeting with your team by preparing ahead of time. Anticipate some of the barriers they will suggest and record them in "Step Three" of your CD-ROM file "BHAGs." Remember, the purpose of this list is to have a target for prayer!

Lift up those barriers and attack them, one by one. Dealing with barriers is how you unlock ideas. Let's assume you've used a meeting—or several meetings—to list all your barriers. The next time you get together, you'll say, "Let's take this single barrier, right here: *transportation*. We're going to *attack* this thing! We're going to take one hour and we're not talking about anything but this. Ready?"

Then let the ideas flow—no limits, no hindrances, no

Dealing with barriers is how you unlock ideas.

boundaries on creativity. You're looking for the one brilliant concept that will (immediately or eventually) make that barrier go away.

It's not exactly brainstorming. You don't say: *What about this? Have we tried that? Oh, that doesn't work.*

No. You attack it. In other words, you take all the reasons that you think you can't beat that thing and you list them all out. And you force onto the table every idea on how to deal with transportation. Get them all out there without judging any of them. We could try this, we could try this, we could try this . . . let the process go to the end. The very end. Go until you've got a big list of possible solutions and don't dismiss a single one.

Now look at all the different possible scenarios and start producing what I call *brain sweat.* You're forcing your brain to attack something that seems impossible to resolve. It will feel as if you're pounding a brick wall and there's no way through. You're pounding and pounding, and forcing your brain to attack instead of saying, "There's no way."

In my experience, something amazing happens then, though it may take several hours, or even several days. At some point, someone will suddenly say, *"You know what? If we did this . . ."* and—eureka! The solution suddenly emerges! I can't tell you how many times we've been in the middle of our planning meetings, and in the midst of a brutal attack on a barrier—when we're all becoming thoroughly fatigued and frustrated—there it is. The breakthrough.

It's been a puzzle, and the pieces suddenly fit together. And maybe it doesn't take any money after all!

Most often, you don't need money as much as you need *ideas* from people who know how to work the creative minds God has given them. (Of course, if you really do need money, gather those folks to you. Who better to help you crash that barrier?)

Breakthrough ideas. These are what you are hunting for. One golden idea could be worth a million souls or a million dollars. People think they need dollars, but they are wrong. They need ideas from heaven that will inspire people and change lives!

Breakthrough ideas unlock solutions. Wow. Those are the ideas that carry you through from dreams to action, traversing all the steps in between.

Not every idea is a golden idea, but when you get one, it could mean a lot of fruit for the kingdom of God. The key is to attack barriers *one by one.* You can't hit them all at once. But if you prioritize and clear away the ones that have annoyed you the longest, you'll have some breakthrough ideas staring you in the face as a result.

Yes, it's hard work. You've got to wrestle and you've got to sweat. But in the end, through the *people* God gives you, God will give you the *ideas,* too.

WHO'S THE REAL COMPETITION?

As you think through your BHAGs, here's a wonderful and quite relevant passage of Scripture to keep in mind—

Jesus and his disciples went out into the Judean

> One golden idea could be worth a million souls or a million dollars.

countryside, where he spent some time with them, and baptized. Now John also was baptizing at Aenon near Salim, because there was plenty of water, and people were constantly coming to be baptized. (This was before John was put in prison.) An argument developed between some of John's disciples and a certain Jew over the matter of ceremonial washing. They came to John and said to him, "Rabbi, that man who was with you on the other side of the Jordan—the one you testified about—well, he is baptizing, and everyone is going to him."

To this John replied, "A man can receive only what is given him from heaven. You yourselves can testify that I said, 'I am not the Christ but am sent ahead of him.' The bride belongs to the bridegroom. The friend who attends the bridegroom waits and listens for him, and is full of joy when he hears the bridegroom's voice. That joy is mine, and it is now complete. He must become greater; I must become less."

—John 3:22–30

John's disciples had a strange complaint: "Jesus is baptizing and gaining more followers than you are, John!" Did John take up a competitive spirit? (This happens all the time in youth ministry.)

As you develop your BHAGs, keep reminding yourself that it's not about having a *bigger* group than the guy down the street or in the next city. It's about beating our real competition, the devil and all of the millions he's trying to pull into his kingdom with MTV, Hollywood, and Grand Theft Auto video games. That is who our enemy is. It's definitely not each other.

John the Baptist says a person can only have what is given to him from heaven. So why should we try to compare our gifts and our callings and our ministries to others? On the contrary, we can glean all kinds of great ideas from other youth ministries who are faithfully following God's will. And we can offer to help those around us.

Then, when someone comes to you as they did with John—and they tell you that Joe Youth Pastor has a *much* bigger group—you can praise God for His goodness and grace in Joe's life. You can refuse to let a competitive spirit hurt your own ministry. All of us together are attending the wedding, but Jesus alone is the Bridegroom.

Develop your BHAGs, figure out what they'll need, and attack your obstacles. Don't worry about what others are doing, or how much. This is God's call on your life. Live His specific vision for you.

1. Brent Schlender "How Intel Took Moore's Law from Idea to Ideology," *Fortune*, November 11, 2002.

Notes

Organizing and Managing the Plan

You have your mission statement, your core values, and your BHAGs. You're forming a team, and you're building planning time into your schedule. Now let's move on to the next step in turning your dreams into reality.

"That's a lot to do!" you shout, "Where do I find the time?" Obviously this all takes time. If you will actually implement the very practical, hands-on, proven steps I suggest in each chapter, you will impact many teens in your region. Not only that, you will save yourself much time and energy in the process. Trust me on this: the results will be worth it! You will see how in this chapter.

In my ministry, as I learned how to work planning

How do I stay on top of the present in order to find time to plan for the future?

into my schedule, I recognized that there are two categories of time: (1) time to manage the *Now Plan* (for maintenance), and (2) time to invent the *Future* (for growth). This chapter will deal with organizing and managing the plan you have developed so far. Chapter 11 will deal with inventing the Future.

Understanding and using these two modes of time will help the Youth Specialist plan for the future and avoid burnout. National statistics show that youth workers are resigning from churches on an average of every 18–21 months.[1] Clearly, we all need to develop a rhythm in our lives that refreshes us and carries us along in faith, productivity, and peace. That way, we can keep pursuing our dreams. Our BHAGs won't burn us out; they'll fuel us.

The *Now Plan* helps us do this through a kind of compacting process. That is, it helps us take everything we're doing right now and compress it into a smaller part of our time, so we have more time to plan for the future. At Teen Mania, we call the *Now Plan* "Friday's Payroll." It's everything that must happen to keep the wheels turning and the ministry going.

ORGANIZING THE NOW PLAN, STEP BY STEP

As we wrestle with ever-increasing demands on our time, the question on all our minds is, *how do I stay on top of the present in order to find time to plan for the future?* Let's look at the answer in six steps:

1. Determine what's absolutely critical. As you look at your BHAGs for the next 12 months, ask yourself, *What are the five or six areas absolutely critical to your success?* Carefully think this through: "For me to even have a shot at accomplishing this BHAG, what *must* succeed?" Or put it like this: "These six things must not fail . . ."

We call these Critical Success Factors. They are the things that absolutely must happen, no matter what. Everything else can fail, but these *cannot* fail because everything else is built upon them.

Often, our problem is that we spend a lot of time and energy ensuring the success of many things—but they aren't the critical things! The remedy is to realize that some of the things taking your time must be pruned away. We hang on to too many ministry obligations out of tradition. If a certain activity has nothing to do with your mission statement or your BHAGs, it is time to let it go.

How do you decide what is critical? Can you read it in a book? Consult with a genius? Choosing the Critical Success Factors is the task of the leader—*you* must choose. You can ask others or read books to gain insight, but every ministry and vision is different and ultimately *you* have to make the decision. Remember, you do have the Holy Spirit to help you; you're not alone!

At Teen Mania we use a process of identifying those elements that are vital to the success of our ministry and monitoring them to be sure we stay on course. Go to your computer now and open the CD-ROM file

"Organizing." This page details the planning process we use to list and track these Critical Success Factors.

Let's talk in practical terms now. Let's say your BHAG is to have 120 on-fire teens in your group by the end of the year. You have 10 kids now, and you want 12 times that number by the end of the year. Therefore, a factor crucial to your success will be to get more people to come. I know that sounds pretty simple, but if everything is great week after week, but no one comes through your doors to see it, then you will never reach your BHAG. You have to find a way to get people through the door. This, then, is your Critical Success Factor #1: *Get them in the door.* It's critical, so write it down.

At this point, you have only one factor to focus on, not 95, so you can probably handle a couple more. Let's say you have 40 new kids coming each week but they're not committing their lives to Christ. They are all bored, and during your sermon they pass notes instead of taking notes. Yes, they are coming in the door, but you're not engaging them in the things of God once they are there. How can you capture their hearts for God when they come to your meetings? You do that by having amazing youth services. Put that down—Critical Success Factor #2: *Produce great youth services.*

Now you have a great youth service, and you have people getting saved. But nobody is following up with your teens. No one is helping them get strong. Kids are coming in, getting rocked, and then heading right out the back door. So you must write that down as critical to achieve your BHAG—Critical Success Factor #3: *Do great follow-up.*

Your Critical Success Factors may be different than these. But whatever they are, they'll focus you. They'll make you chop your calendar to pieces and cut out the useless wheel-spinning that's unrelated to the mission. Monitoring these three factors will eventually make you admit: "There is too much work for me to do by myself. I must develop others around me to take responsibility." Write it down! Critical Success Factor #4: *Develop leaders who can take responsibility.*

Let's stop here and open Resource #1 on your CD-ROM. As you can see, this page helps to identify factors critical to the success of one of your BHAGs. It is the work of the leader to figure out these factors and weigh the importance of each one. Write the first BHAG you want to work on in the space provided, and list its Critical Success Factors below it.

2. Turn your Critical Success Factors into your job description. Let's assume you have listed five Critical Success Factors for your first BHAG. These five areas now become your *job description.* Summarize them into one statement and record it on this page. This, and only this, is the specific work you will spend your time doing as a youth pastor. Duplicate this page and follow the same process for each of your other BHAGs. The results of this think-time will be the foundation for your successful youth ministry!

Now that you have identified the Critical Success Factors for each of your BHAGs for the year, determine concrete, measurable goals for each factor, broken down by week and month. Why measurable? *What you measure is what actually gets done.*

Now open Resource 2 on your CD-ROM and look at the illustration called "Getting to My BHAG." This is a helpful goal-setting tool. I will use the example from earlier in the chapter. My BHAG is: *"I want to have 120 on-fire teens in my group by the end of the year."* The first Critical Success Factor is: *"Get them in the door."* What are the concrete, measurable goals to accomplish this?

To begin with, I must ask myself: "How many people do I need to get in the door, and what percentage need to get saved and stay in order to end up with 120?"

Let's break it down to make it easier: "If I have 40 kids visit every month, then 12 times 40 is 480 kids visiting by the end of the year. Forty visitors per month is 10 per week. *Notice that I've written "10" in my weekly goal box.*

Now out of 480 kids who visit, could I lead half of them to Christ? Yes, I think so. That would be 240 new believers, or five per week. *I've written "5" as my weekly goal.*

If I have 240 new believers, could I get half of them discipled? I think I could. I indicated each of these figures on the chart pictured on the next page. Recording these smaller, concrete goals will help me track my progress toward achieving my big BHAG.

Now it's your turn. Go to the next screen on your CD-ROM and look at the blank page, "Getting to My BHAG." Begin by writing the BHAG you wish to work on in the space provided. Then name the first Critical Success Factor on the line below it. Continue by listing the smaller, measurable targets that you must accomplish each

Corresponds with
Chapter 10
in *Revolution YM*

*The following chart breaks
down the Critical Success
Factors used by Ron Luce
and Teen Mania in a week-
by-week format.*

Getting to My BHAG

BHAG: *To have 120 on-fire teens in my group by the end of the year.*

Month:	August									

CSF 1: *Get Them In the Door*
(Critical Success Factor)

	Week 1		Week 2		Week 3		Week 4		Week 5	
	Goal	Actual	Goal	Actual	Goal	Actual	Goal	Actual	Goal	Actual
1. Visitors	10		10		10		10			
2. Salvations	5		5		5		5			
3. Discipled	2		3		2		3			

*Use these boxes to break down your Critical
Success Factors into smaller measurable goals.*

Month:	August									

CSF 2: *Produce Great Youth Services*
(Critical Success Factor)

	Week 1		Week 2		Week 3		Week 4		Week 5	
	Goal	Actual	Goal	Actual	Goal	Actual	Goal	Actual	Goal	Actual
1. Worship										
2. Great Sermon										
Illustrations										
3. Altar Ministry										

week and month in order to successfully hit the year-end
goal. A tally of these boxes will give you a monthly target
to shoot for.

During the month, you will constantly monitor your
progress compared to your written goals. Maybe this
month you are doing great on numbers one and two but

ORGANIZING AND MANAGING THE PLAN

Resource #2

Corresponds with
Chapter 10
in *Revolution YM*

Getting to My BHAG

The following chart breaks down the Critical Success Factors used by Ron Luce and Teen Mania in a week-by-week format.

BHAG: To have 120 on-fire teens in my group by the end of the year.

Month: August

CSF 1: Get Them In the Door

(Critical Success Factor)

	Week 1		Week 2		Week 3		Week 4		Week 5	
	Goal	Actual	Goal	Actual	Goal	Actual	Goal	Actual	Goal	Actual
1. Visitors										
2. Salvations										
3. Discipled										

Use these boxes to break down your Critical Success Factors into smaller measurable goals.

Month: August

CSF 2: Produce Great Youth Services

(Critical Success Factor)

	Week 1		Week 2		Week 3		Week 4		Week 5	
	Goal	Actual	Goal	Actual	Goal	Actual	Goal	Actual	Goal	Actual
1. Worship										
2. Great Sermon										
Illustrations										
3. Altar Ministry										

are falling behind with number three. *Then that is where you need to spend your time.* Repeat this process for each Critical Success Factor related to this BHAG. You can reproduce this page and line them up side by side on a table or tape them to the wall. (Several extra blank charts are available to you in this part of the CD-ROM.) This will give you an instant overview of the year, as pictured in the last page of Resource #2. You will see at a glance whether or not you are on track to meet the BHAG.

The chart pictured on page 192 includes a sample BHAG and Critical Success Factors (CSFs). You will incorporate your own BHAG and CSFs when charting your plan on the CD-ROM.

Depending on your BHAG, there are several other areas to think about that may be critical to your success:

- developing teen leaders
- adult volunteers
- worship team (to create dynamic services)
- drama team (to help with great services)
- missions recruitment (to make changing the world a norm)
- sermon topics

It is important to remember—especially when considering sermon topics—that some of your BHAGs should have to do with *what qualities you're trying to invest in your students*. If you want kids with servants' hearts, kids who love to worship, and kids who reach out to others, then that will dictate what you preach about. You will spend a month emphasizing giving, or missions, or exploring and meeting the needs of people around you.

One advantage to carefully planning and charting your BHAGs is that you will be continually thinking in terms of the big picture and long-term goals for your group. As you see stories and statistics, object lessons and video clips, you'll be splicing them into your ministry plans. "Oh, that will fit in with October's sermons! I'll save

Your staff, whether volunteer or paid, needs to immediately see that they are functioning in a dynamic environment of great possibilities for multiplying growth.

it in my file so it will be there for me when I need it." Every sermon you do, every nugget you offer, from this point on, should be directly related to your mission statement and to your BHAGs.

3. Use a flowchart to structure your ministry. A flowchart visually lays out how the dream will come to pass. It puts

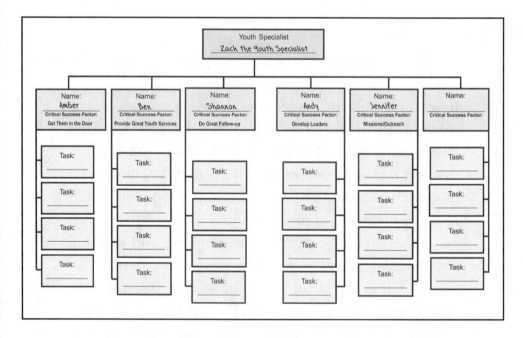

structure to your dream. You are building an organization (even if it's with all volunteers) to accomplish the dream.

You are enlisting others' energy to accomplish the vision that God has given you.

Take some time now to examine the sample flowchart in Resource #3 of the CD-ROM. The row of boxes at the top of the page should directly correlate to your list of Critical Success Factors. If you have five Critical Success Factors, you will fill out five columns, each labeled with the name of one of the factors. (Ultimately, you should have an adult volunteer in charge of each one of your Critical Success Factors so you are not doing it all by yourself. We'll discuss that more in the next section.)

4. Recruit teens and adult volunteers to be "staff" in your ministry. All the blank names in each of the top boxes must be filled by a qualified adult "leader" of that area. When you recruit them, you should show them how their goals relate to the overall BHAGs. You have some smart people in your church, and they'll want to know that if they come and give their time *it will be highly leveraged.* So lay out for them in advance how the work is distributed. Show them the flowchart and where they fit. (We will deal more with recruiting and training your dream team in Chapter 13.)

Help them understand how they fit into the mission statement and your specific one-year goals related to the BHAG. Don't just say, "Here, go to work, bring in visitors." Instead you'll say, "I want you to understand the big picture. While you are working on bringing in the visitors, we have other people working on the services, and others on outreach." Your staff, whether volunteer or paid, needs to immediately see that they are functioning in a dynamic environment of great possibilities for multiplying growth.

Naturally, they won't do the job exactly as you might do it. They might do it only 80 percent as well as you could. That's okay! *If you have five people working at 60 percent, that is 300 percent more manpower than what you have by yourself.*

5. Work with your staff to develop their Critical Success Factors. You need to take charge of the factors critical to the success of your big goals; so do the people on your staff. As leader, your job is to show your staff how to do this. Suppose, for example, you have someone responsible for Outreach. Her job is to get 40 people to attend meetings every month. So print out a blank copy of the Youth Staff Member form, (Resource #4 of the CD-ROM) give it to her and ask, "What are the top four things you need to do in order to get 40 kids here each month?"

"Well, I need to have some brochures. I need to have somebody inviting them. I need . . ." Whatever those things are, help her get those things. Do this planning *with* her by charting each of her Critical Success Factors.

Now create a flowchart for her, just like the one you have. Note that *her chart of Critical Success Factors falls organizationally under a single Critical Success Factor of yours.* You are multiplying your ministry!

Help her break the task down still further. Each of her critical success areas must have a volunteer (teen or adult) overseeing that area. This gives all of your teens in your group a place to plug into the vision. (I'll tell you more about how to get the average teen committed to your BHAGs in Chapter 13.)

6. Set up a regular reporting process. By working with each of your "leadership team" members to set the critical success factors for their areas, you now have the structure for a weekly report. You want to keep your finger on the "ministry pulse" week by week, month by month. Don't wait until the end of the year to ask, "How are you doing with your Critical Success Factors?" Instead, tell your helpers, "I want to hear from you on a regular basis, maybe every week or every other week. I want to know how things are going, so I can be ready to help you out, if you need it."

Then if goals aren't met, you can walk through the charts with that person and his team. "Let's look at the five things you needed to do, and let's figure out which of these things did not really work." Your job as a leader becomes coaching, encouraging, and brainstorming with your leaders. Don't ever just ask, "Why didn't you do that?" No, *you* are there to help them figure it out creatively.

You can check the incremental movements toward goals by looking at the Critical Success Factor tasks that are completed or not completed. For example, if your goal is to get 40 visitors per month, and you're only getting 30, go talk with that leader. Maybe one of her CSFs was to print a thousand flyers a month and pass them out. You can ask, "Did you actually print a thousand flyers?"

You might hear: "No, I only printed 500." That could be why people aren't coming—they don't know about the meetings. Talk about it. Adjust.

Or maybe she answers: "We had them printed, but they weren't distributed." Okay, then what needs to change so that the distribution takes place? Talk about it. Brainstorm.

With this kind of process, people can see which part of their plan is failing. They can pick up on trends and take proactive actions. Receiving regular reports from your staff will help you monitor progress and the overall ministry trends. Adjust accordingly.

Are you starting to see the picture here? You can accomplish much more by enlisting others in the dream and showing them how their role helps to accomplish the BHAG. In doing this you have just redefined your job description. Instead of running around like a chicken with your head cut off, you have a team of people each doing his or her part of the vision. You have multiplied yourself and are saving a lot of time and wear and tear on your body (as well as on your family!).

So, that is how you organize and manage the *Now Plan.* It will help you define where you need to spend your time. You will cut down on busywork activities and focus your energy on the things that count—the factors critical to the success of your BHAGs. The people who work with you will put their time into their areas of critical success. As a result, you can chart your progress and *multiply your ministry*! I think a miracle is about to happen in your youth group!

1. "Our Passion," Youth Link Ministries,
http://www.youthlinkministries.com/ (accessed October 25, 2005).

CHAPTER ELEVEN

Inventing the Future

We've gone deeply into the mechanics of the *Now Plan* in the previous chapter. But what about planning for the future? You have to do more than maintenance to win a generation. Here at Teen Mania, we call it "Inventing the Future." Hopefully, because of the way you're now organized, you will have time in your schedule to regularly *Invent the Future*. If not, you must make time. A big part of the leader's job is to develop the plan for the future. No one else will be thinking about it more than *you*, so if you don't, they won't.

You have to do more than maintenance to win a generation.

You will not do large things to impact large masses of teens without extensive future planning.

Here at Teen Mania everyone on staff has two jobs—one is to manage a *Now Plan* for "Friday's payroll," the other is to *Invent the Future.* A staff person's job is *not* to just keep things going. The other part is for him or her to spend significant time figuring out how to get where we really want to go. The higher you are in the organization, the more time you spend *Inventing the Future.* Remember, the larger you want your ministry to become, the more you have to spend time doing future planning. *You will not do large things to impact large masses of teens without extensive future planning.*

MAKE INVENTING THE FUTURE
A REGULAR PRIORITY!

Here's a scene snapshot from the Gospel of John: "*Jesus and His disciples went out into the Judean countryside, where He spent some time with them, and baptized*" (John 3:22) (*emphasis added*).

Now isn't this interesting? In the middle of Jesus' busy life and ministry, He pulls His disciples aside to spend time with them. Together, they withdraw to a lake while a large crowd follows them.

We see this "withdrawing-with-disciples" strategy again and again in the Gospels. Jesus' model of pulling His dedicated followers aside drives home an important point for us today: *We must deliberately set aside time in our lives to plan together for the future, or we will never do anything huge.* I invite you to take note of some basic guidelines when spending time with "your people," as Jesus did.

Spend time away with your leaders to talk about the big plan. Make it a priority to get away with your leaders and adult volunteers to think about one thing and only one thing: *The Big Plan.* Just that, and nothing else. If Jesus could take time out of His busy schedule to do it, certainly you can.

At Teen Mania we take one or two days per month for the leadership team and me to spend the whole day together. The only thing that we talk about on that day is . . . *the future.* It doesn't matter that there are fires to put out or that the walls are about to crash down around us in our practical, day-to-day problems. On that day, we don't care. We talk *only* about the future. Sometimes we'll meet here on our campus and other times we'll meet at a lodge or retreat center and make it a long weekend.

At these *Inventing the Future* meetings, we don't talk about our plan of action for the next 12 months—that's discussed at our regular weekly meetings. When we invent the future, we talk about *more than one year* down the road, maybe even three or five years from now. Our agenda will

> **Make it a priority to get away with your leaders and adult volunteers to think about one thing and only one thing: *The Big Plan.***

have to do with huge BHAGs that we haven't tackled within this year's plan. For example, we started planning for the Silverdome three years before the actual event. We were inventing the future far in advance. Only after talking about it and researching for a year and a half did we actually announce our plans to the world and invite teens from all over the nation for a weekend stadium event.

Make the agenda crystal clear. So what do we do on those days? We come in with a clear agenda, ready to work. I give everyone an agenda in advance and tell them to bring ideas to the table about a specific topic. This is the work of a leader. We, as leaders, have to tell our people, "I am pulling from your brain the creative ideas that we need in order to plan well. I want you to come ready." Then the team will bring ideas to the table, backed by all the research for those ideas, so that *they present well-thought-through opinions.*

This is key. We don't want our inventing-the-future plan to get sidetracked by random opinions and off-the-cuff notions. We want some meat on those bones! "Tell me *why* you think we should do that." Let your idea-givers also provide the backup, the research, and the thought processes behind the opinion—and then trust their opinion when it is shown to be worthy.

Always give homework assignments. As you dream and think outside the box, ask your staff/volunteers to help gather information needed to move your goals forward: "Between our once-a-month meetings, everyone has a homework assignment! I need to know . . ." If you are thinking about holding a fall youth rally, one person might research which other youth ministries have done big events in September, what kinds of things drew kids, and how many kids came. If you need a band, someone else can research what bands may be available. Maybe you need an auditorium in your town. Assign someone to research what facilities are available.

At the next meeting, you will come back and ask, "What have you learned during this research time?" When everyone brings their items to the table, you can put it all together, think and talk through it, and let it spark new ideas. Then, you can begin to dream outside the box again.

Ideally, you don't want to waste time. This way of approaching the future is to share the work in order to multiply your efforts. In addition, peer pressure is a healthy motivator for everyone to complete assignments. No one wants to be the slacker who leaves things to the last minute or comes unprepared!

Once you've assimilated all the information, you can also identify holes in your data and see what information is still missing. What new questions does the research raise? When you leave that meeting, hand out new assignments for next month, so that when you reconvene you will be that much closer to seeing the BHAG become a reality. Essentially, you're still asking, in many different ways, the planning question we used earlier: "What will it take to accomplish this dream?"

Operate within the fiscal year. We operate according to our fiscal year, which is based on the school year. I think that most youth ministries should, since so much of what we all do revolves around and begins with the school year.

When we start our new year in September, we have already been thinking about that year for at least 12 months, discussing it each month in order to be ready. As we implement the plan for the new year, we also start the planning process for the next year. Let me give you a peek at the itinerary of each monthly *Inventing the Future* meeting:

- *September–December*
  We dream way outside the box for the next three to five years.
- *January–March*
  We back up and say, "Well, if we are going to be there in three years, what will we need to do starting this September? Where do we need to be at the end of this year? For this year, what will our BHAG need to be to achieve the three-year goal?"
- *April–June*
  We plan meticulously what each department will have to do month by month to accomplish the next year's goals.
- *July–August*
  We do the final preparations to launch the new year in September that we have been working on steadily for the past 12 months.

We look at each month, understanding where we need to be in the planning process so that, by the time April and May roll around, we have a very clear picture of what that September will look like—and what the whole coming year will look like.

We are normally looking three to five years ahead,

asking: Where could we *be* then? What does *that* picture look like? What could really be happening *then?*

THREE STAGES OF PLANNING

As you think about *Inventing the Future,* you'll have three steps of planning.

1. The Strategic Plan. Simply put, the Strategic Plan answers the question, "What strategies are you going to implement to achieve your BHAG?" In other words, if part of your BHAG is to draw 100 or 200 visitors each week, what strategy will you employ to get them there? There are many strategies that could work. You could do a big event with a band. You could do a contest with teens, like the "Great Commission Competition." (See Appendix.) You could make young people themselves the evangelizers. With any part of your BHAG there will be a number of methods to accomplish the goal. How do you choose which strategy you will use?

Obviously, you can look at what other people have done successfully. Don't, however, fall into the trap of thinking that if you do what someone else does, you will automatically be successful too. You have a unique community, unique visions, and unique teens. So these ideas may work or they may not. How can you tell? Glad you asked!

You can run tests. Running tests is how you can prevent a scenario like this from playing out . . .

You can test an idea by testing each of its aspects or assumptions.

"Well, I really feel in my heart that we need to have an event. If we do this and this and this, I know we can get 500 kids there. I just know it!"

So you spend wads of money, bring in a band, and do all kinds of things that you just *know* will work. And you get 100 kids there. Out of the 100 kids who show up, most are already saved, but three get saved. Then you say . . .

"Oh, I know we still owe the church $1,500 because we lost money on this event, but I don't know where we're going to get that money. I guess we'll have to work for the next year to pay the church back. But if it was for the sake of even one soul it would still have been worth it."

Foolishly, we justify a lot of things we do for that proverbial "one soul," don't we? Yes, every soul is important, but that's not an excuse for us to be bad stewards of our time and resources. Testing an idea before it is implemented will help you be a good steward.

All successful enterprises test their potential ideas. They try a new burger or sandwich in various cities, run the ads, track the sales, and find out whether anyone will buy it before they commit big bucks to it. If it fails, then that particular product won't be added to the menu.

But how can we do this type of testing in our ministries? Let me suggest that you can test an idea ("I want to do an event where a lot of seeking kids are going to come and hear the Gospel") by *testing each of its aspects or assumptions.*

In the example above, you might first test the band. Run the band's name and its style of music by many of your teens and others in the local high school. If most of your potential market says, "Yeah, that was really great for . . . *the*

'80s!" then you probably won't want those guys to come play for you. It's no fun working hard only to find out later that "no one around here even likes the band"—you were the only one excited. So you do a test, take a poll, or start a focus group to find out what your potential market thinks.

Second, you might test your ideas about "how we'll get kids to attend." We do a lot of "testing" at Teen Mania. For example, maybe you're thinking, "If I put posters everywhere, call every kid in town, and run advertisements on the radio, then that will bring a thousand kids to our event." So you put posters all over South Mall, which *sounded like* a good idea—but none of the kids hang out there. You didn't know that. You got 20 kids from your youth group to make 30 calls per day for x-number of days, but those kids decided not to come.

Instead of calling 1,000 kids for your big event, what if you tested like this: "Let's try a 'medium' event on a regular Wednesday night and let's call 100 kids. We'll get some kids to make the calls, give them an exact script and see—out of those 100—what percentage actually shows up."

You might find that 50 weren't even home, 20 of them hung up on the caller, 10 of them said maybe, another 10 said, "on a cold day in hell would I come," and 10 said they were excited and would, indeed, show up. Seven actually showed up at the event.

Now you have some data you can use to predict results. You know you called 100 kids, and seven showed up. Part of your learning would be that for every 100 calls you make, seven will show up. So if you want 100 teens,

Ongoing tests help you put together a strategic plan that you can have confidence in.

how many calls would you need to make? You do the math. That's why you run a test: to see if that effort will actually work and how much of it you'll need to apply to get the results you want. Conclusion? Don't expend all the energy and all the money on the wrong strategy.

Here's another example. Suppose you think it would be just great to run ads on the radio, so you go to the church board and ask for $3,000 to run the ads. After you've run hours of ads you find out that none of the kids listen to that radio station. You seemingly did everything right, but you end up with a lame turnout as a result. Could you have tested the idea first? Could you have asked around to make sure which radio station the teens listen to? Sure!

Ongoing tests help you put together a strategic plan that you can have confidence in. By the time you execute your plan, you can be pretty confident—at least 80 percent sure—that the efforts you're exerting are going to work and actually produce the result you envisioned. You can roll out your plan to everybody—detailing the destination—and have great confidence that you will really arrive. You tested the ideas enough to know that if you do this and this, you will probably get *this* result.

Remember, in life we don't get graded on our intentions; we get graded on our results. We don't even get graded on our efforts toward what failed. Therefore it makes sense, doesn't it, to find out through a testing process whether a plan will likely work?

"But Ron, how can you be so mean?" I hear you say. "People are *really* trying here, spending a ton of time and energy. Can't you give them some credit?"

My response: "Is it really mean to want people to be productive with their lives?" Think about how Jesus put it:

> "Again, it will be like a man going on a journey, who called his servants and entrusted his property to them. To one he gave five talents of money, to another two talents, and to another one talent, each according to his ability. Then he went on his journey. The man who had received the five talents went at once and put his money to work and gained five more. So also, the one with the two talents gained two more. But the man who had received the one talent went off, dug a hole in the ground and hid his master's money.
>
> "After a long time the master of those servants returned and settled accounts with them. The man who had received the five talents brought the other five. 'Master,' he said, 'you entrusted me with five talents. See, I have gained five more.'
>
> "His master replied, 'Well done, good and faithful servant! You have been faithful with a few things; I will put you in charge of many things. Come and share your master's happiness!'
>
> "The man with the two talents also came. 'Master,' he said, 'you entrusted me with two talents; see, I have gained two more.'
>
> "His master replied, 'Well done, good and faithful

servant! You have been faithful with a few things; I will put you in charge of many things. Come and share your master's happiness!'

"Then the man who had received the one talent came. 'Master,' he said, 'I knew that you are a hard man, harvesting where you have not sown and gathering where you have not scattered seed. So I was afraid and went out and hid your talent in the ground. See, here is what belongs to you.'

"His master replied, 'You wicked, lazy servant! So you knew that I harvest where I have not sown and gather where I have not scattered seed? Well then, you should have put my money on deposit with the bankers, so that when I returned I would have received it back with interest.

"'Take the talent from him and give it to the one who has the ten talents. For everyone who has will be given more, and he will have an abundance. Whoever does not have, even what he has will be taken from him. And throw that worthless servant outside, into the darkness, where there will be weeping and gnashing of teeth.'"

—Matthew 25:14–30

This is important stuff from our Lord! It's life or death for His servants. Don't forget about the man who was given the one talent and buried it. Scripture calls him a wicked and lazy servant. You see, the Boss (for us, that's Jesus) expects His servants to be productive. Why? Not because He's mean. It's because deep in His heart He's saying: "I love you and want you to do something productive with your life."

Jesus doesn't want any of us putting out massive efforts that don't pay off. Our job as leaders in the strategic planning process is to ask our staff people, "Have you actually *tried* this and this and this? If not, how do you *know* it will work?" That's a lot different than talking about what they *feel* will work.

At this point, fill out the CD-ROM file titled "Strategy." This will give you a chance to strategize the best ways to go about accomplishing your BHAG.

2. The Operational Plan. Look at the flowchart in Resource #3 again. This is a simple device that graphically displays how you will accomplish your operational plan day by day. It ties people and resources to your strategies and specifies *when* and *how* they will come into play throughout

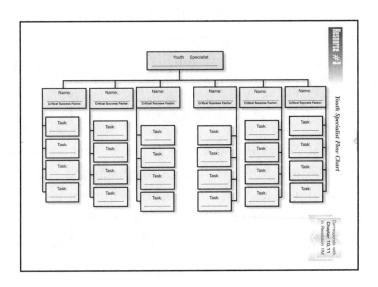

Remember that as you do this "unglamorous" work of planning, you will achieve more ministry impact than you ever thought possible.

the year. What are the critical success factors for each area? Are you still on target to achieve those goals each week? The flowchart tracks these critical operations for you.

You don't have to be a genius to develop this kind of operational plan, but you do have to sit down and chart things out. To be the most effective, you'll need to be sure that everyone is aware of the accountability tied to his or her specific tasks (which means you'll also need a process of "checking in"—which means regular, updated progress reports). Make the chart accessible to all.

Your operational flowchart takes all the goals and strategies that you know are going to work and divides them into "buckets of responsibility"—who will do what, and when. It figures out what this "execution machine" has to look like if it is to make your strategic goals actually happen. This is the operational plan. Once you plug in your volunteers and all the other resources, you can probably hit your strategic goals.

3. The Financial Plan. This is the subject we all hate to talk about. Money. But it's time to attach dollars to all those initiatives you have been planning, and put a budget together. How much do you have in the revenue stream? Not much? Don't worry and don't be discouraged! Do be realistic.

Sometimes we would love to accomplish a certain strategic plan—we can see how well it would work—but it is just going to cost too much. We can't afford that many staff, or that many brochures. So we crunch the numbers a little more and figure out what we must spend and what we think we could get donated by someone else. We go back and change the operational plan a little—this might work with fewer staff, more volunteers. Or we just try to do something a little smarter.

It's a back and forth process when you work with the finances. Try to creatively balance the operational and financial plans.

Inventing the Future must be a regular priority from now on if you are to continue to pursue the dreams God has for you and your youth ministry. When you make time for it, all your volunteer staff will make it a priority as well. Remember that as you do this "unglamorous" work of planning, you will achieve more ministry impact than you ever thought possible. The lives you touch will make it worthwhile.

Notes

CHAPTER TWELVE

Funding Your Plan

"If I just had more money I could . . ."
How many times have we said or thought those words? Too often the youth ministry budget is the bottom entry of the church budget—if it's on there at all.

Most of the plans you have developed will take some serious cash to get off the ground. Don't just sit there paralyzed because you think you'll never get that kind of money; if this is God's dream, He will provide. Still, that doesn't mean you should sit around waiting for provision to fall from heaven. There are many things you can do to prepare to receive the blessing of the Lord.

All youth pastors have become experts at fundraisers like car washes and bake sales. I am not going to talk about any of that here—there are many more creative, fresh ways to gather resources for your youth ministry. It costs money to reach teens. It makes me so mad that the world spends

Don't just sit there paralyzed because you think you'll never get that kind of money; if this is God's dream, He will provide.

billions to reach kids through rock 'n' roll and television, while most youth ministries are on a shoestring budget and can't even afford new curriculum.

Once my daughter Charity was in the kitchen with my wife, Katie. Charity was singing, "If you're happy, and you know it . . . " and Katie was doing the motions. "If you're happy, and you know it, stomp your feet." Several verses later, Charity wanted to see how far she could push it, and sang, "If you're happy, and you know it, give me a dollar." Katie stopped doing the motions.

Too many of our youth fundraisers are the equivalent of this song. We do a lot of activity, make a lot of noise, and end up with little to show for it.

Let me give you some practical steps to getting resources.

THE DREAM COMES BEFORE THE MONEY

Some people think, "If I only had money, then I could dream something great for God." In reality, if you had the money before you had a clear dream from God, you would waste it! Your lack of money isn't what's holding you back; your lack of a dream is. If you will do the planning work of a leader that we've talked about, the money will follow.

How does God lead you? First, He gives you *the vision*, then He gives you the *PRO-vision*. The first step is having the dream.

Think of the example set by Mary in the Bible. When the angel told her she would give birth to the Son of God, she responded with instant acceptance. She didn't say, "Lord, I'm unmarried and have no means of financial support if I have a baby out of wedlock." After she gave birth, the wise men came from the East with gold, frankincense, and myrrh—gifts which would support Mary and Joseph.

The gifts come after you've committed yourself to God's dream. God's provision *will* come. And it will surprise you. It may be countries and months away, but it *will* come into your life when you need it. Don't wait for the camels to get there before you agree to His dream.

Think about it. What ministry have you ever known that started because they had a ton of money and didn't know what to do with it all? It almost never happens that way. Many people believe that if they worked at a megachurch the pastor would give them a lot of money and they would have a big youth group. Let me set you free from that myth.

First of all, those youth pastors at the big megachurches don't necessarily get big budgets. Let me give you a rule of thumb: in general, youth budgets are determined by the proportion of youth in a congregation, not the size of the church. And youth, on average, make up only 10 percent of a congregation.

Secondly, don't fall into the trap of thinking that your group is in competition with other churches. Instead, ask

First, He gives you the vision, then He gives you the PRO-vision.

yourself how you're doing within *your own church.* "Why don't I even have all of the kids that are in *my* church?" This is a good question for us all to ask.

When answering this question, first figure out what it's going to take to capture the hearts and attention of the kids in your church. But don't stop there. Begin to dream of all the other kids that God has called you to reach in your town. That's what building a dream is all about. Ask the Lord who He wants you to reach and how best to reach them. Remember that if you are only reaching the kids whose parents go to your church, you're not gaining any ground.

Once we have the dream, how, then, do we grow this thing? Philippians 4:19 says, "My God will meet all your needs according to his glorious riches in Christ Jesus." If you get God's vision, isn't it in His best interest to supply the needs for His dream? Do you think He is going to tease us and *not* give us His provision? Of course not!

DEVELOP A BUDGET FOR THE DREAM

Open your Bibles and turn with me to Luke 16. This parable of the shrewd manager is one of Jesus' most difficult parables. I have a real love/hate relationship with this passage. I love it because Jesus said it, but I hate it because the punch line in verse eight stings:

> *"The master commended the dishonest manager because he had acted shrewdly. For the people of this world are more shrewd in dealing with their own kind than are the people of the light."*
>
> —Luke 16:8

The master commended his steward not because he was dishonest, but because he was shrewd. This indicts most Christians. People of the world who make meaningless widgets are smarter with their money than the people in the kingdom of God. People who make toothpaste and soap put together better budgets than many ministries—and budgeting is about being shrewd. Sure, deciding sermon topics and the theme for this year is very important. But at some point we have to take the dream and reduce it down to how much it will cost. That's the work of a budget. There are two parts of a budget:

- *Operational costs* – These are ongoing costs that you want to keep as low as you can.
- *Capital costs* – These are one-time costs, like building a youth room or purchasing a sound system.

Do you think that having a large budget is something to brag about? It isn't. I believe in the "biggest bang for the buck"—the greatest number of souls for the fewest dollars. Your goal is to keep the operations and ongoing costs as low as possible. If, for example, you want a youth center, you must factor in how much it will cost each month—lights, bills, and rent. Lots of outreach attempts like this end up closing because no one thought about the monthly costs. Will businesses rally to support it? Will your pastor? A budget will help you project monthly costs.

In the midst of doing your budget let me encourage you to classify items as Needs versus Wants. Sometimes the things you think you "*need* to have" are really only a preference. They would be cool, but they're not necessary.

Careful evaluation of ministry items in terms of need will help you stretch your budget dollar.

Go to the CD-ROM file titled "Funding Your Plan." Start planning your budget by filling out the first two pages.

Once you've figured out your one-time and ongoing needs, track your budget very closely—did you come in behind or ahead of budget? We do this at Teen Mania. I know this seems obvious, but many times people only think about ministry and not how to measure whether they stayed within budget. The crunch comes when the pastor comes in and says you're over budget, and you can't do it

anymore. We must be more shrewd than most "people of the light."

I am a simple guy, but when my wife and I started Teen Mania 19 years ago, we had a big dream. We didn't have any money, so we did what every ministry does: we wrote a letter to every person we knew—120 people. Every day we ran to the mailbox, just knowing that God would fill it with cash. But nobody sent anything!

We were reduced to living off the offerings of teenagers at the churches we'd visit (and there weren't many teenagers). We lived on a couple of hundred dollars a month. We stayed in people's homes and spent as little as we possibly could so we could buy some paper to print more letters and brochures. But even as we lived by faith, we were shrewd. We didn't rack up more expenses than we had money coming in.

The church cannot operate on the principle, "Oh, Lord, we will be able to keep the doors open as long as you send a generous donor this month." You won't hear Motorola or Proctor and Gamble say, "We hope people will buy this product and if they don't, we'll have to lay people off." They don't want to go out of business, so they plan ahead. They watch the economy. Sometimes they take financial risks, but only after they've researched them thoroughly. They are shrewd when the economy goes down and consider the long-term health of their organization. We must think the same way in our ministries.

Every budget needs to track the money coming in and the money going out. You know where the money will go *out*—that's your dream. You also need to figure out where the money will come *in*.

THE FOUR SOURCES OF MONEY

Teenagers. Some of you may think teenagers don't have money. Yet, the average teen spends $50 per week. Teens worldwide spend $100 billion per year.[1] They have

> We put our money wherever we think it has value, so a ministry has to prove that it's worth a teenager's money.

It's no longer merely "throwing money in a bucket;" it's being part of a vision.

money. Some earn it; some get it from their parents. But where do they spend it?

We put our money wherever we think it has value, so a ministry has to prove that it's worth a teenager's money. Otherwise, why would a teen want to give up his daily pizza, her designer jeans, or his movie tickets? Most teenagers have not been taught to give. You've all seen adults curl in the fetal position around their wallets when the senior pastor takes an offering. That attitude does not teach teenagers to give. When a mom hands her children a quarter or dollar to put in the collection plate, they don't learn giving; they are just transporting someone else's money!

We have to teach teens to be givers while they're young. The way you shape your kids now will have lifelong results. Teaching teens to be generous won't happen with one sermon; it is a continual education. Each week you should take an offering and teach them a little bit about giving. Talk about Scripture verses that link generosity with God's blessing. Tell them of times God has blessed you when you have given for a big need. As Youth Specialists, we must raise up a generation of generous people.

Your dream must be clear to your teens. People are motivated to give when they see where their money is going. If you say, "We're going to build this youth center, and then we want to grow to 200 kids," they'll be excited to be a part of something. Think about the football coach who tells his team they're going to win the championship. They'll have to work hard, run until they drop, and practice six nights a week, and *they do it!* Every time you take an offering, give the vision. You've changed the value of your ministry in their eyes. Now they have to decide between spending money on pizza or changing their generation. It's no longer merely "throwing money in a bucket;" it's being part of a vision.

What can you tell them they'll receive in return? God will bless them. They'll get a sense of godly pride. They'll be excited to give money to Jesus to reach their generation.

Some of you might think I'm way too optimistic about teenagers' generosity. Yet, I can tell you story after story of youth pastors who have trained their group to give. For example, Scott Gurule's youth group (I'll be talking more about Scott and his group throughout the chapter) had 40 people when he started to teach them to give. In less than three years, the group grew to 400 people and the kids themselves gave the money; they didn't rely on fundraisers.

There are two ways you can raise money with your kids—doing fundraisers or teaching them to give. If they give, God will bless them, and they'll have more to give. They get better jobs and promotions. Mom and Dad bless them. The kids in Scott's youth group gave $55,000 their second year. They built a totally cool youth room. They couldn't wait to bring their friends to it, because it was *theirs.* They had ownership because they learned to give.

Teenagers are your first source of funds. Don't overlook them.

Parents. I really encourage you to have an ongoing relationship with the teens' parents—meet with them once a month, twice a month, whatever. Get them together, not just to take an offering, but to help them understand where you're going and what the dream is. Talk to them about the hot issues teens are dealing with. Talk to them about what you're preaching on for the next month or two. Give them your sermon notes in advance. (Wouldn't that be amazing if you actually prepared that far in advance?) "I just wanted you all to know what I'll be talking about, so when the kids come home, you can ask them about these things." A partnership with your kids' parents benefits everybody.

If you can have an upfront discussion with the parents about why you care for their kids and what you're going to do for them, it will knock them to the floor. Parents will appreciate being included, and they'll respect your plans.

Lay everything out for them. "Here is our vision—we want to have a youth room and double in size . . . You and your children stand to benefit the most from this ministry. Now, I know you already tithe to the church. But if you'd like to be a part of this vision and help not only your kids, but also the kids in this community, would you consider giving a one-time gift—or even an ongoing offering—in addition to what you're already giving? It's important, because the new vision and direction for this group will help your family directly."

I know youth pastors who have been very successful in generating offerings through the parents by making parents realize that youth ministry is not a Christian babysitting service. For this, as we discussed in an earlier chapter, you must carry yourself like an adult, and not an overgrown teenager. If they think you're a goofy guy, they won't believe in your vision or fund it. They might throw a couple bucks at you, but you don't need a couple bucks. You've got a massive dream. You need some people to sell their boat, cash in some IRAs, or something big.

Do some comparison spending for them. Talk about the parents whose kid was having troubles, so they sent him to a psychologist for three years. That costs a ton of money, since insurance doesn't always cover psychiatric help. You're cheaper than a psychologist, and you're great preventive medicine!

So far, you've seen how you can get revenue from teens, from parents, and now (trust me; you're going to love me for this one) from outside sources.

Sources outside the church. We've been dream building, planning, and brainstorming. What kind of outside help does it take to accomplish your dream? Write down all the things you need and attach a price tag to them.

Now here's how you go about getting that price tag covered. On nice stationery write a little bit about your dream, all the things you need, and how much it's going to cost. Print copies of it and make sure they look good. Then carry that paper around with you EVERYWHERE you go. Day or night, don't leave home without it.

Then, when you get in conversations with people, and they ask you what you do, say, "Oh, I'm glad you asked. God's given me a heart for the young people of our region, and He's going to reach this generation. There are kids that are hurting and broken, and we're going to bus them off the streets." Whatever your vision is, don't be afraid to share it. "We're going to have vans and multi-media, and we'll pray for hurting kids and encourage them through our service."

You'll have to tailor your pitch depending on the person you're talking to. If he's not a Christian, you can still tell him the heart of what you're doing. Just don't use phrases like: "And the power of God . . ."! You don't have to express it like that. Simply say, "We're going to help a lot of hurting kids." Then share some stories or stats.

If you do this, you'll shock people into forwarding your dream. If you're walking around with a dream, you're weird. Most people don't have a dream and a vision of really doing something with their lives and helping a lot of other people. When they see you exuding this vision, they will be so enamored by what you're doing that they'll say, "Wow, that's awesome. Is there anything I can do to help?"

Trust me. People want to follow someone who's dedicated to a dream. People talk about leaders who have "charisma." They think it's something you're born with. But charisma is just a fancy word for someone who's "sold out for a dream." When people hear your well-thought-out and consuming dream, they'll want to help.

Help—a very interesting concept. People really care about kids; they just don't know what to *do*. When they find someone who knows what to do, they'll ask what they can do. You could say, "Well, just pray for us, brother." But is that all? Yes, you need prayer; you also need money. Instead say, "I'm glad you asked. As a matter of fact, I just happen to have a sheet right here that describes some things you could do to help. A bus, a van, a video projector, a PA system . . . would help. Lots of things would help because we care about these kids."

You're going to be talking to businesspeople. These people are mature and know how to run finances. They're impressed when they see someone who says more than, "I wanna reach kids." Anyone can say that. Instead, you say, "I want to reach kids, and I *know* how to reach them. I have a plan to do it. If I can just get these specific resources, then we can do *these* great things to help them." When businesspeople see your vision and plan, they'll be impressed with your ministry—and they will write you checks!

Here is a personal testimony. Once, I was meeting with the president of a corporation. I had heard that his company tithed and gave money to good causes and was hoping that subject would come up. If it didn't, maybe I could help it come up. So I asked him a bunch of questions, and at some point I said, "I heard your company tithes."

He said, "Well, as a matter of fact we do. We look for different needs and this and that . . . is there something going on?"

"Yeah, we're building dorms on our campus and reaching these kids." I went on describing my vision.

He said, "Well, maybe you could put something together and send it to me."

I instantly replied, "As a matter of fact . . ." and I pulled out the packet for him. He opened it and read all the charts and looked at the projections of how many kids we could reach. Then he turned it over and saw the exact needs we had—something like $700,000 to build a dormitory. He examined it all.

Finally he said, "Well, I can't commit to you now; I need to talk to the board of directors, but I'll tell you that we will do something." I was content; after all, something is better than nothing. About a month later he called me up and said he'd met with the board. "Remember your presentation?" he asked. "We're sending you a check for $300,000."

Thank the Lord I just happened to have a packet to give to him that day. I'm telling you that it works when you get your vision together and make a nice-looking presentation.

So how do you meet these people? You knock on doors, or you go door-to-door to local businesses. Sometimes it just comes up with people you meet. Don't limit yourself to Christians. Even secular people want to help their community.

Sources within the church. This is usually the only place that pastors look for funds, yet this should really only be bonus money.

Let me tell you a little more about Scott Gurule, the youth pastor who taught his kids to give. He drew a line in the sand with his pastor. The church was giving him a budget of $500 a month. It was a church of about 2,000 people. He said, "We're never going to reach this whole community on $500 a month." (I know some of you are thinking you'd be very happy with $500 a month.) So he went to the pastor and said, "Thank you for your kindness, but why don't you give it to a missionary somewhere or some other charity. We're going to teach these kids how to give. They're going to reach their own generation."

He taught his youth to give, they gave, and their group grew tenfold. So, if you get money from inside the church, terrific. That can be bonus money; but don't think that your whole destiny depends on whether the church is generous or the pastor decides to put youth ministry in the budget. God will fund His own dream.

On page three of the CD-ROM file "Funding," dream about how you are going to begin pulling in and tracking the revenue you need.

Regardless of where you find your funding—from one of these sources, or a combination of them all—there is one overriding thing you must do.

SUBMIT YOUR BUDGET TO YOUR PASTOR

Submit everything to your pastor—your dream, your vision, your goals, and even your budget plans. Don't go to anyone to ask for donations until your pastor is onboard and behind your ministry. Tell him your dream and vision and make sure they are in harmony with the church's

Submit everything to your pastor—your dream, your vision, your goals, and even your budget plans.

Budgeting is the leader's job. You have to have the dream and find the resources.

vision. If they aren't, then you need to rethink them and make sure there is full agreement.

You need to get your pastor and the people in your church excited about reaching kids. "How can I help them catch the vision?" you ask. Understand this: people care about young people; they just don't know how to help. People who aren't even saved care about young people. I have seen grown men cry and say they want to help young people, but they just don't know what to do. You need to show them *how* you plan to do it.

First, you tell them stories of real-life broken kids who are hurting. Don't just go in and say, "Pastor, we want to do this huge thing that's never been done before. What do you think?" Be wise.

Instead say, "Pastor, I've really been thinking about the young people in our community. You know Josh Taylor, the young man who is dealing with . . . ? My heart really goes out to him. And I just found out this week that a dozen girls in the local school are pregnant. My heart would like to do something to help them too. What do you think, Pastor?" Help him see the lives that are really hurting. "Did you know about the kid who tried to commit suicide? Maybe there's something we could do . . . "

Stories open people's hearts to help. Once your pastor asks what he can do, then you can share the vision of opening a youth center or a place where kids could come each Wednesday that they wouldn't be ashamed of. Don't present it as a big thing that *you* want to do, but as your understanding of God's heart for these kids. Don't expect it to happen all at once. Share a couple of ideas at a time. Allow your pastor to grow with the plan. Make sure he is in agreement before you go and get your money.

One last thing: I encourage you *not* to ignore this stuff about budgeting. I know a lot of youth pastors hate talking about money. "Wouldn't it be great if we could just have the dream, and someone else gave us the money?" No, this is the wrong attitude.

Budgeting is the leader's job. You have to have the dream *and* find the resources. It's not an added burden for youth ministry; it's one of the many parts of youth ministry. If we care about kids, we must find a way to reach them. Part of that way is finding the resources. When a person wants to start a business, she doesn't say, "If only I had the money." No, she puts together a plan and finds a way to finance her business—she borrows from Uncle Ted, or goes to a venture capitalist.

Now is the time to start budgeting. Use page four of the CD-ROM file "Funding" to help you get started.

Our business is touching lives, and we must find resources as well. Our commitment means we will find the resources to finance the dream. Without the resources, the dream will never become reality. Lives will never be saved or changed.

I know a youth ministry in which the youth pastor started with 26 kids, and a year later he had 260 kids. He created a center right on the church grounds without receiving one cent from the church. They raised all $66,000 by doing the very things that we've talked about here. It was an incredibly cool place complete with video games and a café. You too can accomplish dreams this big.

We'll close this chapter on *Funding Your Plan* by looking again at the example of Scott Gurule, the youth pastor in Tucson, Arizona.

> *Scott Gurule taught his youth group to give. And give they did. As they became generous and gave, God began to bless them. They grew in numbers from 40 to 400 in just three years, and raised $120,000 in about a year without selling candy bars or washing cars. They built their own youth room and bought sound and lights, which in turn helped to facilitate their vision to reach more teens.*

Let's look at some of the key things Scott taught his group that convinced them to be generous. You will discover exactly what he did to mobilize them, and you can implement these same principles in your youth ministry. Watch God do incredible things through your young people as they learn how to be givers.

When Scott started as a youth pastor in Tucson, the church gave him a budget of $500 a month to run a youth group. But God had given Scott a vision for a youth *ministry*, and he knew there was no way he could build the thriving youth ministry he had in his heart on that amount.

Youth *ministries* (some call them youth churches) are self-supported (youth *groups* are supported). You have to sow before you grow, go, or glow. Think about it. Teens spend over three billion dollars a year to buy balls for sports. Girls spend over seven billion dollars a year on make-up and clothing. They *have* money to spend.

So Scott began to build the values of giving and generosity into his group. He talked about all the different offerings in Scripture. He showed them what God had to say about the practices and attitudes of giving offerings in the Old and New Testament. When he taught the young people how to sacrifice, and the difference between a tithe and a sacrificial offering, they went nuts.

God is looking for a generation of givers! We have to change the way things are done. People may have different thoughts on how tithing should work, but we cannot escape the fact that we are called to tithe of our firstfruits.

These are some of the things Scott instilled into his students:

- *No loud offerings* – We shouldn't tip God like He's a cosmic bellboy. Don't throw in quarters unless that really is the best you can give. Scott refused to do car washes or candy sales to raise money. Those are paltry things. God has put wealth in this generation, and the shrewd manager will use the wealth. Some of the youth who didn't have any money put their drugs in the plate, because that was all they had. God won't release what is in His hand until you release what is in yours. Scott's adult leaders were required to be givers to set an example. Tithing and sacrificial offering became the name of the game. The youth ministry last year gave $58,900 with 400 kids.

- *Give up something* – Teach young people to fast. He asked them to give up their snack food to fast and pray. This gave them the money to tithe into the youth ministry. These kids have money and his youth budget was proof of it. He said, "Next year we're going to have a youth conference, and it will be free because you all will finance it." They got behind it and they did.

As a Youth Specialist, you have to be prepared to change your kids' and your church's attitudes. Demand more of them, and they will step up to the challenge. Don't be wishy-washy about money just because "youth guys" hate to talk about money. You are a Youth Specialist, and you will do whatever it takes to achieve God's dream.

1. Zollo, Peter, "The Cosmetics Category: Talking to Teens," American Demographics, November 1995, http://www.ecrmepps.com/Expose/V3_3/V3_3_A8.asp (accessed October 25, 2005).

PART C

Build It!

CHAPTER THIRTEEN

Building Your Dream Team

Why do you need people to assist you in the vision? Some of you already know why: *"Because I'm gonna die if I don't get help!"* One of the main reasons youth pastors wear themselves out is that once they get their vision, they try to do it all themselves. We all know the old saying, "If you want something done right, you've got to do it yourself," and that's what too many of us try to do. The truth is, we can only do it by ourselves for a little while before we're delirious and our family falls apart. I believe we can have a healthy family and a great ministry at the same time, but the key to having both is to surround ourselves with a team who will buy into the vision and pour their guts out to bring it to fruition. A *dream team* of adult volunteers and teenagers around us will help us accomplish the vision.

If you think you can accomplish the vision by yourself, then your vision is not big enough.

I can hear you object: "It probably *is* better to work with a team, but it's so hard to feel like you're always begging people for help." Let me assure you, it's infinitely harder to achieve God's dream by yourself. Let's look at this issue a little closer.

WHY DO I NEED A TEAM?

Because this vision is bigger than you are. If you think you can accomplish the vision by yourself, then your vision is not big enough. I talk a lot about vision and building ministry because I believe that *Jesus didn't die for 10 quality people, He died for the world.* It doesn't matter how big your church is, or how big your town is—*your ministry can and must grow.* Why do we need workers? Our vision demands it. It will take a lot of work to reach this generation, and we need help.

Because your group will grow. This is a good thing. You want your group to get to the point where you *can't* handle them all. Your ministry will generate a variety of roles for adult volunteers to assume. You've got to raise up a group of people willing to help administrate different parts of the vision. It's not just about you and a group anymore. Once this thing starts growing, you have to have people who are willing to roll up their sleeves and get in the trenches. The good news is that when people see a vision in progress, they're eager to help. And you'll need every one of them.

Because the vision harnesses people's energy. As we mentioned in an earlier chapter, Proverbs 29:18 tells us that God's people need a vision to harness their energy. Without vision, people cast off restraint. You know this is true. You've seen what happens when kids have no vision from God to bridle their energy—they get into sports, drama, choir, drugs, or gangs . . . with a passion! Adults aren't much different; they just do other things with their energy—take a second job or work hours of overtime to buy a bigger house or bigger car or bigger something else. We have a ton of believers sitting in church with no vision from God to harness their energy; instead they let the world harness their energy. If they are going to use their energy somewhere, it should be used for the kingdom of God. So in a very real way, though they don't even know it, they have a need. *They need to have their energy harnessed.*

I want to show you how to build your dream team. What kind of people do you want to choose? What kind of people *don't* you want to choose? Let's break it down.

When people see a vision in progress, they're eager to help. And you'll need every one of them.

WHO SHOULDN'T YOU CHOOSE
FOR THE TEAM?

Somebody is better than nobody, right? Wrong. You don't want to get just anybody who will say yes. You want handpicked people. A bad volunteer can bring poison to your group that will hurt your ministry, not help it.

You may already have inherited bad volunteers because they were already in place when you got there. Now you're stuck with them. Here's what you don't want in a team member:

Adults who always compare you to the last youth group leader. Can you imagine if everybody had kept complaining to Joshua, "Moses always used to do it *this* way"? You do not need people like that. You might justify their involvement because they've volunteered in youth ministry for 10 or 20 years. But if they're stuck in how it's always been done, they'll never hear your vision for how it *could* be done.

You might think, "At least they're helping," but are they really? It only takes one person pulling in the other direction to ruin all your momentum. You will try to get people fired up, but they will be sucked back down with "how it used to be."

People who are disloyal. People who are disloyal agree with everything to your face, but then you hear that they are saying other things behind your back. You simply cannot operate with that. It's unacceptable under any circumstances.

Adults who have their own dreams for youth ministry. As you look for a team to assist you with your vision, you will sometimes find people with a vision of their own. They'll say, "I always thought that we should do this or that." They'll have their own ideas of what the youth ministry *ought* to do and what direction it should take. *There is room for only one vision at a time.*

Some might think it's arrogant for a youth pastor to say, "We only need to have *this* vision." No, it's not arrogant; this is how God does things throughout the Bible. He chooses one person, a man or a woman, gives him or her a dream, then gathers people around that leader to support the dream and vision. The leader doesn't call a committee, and he doesn't vote on things. These are godly principles.

People might bring baggage from a previous youth group: "We always voted on things like this, and I think we should go in that direction." You should respond with, "That's fine, God bless you; go start a ministry and do that. I don't want to stifle you at all. In fact I want you to be free to do those things." You don't have to fire anybody, just set them free. "But he's a deacon," you say. Oh, well, that's a different story. Now, obviously, you'll need to get your pastor's support to set him free. The point is that you can't have a bunch of nay-sayers pulling you back.

Yes, you need a team to volunteer and support you but you need them to support *you*—not their own agendas. Their role will be to help you brainstorm how to make the dream that God has given you into a reality.

Remember, for whatever reason, the adult with a dream of her own is not the leader of the youth ministry;

God chose you. Before you came, the pastor could have chosen her, but he didn't. For whatever reason, God didn't think she was ready yet. If He had, she would have had the opportunity to implement her own vision.

If you find people like this, and they are not able to support your vision with word and deed, you will have to let them go. If you don't, they'll try to run your whole ministry. For whatever reason, these adults are not leaders of their own youth ministries; God chose you.

Remember the example of Absalom, in 2 Samuel 15:2. While his father, David, was king, Absalom sat outside the gate and said: "You know, if I were king, I'd do things differently," and, "If I were king, I'd fix this or that." Eventually it split the kingdom. If you have an Absalom in your group, it will prevent you from doing effective ministry. You don't want this. *"Someone" is not better than no one in this case.*

People with too much extra time on their hands. You might think this doesn't make sense. Don't people with extra time have more time for ministry? Here's the problem. There's usually a reason they have so much extra time. *Nobody else wants them either.*

The people who don't have any time, *they* are the people you want, because they are the people that *everybody else wants.* Everyone else wants them because they get the job done. They make things happen! Your job is to prove to them how your dream and your vision are more important than all the other things that they've been asked to commit to.

Because these are productive people, even if they give you only a little bit of time, it'll be more valuable than somebody who gives you a lot of time but doesn't have the right motivation. These individuals have to constantly be reminded, pumped up, and asked over and over again to do things. By the time you've told them 10 times how to do the job, you could have done it yourself.

"Why didn't anybody tell me this before?" you ask. "You've just described three people on my team! Now what do I do?" If I have been describing people in your group of adult helpers, then you may need to start thinking about how to release them from your ministry.

How to "set free" adults who don't help your ministry. I have never fired anybody, but I have had to set some people free. Always give people a chance to change problem behavior (and be thankful when they take it). Giving them that chance means you must be willing to confront them. Then, if they don't change, you have to confront them again and get even tougher. Few people enjoy confrontation. I don't like it. It's not natural for me to confront, but I recognize that confrontation is part of leadership, and, when people respond positively, it can be the catalyst for positive life-changes.

So give them the chance. Explain the vision. Explain how their behavior doesn't move it forward. Be as positive as you can, and then watch them. Some will make changes but I guarantee there will be others who won't respond. Oh sure, they'll *say* they will, but before long you'll see the issue crop up again, and at some point you'll have to direct them to express their energy and desire to minister in another way.

Your goal is to move toward your dream, and to speak the truth in love.

Let's be clear on this issue: this isn't being mean. You've given them the chance to respond, and it's godly for them to be loyal and learn submission. If they can't or won't, then you can't keep struggling with them forever. Love is more than mere kindness. Kindness tries not to hurt anybody's feelings, regardless of truth. Love demands honesty, spoken as gently as possible. Your goal is to move toward your dream, and to speak the truth in love as you release these people from a dead-end situation.

WHO SHOULD YOU CHOOSE FOR THE TEAM?

Now, let's look for the *right* qualities in leaders. Paul reminds Timothy of these very traits when he says, "And the things you have heard me say in the presence of many witnesses entrust to reliable men who will also be qualified to teach others" (2 Tim. 2:2). What is the first characteristic Paul finds so important in men who are going to teach others?

Qualified. First, they need to be qualified. They need to have an ability—a talent—for something. This means you must be discriminating about the people you pick for different parts of your ministry. Just because someone wants to help, doesn't mean they should. Too often we enlist people who don't have any talent and let them lead worship anyway. Then we wonder why we have bad worship!

I remember when I was first saved in high school. I was learning to play the guitar and was always begging to lead a song during worship. I was terrible, my voice was rotten, and so they never let me.

I'm so glad they kept saying no. It forced me to practice more, which was a good thing. But it also helped me realize that music wasn't my calling. We're not all good at everything. I'm not saying that your helpers need to be perfect at the things you're looking for. You can train them and they can improve, but they need at least some aptitude before you throw them into a position outside their skill sets.

Consider making some kind of application form that includes an inventory of skills and abilities, so you can assess a person's experience. If, for example, a woman writes for her company newsletter, she may be a good writer for fliers and brochures. Find out each person's experience, and match his or her skills to the roles you need.

Faithful. You've got to find somebody who's a faithful Christian. You want someone of proven Christian character. You don't want somebody who just started coming to church. 1 Timothy 3 tells us that a leader "must not be a recent convert" and "must first be tested." You need to know that they've been faithful in their walk with God and are deep in the Lord. It scares me sometimes that churches don't do enough of a background check on people. It's wonderful that they're really excited about

Faithfulness is more than perfect church attendance every week. It is pursuing God, reading the Word, living true to God's promises and convictions, and growing in faith.

God, but if they've only been saved a couple of months, what happens if they fall away? Do you realize what that could do to your kids? Everything you've been working for could be blown away.

I see this problem in Christian music. A talented band signs with a label, but they don't have a proven track record of faithfulness. Then, when they become famous, their character falls short; they blow it, fall away, and their fans are disillusioned with the faith. We need to look for people who are faithful and strong.

We need to be careful not to cheapen what faithfulness means. Faithfulness is more than perfect church attendance every week. It is pursuing God, reading the Word, living true to God's promises and convictions, and growing in faith.

Besides their faithfulness to the Lord, will your leaders faithfully represent *you*? When an artist paints a portrait, the best compliment you can give him is that it's *a faithful representation*. When you talk about leaders—your dream team—they need to faithfully represent you—your heart for kids, and your heart for God. Whether it's on a Wednesday night, or all of the rest of the week, if they're part of your team, they have to represent you well.

Equally yoked. Your Dream Team should be "equally yoked." My interpretation of "equally yoked" means we are on the same wavelength.

If, for example, you cast the vision to your leaders, "I want 100 kids in this group this year, 200 next year, 400 the year after, and we want to save a generation!"—your leaders should be on the same page as you are. But if your leaders say, "As long as we have 10 on-fire kids, we're pretty good with that," you're definitely still family in Christ, but you are *not equally yoked.*

Or, let's say you are passionate about breathing life into young people so that they can save their own generation, but your team thinks the best you can hope for is that they don't have sex or do drugs. You are *not equally yoked.*

What we're talking about here is philosophy of ministry, what you're passionate about. You will not always readily find people who are equally yoked, and at times you may have to breathe some of that into them. That's okay. They'll change. Ultimately, though, you've got to be equally yoked with your dream team.

Good character. You can see in 1 Timothy 3 that God wants leaders to have character. In fact, He is more serious about that than we are. When you're a leader you can help a lot of people, but you can also hurt a lot of people. The more opportunity you have to help, the more opportunity you have to hurt. Look at the example of Moses. Remember, he was leading the children of Israel, a group of about three million. Some youth group, huh? The

God is looking for people with character and self-control.

group was thirsty, so God said, "*Speak* to the rock." And what did Moses do? He *struck* it in his anger, and as a result, God wouldn't let him go into the promised land. There's a huge principle behind this thing. God expected Moses to behave better than that. If Moses was going to be in charge of the group, he needed to be a trustworthy leader—not one who was ruled by his attitudes and impulses.

The same principle holds true for leaders in youth ministry. God is looking for people with character and self-control. He demands a high level of character and holiness in the small things and big things in their lives.

Take some time now to think about the names of some people you might want on your leadership team. Go to your computer and open the CD-ROM file titled "Dream Team," and begin to list those names as you prayerfully consider each one.

HOW TO RECRUIT THEM

Now that you've spotted the kind of people you want, with the qualifications you need, how do you get them to sign up?

Pray. But pray discerningly. Write out the job description and then ask God, "Who would be the best person for *this* role?" Even if they don't know you're praying about them—even if they don't know you want them—write their names on your flow chart. "I want this person for this, and this person for this." Pray, "God, give me the opportunity to talk to them, because I know that they've done these kinds of things in the past and they'd probably be good at this." Then pray for Him to open their hearts to helping you. Once you've done this, you can approach them.

Do not just ask them if they will help you with the youth group. As we've talked about before, these people are busy; they need to see a reason to spend their precious time on your ministry.

Don't forget you're looking to build a "dream team," not just an hour-a-week babysitting service. You need to get to know these people yourself before you recruit them. For both of these reasons, your next step is . . .

Get to know them. Maybe you don't know them that well. This is okay. You don't always want to ask your closest friends to help with everything. You need to get other people involved in your ministry for it to grow. So take them out to lunch, interact in a social setting, etc. Start with small talk, but be ready to move on to your purpose.

Share your vision. After you've gotten to know them, say something like, "I've got some things on my heart I'd like to share with you and see what you think." Don't be afraid to get passionate. This is like fundraising. Just as people will contribute money to someone with a huge dream, these people will be more likely to volunteer if you are excited about what you're doing.

Explain why they're important. Once you've shared your dream with them, get specific about how you see their role. Tell them the strengths you see, and why you

You will find a whole army of people with a heart for the kids and a willingness to embrace your vision.

think they would be vital to the vision.

You don't even need to ask them to commit to "until death do us part." Just ask for a short-term commitment. "If you could help me for three weeks in this area," or "just two months over here." Hopefully they'll say, "Sure!" Then once they are done with the three weeks or two months, you can get together again and say, "Well, you've done a great job, you've really become part of the team. Do you feel the Lord's calling you to keep going?" Either God will touch their hearts for young people, or they'll have learned that youth ministry isn't where they're called to be. Either way, it's a win-win situation.

Ask them to help the teens, not to help you! It's hard to ask people, "Will you help me out?" But if you're talking about the kids, and the vision of reaching more of them, that's a lot easier, isn't it? This isn't about you. Point the focus away from you and more toward the vision. Your goal for these leaders is first, for them to get a heart for the kids, and second, for them to embrace your vision. After a trial period, they should be incredibly excited about what you're doing.

Don't feel like you have to settle for just anyone who will show up. You will find a whole army of people with a heart for the kids and a willingness to embrace your vision.

So keep praying for God to raise up the leaders that you'll need for your dream and your vision.

TURNING THEM INTO A TEAM

Just because you've gotten your leaders to show up doesn't make them useful. It's what you *do* with them once you have them that will make them useful. Compare it to a sports team. The 2004 U.S. Men's Olympic Basketball Team had a lot of star players on it, but there was no teamwork. So they lost. They lost to a bunch of teams with mediocre players and great teamwork. Where does teamwork come from? The coach. In this case, you. Once you've assembled your team, don't worry about how impressive they may or may not seem from the get-go. You are going to pull them together into something fantastic. What does it take for a team to become a dream team?

A vision for themselves as a group. You've already given your team a glimpse of your vision for youth ministry. You've answered their questions: How big will it be? What's the nature of our youth ministry? What has God put on our heart?

Now you have to share your vision for the team. *What is this team about?* Just like a coach, you have to create the atmosphere in which this team will work. Here are some good examples of what any ministry team should be about.

We'll have fun together. It's not going to be all work. Ministry needs to be enjoyable. This doesn't just mean, "Okay, let's all play a game." But your focus must be more than, "Did you do this job? Did you do this job?" Ministry

When a team has fun together, it creates energy.

is about more than just getting the job done; it's about having fun while you're doing the job. The relationships you build are part of the vision. "You know what, this is the kind of team we're going to be: the kind that has fun together." When a team has fun together, it creates energy. We'll talk about that more a little later.

We'll be competent. One person is good at one thing, and another is good at something else. We'll all do our jobs well, and together we'll make this a great team. That includes pulling together toward the same vision. As a leader, you don't need to stress that they be loyal to *you*, but that they be loyal to God's vision for the group, as revealed to you because the end of that vision is people; it's lives. You're asking them to get sold out for the vision and pursue it with excellence.

We'll be a community of trust. The meaning of trust here is two-fold. First, there is the sense of sharing the same basic values of honesty and integrity—which we can almost take for granted. But trust also deals with having confidence in each other to fulfill different roles. It's not about who gets a certain position. We are different members of the body of Christ, and each of us will serve in different ways. We don't ask, "How come he's in front more than I am? How come they get to do *that* ministry?" It will take some problem solving. The team has to work together to figure out how to get something done and maximize everybody's gifts.

I would definitely recommend that you and your team go do team-building events together—high ropes, obstacle courses, etc. These events help your team to bond and build trust and learn how to operate as a team. You can look in the phone book or call some different camps.

We'll challenge each other. This is an environment of stretching each other without threatening each other. Ideas will come from different people. An idea can be discussed, modified, or ultimately rejected. People need to be affirmed, and never rejected. This means that people can't afford to identify themselves with their ideas. You'll be doing lots of brainstorming with your team, and lots of things will be thrown out there. We want to challenge the way we think, not who we are. We're just trying to refine our ideas and make each other better. Amen?

We'll personally care about each other. We will get the job done, but not at the expense of each other. We don't just care about the vision; we care about each other as we walk toward the vision. We care about each other's personal growth. Are we really growing in the Lord, or are we just kind of strung out and barely having quiet times ourselves? People need to commit to each other enough to look each other in the eye and say, "Hey, what's really going on? How's your family doing? How's your walk with God going?"

As the leader, it's your job to cultivate this atmosphere. Start the process by spending a little one-on-one time with them. It's so easy for them to feel that all you want out of them is their hard work and time. You need

Ministry isn't about glory. It's about creating a team with whom you can share the victory.

to go the extra mile to show that you care about them. Maybe you don't know someone that well; maybe you inherited her from the last youth pastor; maybe he was forced on you. Doesn't matter. Be prepared to invest yourself in their lives.

IDENTIFY THE PURPOSE OF THE TEAM

Vision and purpose are two different things. The vision means what kind of team you're going to be—your "atmosphere." Purpose means, "Why are we here? What will we accomplish?" You must define purpose. Well, the purpose is to accomplish the vision. How do you do that? You have to work.

But work on what? The purpose of your team, essentially, is to figure out how to accomplish the vision, and then do it. Each person you invite onto the team needs to be able to see where he or she fits into the vision. For

example, is she on the drama team or does she lead praise and worship? If you achieve your dream, it will be because your leaders did the work behind it.

Take the next few minutes to define your team's purpose. Use page two of the CD-ROM file "Dream Team" to guide you.

Some leaders are not very secure and want to get all the credit. A confident, well-balanced leader doesn't care who gets the glory. It's not about you. It's not about your individual leaders. It's about God and His dream.

It's such an empty feeling to have a victory all by yourself. Once, an Olympic runner who had won several gold medals was asked, "Of all the gold medals that you've won, which one was the sweetest?" She said that it was the one relay for which she won a gold medal. "But why?" She answered, "Because I got to share the victory with three others."

Ministry isn't about glory. It's about creating a team with whom you can share the victory. It's "we," not "me." They're there to assist, advise, and labor with you.

This is the purpose of your team—figuring out the "how" of the vision.

DEFINE CLEAR EXPECTATIONS

Laying out the expectations helps to define the relationships of each team member. You need to be clear about the expectations you have of them. They need to be clear of the expectations they can have from you. If you don't clarify expectations, your team will always let you down, because they didn't even know what you were expecting of them. Here are some possible expectations:

Count the cost before they join the team. They're not just coming to show up. "We're about building a vision, building a ministry, reaching a whole generation and I'm going to need your heart, I'm going to need your sweat, I'm going to need your time. I need you here. I'm expecting that when you committed, you counted the cost. And I will not keep begging you to do this." Before a recruit enlists in the army, he's a volunteer. After he enlists, he's committed. It needs to be the same in youth ministry. You can still show compassion and understanding, but raise the bar on expectations.

Have an active walk with God. Your team needs to have its quiet time and grow in the Lord. Members need to keep a strong walk with God. They need to be faithful. Yes, this means faithful attendance, but more than that, they need to faithfully represent you. There is another very realistic expectation: expecting your team to read and to grow in God.

Bring work to the table. People often think the only time they have to work is at the meeting. "I'm showing up, isn't that enough?" No. I need you to work in between meetings. Maybe it's research, maybe it's planning, maybe it's making phone calls about the projects that we're working on. Meetings should become times where you discuss the work that's already been done. You're not there to babysit them. "Did you do your work? Please come back!" You shouldn't have to call them a million times to make sure the work gets done.

Other expectations for meetings: be on time; bring your best; be ready to think; be bright and alert; contribute.

Communicate with you. You know there shouldn't be any logjams. If something's not going to work out, then your team needs to e-mail, call, or let you know as soon as possible. Most of us have a pager, cell phone, or answering machine. When you figure out communication within your own ministry, it will diffuse 90 percent of all the confusion.

WHAT SHOULD THEY EXPECT FROM YOU?

These are the things you should be able to tell your team:

I will be the leader. "I will take responsibility." "I will set the standard." "The buck stops with me." "I am the leader."

I'm going to keep my heart with God right. Tell them, "I'm not going to be two-faced with you; you're going to see the real me. I'm not going to pretend everything is great when I'm digging myself up from the bottom of the pit. I will be sincere with you." Some things that go unspoken shouldn't go unspoken. Tell them to hold you accountable. "You can ask me anytime, 'Are you growing in the Lord?' If I'm growing, I'll tell you; if I'm not, I'll thank you for getting me back on track."

I will help you. "You know, you may not get everything right. That's fine. If you mess something up, I will coach you through it. I'm going to help you get better and as a result you'll make more of an impact on lives." That's what it's about. Helping your leaders make an impact on lives. A lot of people feel insecure and don't think they can really help. Suddenly, when they're part of your team, they'll be able to do a lot of things. Why? Because you believe in them and help them grow.

When you have questions, you can expect to hear back from me. You're not just going to go into an endless spin. "What about this, what about this?" Expect to hear back from me. I will respond to your questions. When you have a cry for help, you don't know what to do, you have a question, you can expect me to respond. You'll hear back from me when you have a question.

I'm going to be an encouragement to you. "I'm going to inspire and encourage you." One of the great coaches said, "My job is to get guys to do what they hate doing, so they can become what they've always wanted to become." There will be times when your leaders are frustrated and discouraged. You will help them through those times. We all have to do that. We all have to do things that we don't like doing so much, because it helps us to do the things that we really love doing: seeing lives changed.

Make these things clear. These are your guidelines for your team and for yourself. With these principles of leadership and teamwork in place, you have the foundation for a healthy team.

CHAPTER FOURTEEN

Leading Your Dream Team

So, you have the group, you've given them the vision, the purpose, and you've clarified the expectations. What do you actually do when you meet? What can you do to make this team proficient? To make it a high performance dream team? Well, let me give you some detailed things to actually do.

BEFORE THE MEETINGS

You need to prepare. This is the biggest challenge for leaders: we have to prepare for meetings. We all know we need to prepare to preach, but how many times do we excuse ourselves from preparing for a meeting with our team? "Oh, this is just a small group meeting," we say.

Thinking like a leader is about more than just getting these people to do a job. It's about pouring into their lives.

Listen carefully. You probably need to prepare more for those meetings than for preaching, because the impact you have on your team in a meeting will have a greater impact than any of your sermons. You're shaping the team who's building the ministry.

What do I mean prepare? Ask, what do I need to bring to the table to make sure it's worth the team's time? I've told them to come to the meeting prepared. To honor their time, I also must be prepared.

Make a deposit. Don't ever meet without depositing value into your leaders. The temptation is to think logistics and nothing else: "We've got a retreat in a month. Who's driving the bus? Who's doing this or that?" If that's all you focus on, you'll drain them dry.

Thinking like a leader is about more than just getting these people to do a job. It's about pouring into their lives. The more you personally deposit into them, the more they'll love you, the more loyal they'll be, and the more they'll feel like a better person around you. Not only is this good for your leaders, it will bear great interest in a heart for ministry. What else can you do to prepare for the meeting?

Prepare for the work that needs to be done. Think about how you are going to run your meeting. You need an agenda or a format that is more than just, "Here's a pile of work, okay, let's attack!" You need to decide what are the priority issues to cover at this meeting. In what order should they be discussed? What are the decisions that need to be made? At our meetings, we try to think about one work item at a time, and think it through together with time for each person to bring ideas to the table. Then we take a break and tackle the next area.

As we've mentioned before, part of preparing for the meeting is making sure that everyone else brings their homework—research items that you've assigned them beforehand. You can schedule a meeting for every day of the week, but if people haven't done their homework and brought it to the table, then you won't have a productive meeting.

Make sure you have the authority to get the job done. If you're meeting about something specific, and you've spent a lot of time planning for it, you'll want to be sure that you've got the authority from your pastor to tell your team, "Go with it." If you don't, you'll end up wasting your time and a lot of other people's time.

Be strategic about who attends the meeting. Is everybody who's necessary to get the job done present at the meeting? Do you have some people attending who don't really need to be there? Make some phone calls, e-mail, and cover your bases so that the work doesn't get hung up because a key person is missing.

Where and when is the meeting scheduled? When you schedule a meeting, you want to bring forth the best from your people. So if it's going to be a three-hour meeting,

The more you build as a team, the more proficient your team will be and the quicker you'll get to your vision.

you don't want to cram everyone into the back of your VW. Find a place where you will have something to write on, and an environment that produces creativity. If you want high productivity, you'll also want to consider when you will schedule the meeting. Will some people need to leave early? What time will they be the most focused?

Go to your computer and open up again to the CD-ROM file titled "Dream Team." Use pages three and four to help you prepare before each dream team meeting.

DURING THE MEETING

Be psyched. My goal for every meeting that I lead is to have people walk in the door and say, "This is the best place in the world to be. I don't want to be a part of any other ministry. I love being here." Amen! They ought to be so hyped. Not because you said, "Isn't this a great place?" but because they see the vision and they know it's going to happen. "We're going to reach 50 kids next month, and then next year we're going to have 100, and it's going to grow." It's incredible for them to walk out feeling, "Man, I love this place; this place rocks."

It's not easy getting them to that place. They'll see the size of your big vision and think, "Man, this is hard." But anything that's worthwhile is hard, right? So you make it a fun place to be. You give them space to use their energy to change the world and change people's lives. You give them a reason to say, "I wouldn't want to be any other place in the world."

Sometimes getting to that place will be tied to the vision, but it will also be tied to the team. I love the people. We work hard and change lives. Your team will be productive when they begin to love the people they're doing ministry with as much as they love the vision. How does this happen?

Plan team-building time. Earlier, we mentioned the importance of fun, team-building time. Your job as a leader is not just building the ministry; it's about building relationships, too. Listen carefully. The more you build as a team, the more proficient your team will be and the quicker you'll get to your vision. Let me give you some examples on how this works.

You don't have to spend a lot of money to build a team. You can eat together or go out to play laser tag. Go

My goal for every meeting that I lead is to have people walk in the door and say, "This is the best place in the world to be."

There's something about the synergy that happens when you have fun together.

dirt biking, camping, or ride horses. There are all kinds of low-cost relationship-building things you can do.

Let me tell you about one of the first times I did this. I was just starting to understand that we weren't supposed to just work, we also needed to have some fun and have relationships. So, I e-mailed my leadership team in the ministry and said, "Listen, there's a lot of construction down on the campus and we need to get out there with some of those construction workers and just relate to them. So, bring some work clothes; we're going to get dirty together." I'm sure my team was thinking, "What is going on with Ron? He's lost it. We have to run a whole ministry and he wants us to . . . uh, okay, whatever."

So they brought their old clothes to the next all-day planning meeting that we do once a month. They didn't *wear* them; they just brought them. When everyone was there I said, "We'll just spend part of the day just getting out there and relating, so I have a project that I want us to work on. Follow me." They all followed me out of the conference room into a warehouse and opened the door. In the warehouse was a bunch of different dirt bikes and four-wheelers that I had rented. Their eyes opened wide, and I have never seen people leave to change their clothes so fast! Our property in Garden Valley has about 470 acres, and we went out and we rode those dirt bikes through the mud and dirt for hours. We tipped over, we went over jumps, we laughed, and we got disgustingly dirty. We had so much fun, and took a video and pictures of it all.

About noon we were done, went and took showers, and had lunch together.

That afternoon we met and I'm telling you, we had a legendary meeting. We came up with some of the most creative, breakthrough ideas that we have ever had in the ministry. There's something about the synergy that happens when you have fun together. You're laughing, you're trusting, you're sending the signal, "I don't just care about you for the work that you bring to the table; I care about you as a person, and we're gonna be a team in this thing." It was a landmark day in all our minds.

Since then, we've done a lot of other team-building kinds of things. We've hunted together, gone to sports events together, and lots of things that are just kind of off the scale and strange. Recently, we went to the jungle in Ecuador together and visited some tribal people. Some of you may remember back in the 1950s, Jim Elliot and a few missionaries were martyred by the Auca Indians in Ecuador. We actually got to meet the Indians who killed them. It was an incredible experience that none of us will ever forget.

You don't have to leave the country to have legendary opportunities for team-building. You don't even have to leave your town. Do be intentional about finding things that build relationships. When you build that kind of trust and synergy into relationships, you'll get the kind of inspired planning meetings we've been talking about here. All it takes is one idea—one amazing, anointed

Team-building makes ministry a lot more fun, but it also helps you get to your vision quicker.

idea—to break through a lot of the red tape, a lot of the reasons you didn't think you could get there. That's what your planning is about, right? How to get there.

Do whatever you have to do to cultivate an environment for your team that will generate those ideas. It will be worth any money that you spend on the trip, or that outing, or that dinner together, or whatever it is. It is a great investment. Team-building makes ministry a lot more fun, but it also helps you get to your vision quicker.

The power of "What if." As we talked about in earlier chapters, you need to rally your team around the vision and the planning to accomplish it. Don't be afraid to think big, amazing goals, to think outside the box, to think, "*What if* we . . . " There's a lot of power in *what if* thinking. "*What if* this is what God is saying?"

This is exactly what I did when we first pondered going to the Silverdome: "*What if* we filled the Silverdome with 75,000 young people?" You know of course, the first thing my team thought was, "Did God tell you that it was gonna be full?" My answer was, "You know what? This is part of our dreams, some of our goals. Just *what if* this is God's will? If it is and God really does want us to be there, *what do you think it would take to get there?*"

I wasn't saying, "This is God's will." I was asking, "Just *what if* it was? What do you think we would have to do to go in that direction together?" All of a sudden their whole demeanor changed, and so did the conversation: "Well, we could do this or try this. Let's try out this and see if it works." And pretty soon, the whole thing was out of control! It wasn't me pushing, "Come on you guys, I know we can." It was them grabbing hold and saying, "If it is, I think we could try this." Are you following me? The momentum began to come from them instead of me. They rallied around the "What if?" I'm telling you, it has power to get them to buy into the vision. Soon, they'll want to work on the "How."

Talk about the "How." What do I mean by the "How"? There are two "hows." First, "*How* do we get the vision done right now?" That means next week and next month.

The second is broader than that: "*How* do we get the big plan done?" If you have 10 people in your group today, no matter how hard you work this week, you won't have 1,000 people next week. You won't have 500 next week. You may not even have 100 next week. If you want to get THAT part of the vision, you need to start planning things a year or two in advance. This is the part of the meeting where you will do the strategic planning that will ensure the success of the ministry. You'll divide your planning time between the *now* visions and the *future* visions.

Let me give you some tips on how to manage meetings so that these things actually happen.

MANAGING THE MEETING

Establish ground rules. Ground rules make everyone understand up front what you expect of them. They keep people from wasting time, and help maximize the efficiency of your meetings. When people get there, you want them to be there, right? You want them to be focused, not just there in body; you want their minds, their hearts, and their focus too. Let me give you some examples of ground rules that you can use.

- Don't be late.
- Don't interrupt meetings for phone calls unless it's an emergency. Turn off your beepers; turn off your cell phones.
- Don't leave the room once the meeting has started. The point is, once we're here, we're here to stay focused, not to do other things.
- Don't slump in your chair or doodle. These postures indicate lack of interest. Be engaged in the meeting.
- Listen attentively to the contributions of your partners and other people in the room.
- Actively contribute. In Harvard Business School, half of the grade is based on class participation. Forget all the papers and the tests; if you don't contribute during class, you will flunk.
- Focus hard to achieve the group good. It's not about me doing well; it's about everyone doing well.
- Find what's positive and eliminate the negative. Don't simply say, "I don't like that." Find the positive and accentuate that. Then seek to be the kind of participant you expect others to be.

Here's another idea: Don't you hate when people talk about things they've already told you again and again? Then they act like it's the first time anyone ever heard it? Lay the ground rule that anyone may call a time-out: "Time-out. Wait a minute. You've said that before; we've heard that speech." Be careful, people might call a time-out on you. But that's good, because repeating things just wastes people's time.

As the leader, it's your job to run meetings well. If you don't manage them, no one else will.

Define the roles. Make sure you know what your role is as the leader (managing the meeting). Also, help your team leaders be clear on their roles. Sometimes when I'm in a meeting I'll give the marker to someone and say, "Here, you lead this part of the discussion." I want them to be involved and engaged, not just along for the ride, so define the roles within the meeting.

Limit the issues. Don't talk about everything in the world. Choose enough issues to fill up your time and allow enough time for each of them.

Prepare an agenda. Don't just have it in your mind! Write an agenda before you walk in the door.

Be early to your own meetings. I encourage you as a leader to arrive early. This helps with the relationship side of things. "Hey, how are you doing, Sarah?" I'll walk around, rub somebody's shoulder and ask, "What's going on with you?" There's something about touch. Touch shows you care and are involved. You don't have to touch everybody. Just touching two people (in friendly, appropriate ways) creates a positive atmosphere.

Then start on time. It's very important how you begin the meeting. Say, "I'm so glad you're here. We're going to have a great meeting." This is part of depositing value

I encourage you as a leader to arrive early. This helps with the relationship side of things.

Having a good team that you love, respect, and enjoy is the best way to accomplish a vision.

into your leaders. Get announcements out of the way as quickly as possible.

Use the meeting for synergy, not information dispersal. Minimize announcements. Using meetings to distribute information is a bad use of people's time. If you need to disperse information, send an e-mail beforehand. Many youth pastors use announcements to collect their thoughts, since they're just winging the meeting anyway. On the other hand, you've prepared in advance and have valuable things to actually *discuss* with your team. The value of people is getting them together to think and dialogue.

This goes for your leaders as well. If someone is going to report, have her send you the information ahead of time. Forward it to the group. They can read the information before they get there. Then they can be ready to discuss it when the meeting starts.

At the very beginning, state the objectives and estimated time for the meeting. These things need to be clear to all in attendance. If people come in late, don't draw attention to them, just keep going. Make sure that people who come in late or miss a meeting know that it is their responsibility to find out what happened when they weren't there. It is not your responsibility to repeat it all over again to them and be the babysitter.

Periodically, however, restate the meeting objective in order to keep the meeting focused.

Be a moderator, not a partisan. Remain impartial, or at least demonstrate the appearance of impartiality during the meeting. For instance, don't take sides too quickly when people have contradicting opinions. Your value as a leader is to hear all sides on an issue. If you appear to take a side then people will think you're biased, and they will hesitate or hold back from sharing. Stay objective for as long as you can. Try to separate facts from opinions and beliefs.

"I really, really think we should!"

"But why . . . what evidence do you have?"

Watch the pacing of the meeting. Move things along. Don't get so wrapped up in one thing that you run out of time to talk about something important. Be on the lookout for any emotional build-ups. If you know someone gets really passionate about a subject, be ready to try to defuse the discussion if necessary.

Involve everyone. If a team member is sitting there being quiet, don't just let him sit there. Ask, "What do you think, Joe?" Ask his opinion, even though he didn't volunteer any information. He may have a great idea, but you may have to pull it out of him a little bit. Or it might show that he is not prepared, which is good to know too. He'll realize he needs to come prepared next time.

Make people feel important. Affirm people and their contributions. There are two things people on a team need to hear: "That's a great idea," and "You are a valuable part of this team."

Protect the weak. If there are people who don't present strongly in meetings, look out for them. Don't allow others to trample their feelings or ideas. Maybe you need to help them develop in this area, or maybe they don't belong on the team. Either way, you need to protect them.

Be sure to end the meeting. I would encourage you to have a time written down that you *will end* the meeting. It's your responsibility to keep it from going on forever.

Having a good team that you love, respect, and enjoy is the best way to accomplish a vision. Too many churches, not to mention youth ministries, don't take advantage of team ministry. They may have a board of deacons, and a board of elders, etc., but very few actually work as a team to see a vision come about. Victory is so sweet when you have accomplished it through loving teamwork.

Jesus did this with His disciples. He constantly used team dynamics to pull them together, to give them the vision. He taught them lessons, sent them out, brought them back, then sent them out again. He was pulling them into His vision for the world, and their role in it. That is what you must do if you are going to see your incredible ministry vision from God come to pass.

CHAPTER FIFTEEN

Preparing for the Rollout

Now that you have completed so much of the work that a real leader does, it is important to "unveil" the vision in a way that draws people in. By now you have had weeks of praying over and thinking through the details of the new vision, but others have not. You are convinced it is God's direction, but they know nothing about it. In order to complete the vision, you must have people agree with your vision, so how you present it to them (the rollout) will either woo them into the vision or drive them away. Remember, we mentioned earlier God's model for leadership: God gives the vision to the leader, and the leader is called to take the people with him.

How you introduce folks to the vision is crucial. It

How you introduce folks to the vision is crucial. It will, in large part, determine whether or not they'll follow.

will, in large part, determine whether or not they'll follow. It's as if you're unveiling an amazing sculpture that you've carved in private (of course you have had some of your adult and teen leaders helping you with the plan) for a long time. You want everyone to be thrilled about the new direction. Just telling them, "God has put this on my heart. I know we have only 25 kids in here now, but in a year we can have 200," may not do it.

Part of the rollout is making the dream compelling, but also showing them your plan to accomplish it. This makes the dream believable, and not just a fantasy. They have to know you are serious about the direction and that you have done the homework. Some people get so excited about an idea they have for ministry that they talk about it prematurely, and as a result it comes off as a whim. When they see the planning that you and your team have put into it in advance, they will know you are serious about pursuing the dream. Our job as Youth Specialists is to not only give them the dream, but give them a glimpse of how it will happen.

In this chapter, we'll deal with these things that come *before* the actual rollout. Then, in the chapter to come, we'll cover a few important principles to guide you through the period *after* the rollout.

What things must you do *before* your big event? Here are eight things I've found absolutely essential for rollout success:

1. Don't go past . . . your pastor. As Youth Specialists in a church, part of our challenge is to help our pastors understand what God is burning into our hearts—and show that it is lining up with the broader vision of the church. Make sure the pastor is fully on board, because if it is a vision that is going to rock your region, a dream that will really change the community, then you must gather plenty of support.

At all costs, avoid having your pastor find out about things accidentally, through other people. Instead, woo your pastor. Don't just walk in and say, "This is what God is telling us. Obey or perish!"

Instead, very early on in the dreaming process, try something like this: "Pastor, the Lord has really been putting some things inside of me about the direction for the youth for the next year or so. I just want to make sure it lines up with where your heart is for the young people in this church. So maybe I could just share a couple of things with you and see what you think about these ideas."

As Youth Specialists in a church, part of our challenge is to help our pastors understand what God is burning into our hearts—and show that it is lining up with the broader vision of the church.

Most pastors will want to help these kids. We just need to personalize the need and help them understand that it is all taking place *right here in our community.*

Then . . . share those ideas.

Of course, some pastors will resist. You then need to back up a little further and help him develop a heart before you share your plan.

How can you do that? You might say things like: "Pastor, I've done some research about the kids in our high school and this is what I've found . . ." Then tell what you know. It's already broken your own heart to know these things—the abuse, the loneliness, the drug use, the abortion, the sexual experimentation and disease. Who could know these things and not be moved to action? Yet be gentle, submissive, and—above all—exercise patience. You might say something like: "What do you think, Pastor; do you think we should do anything to help these kids in our community?"

Most pastors will want to help these kids. We just need to personalize the need and help them understand that it is all taking place *right here in our community.* "Pastor, maybe we can do some things to help these kids." He then will begin to ask whether you have any ideas . . .

2. Ramp up your teen leaders and adult volunteers. Far in advance, pull some teens in that demonstrate leadership and tell them that God is burning things into your heart. Ask them whether they want to help. Then, when you have your rollout, you'll already have plenty of teens who are excited and behind you—even encouraging others. Pull them into the dream before telling everyone else. You may also get good ideas from these teens. (Note: Don't go to them for ideas about where they think the ministry should go; that is your job as the leader. But you *can* say, "This is where God is taking us, so do you guys have any ideas on how we should get there?" And don't offer any voting control. Just let them give you ideas and then you pray and choose.) You will want to already have assigned them different areas in your flow chart so that organization is in place to accomplish the dream before you roll it out. (See Chapter 13 on recruiting and training leaders.)

Look now at your CD-ROM again. The first page of the file titled "Rollout," asks you to do some thinking about key people who will come alongside you and help as you reveal the new direction of your youth ministry. Ask God to show you people with ideas and enthusiasm! The second page helps you prepare for the rollout event itself.

Don't forget that there's a difference between *having* a plan and *implementing* the plan.

3. Don't start until . . . you're finished planning. Okay, let's back up a minute. Don't forget that there's a difference between *having* a plan and *implementing* the plan. Often people start dreaming about all they're going to do for God, and they get so excited about it that they *start implementing it before the planning is complete.* "Oh, we're going to do *this* and *this* and *this!*" They talk to people before they've thought the whole thing through.

What happens then? A couple of months later you are still putting the plan together and still "sort of" talking about it—with a lot less energy. Naturally, this causes people to lose confidence in your plan and think that you are just a talker, not a doer. Do not start talking about the plan (to the group) or implementing any part of a plan until the planning is complete—until you really do know where you *are* and where you're *going* and exactly *how* you are going to get there.

When you first begin to pull the plan together, it will be a little fuzzy, like an artist's first blotches of paint on a canvas. Who can tell what it will become? But she keeps coming back to it, and eventually we see something clearly take shape. With the final touches, everything is crystal clear. *That's* when it's time to start showing it around.

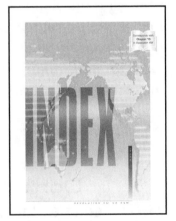

In the Index of your CD-ROM, you will find several letters

and organizational tools that may help you as you roll out your youth ministry plan. Feel free to reproduce or adapt them for your own use.

4. Believe, and make the plan . . . believable. Now you have the plan, the step-by-step process, all laid out in charts with a mission statement, objectives, goals, core values—the whole nine yards. Your next job is to make the vision believable to the kids and to the leaders and parents. You must instill confidence. But here's the key concept I want you to remember:

> *Others may not believe in the plan, but they believe that you believe it will work.*

They see that you believe the plan so much—with so much passion and practical sweat-and-tears commitment—that they are enabled to believe it too. Clearly, you have to believe that the dream is from God. Then it's simple: you pour your heart out.

Whenever a giant new step is taken in ministry, people need to know that the leader really believes this is from God. When we were preparing to move our ministry headquarters to Texas, the numbers all lined up, but my board of directors asked, "Do you believe this is the Lord's direction?" They didn't care if it was logical—if it wasn't God's direction. My leadership team, who would have to move their families if they were to stay in Teen Mania, had to have great faith. Finally I told them, "I have so much faith this is from God, that even if you don't, I have enough faith for all of you!" Based on that, they all sold their houses and moved their families and followed the dream!

5. Tease your teens. Part of a great rollout is creating anticipation in the youth group about what's coming. Make some off-the-cuff statements like, "God has been putting some great things in my heart about where we are going as a ministry . . . oh, I can't talk to you about that now . . . I will tell you more later." Then at another time you say something like, "Oh, guys, I am so excited about where God is going to take us—oh sorry, I can't really talk about that now." Then later you can say, "On this date, everything is going to change. God is stirring me up, and I can't wait to tell you everything. On May 15 (or whatever date) I will . . ."

A couple of weeks later, tease them again, while you are still several months in advance of the rollout. Be clear about this, though: you're not throwing pieces of the vision out there. You are simply building a sense of anticipation. A week before the rollout, that anticipation will include a lot of detail.

If you do this right, it should be a launching pad for your dream. For example, one week before rollout, you could hold a funeral service for your old youth group. Do it right—play a CD with organ music, have a real coffin, wear black. Don't even announce it; just let kids come in and tell them you are burying the old youth group. "Here lie all the old attitudes, the old names, the old program, everything we have done. We are going to bury it all and only take with us what God wants us to take." Write all those "old, dead things" down and throw them in the coffin. Then offer your eulogy: "We are gathered here today in remembrance of . . ." Finally, have someone carry the coffin out and invite the teens to say their final goodbyes.

Kids won't know what to expect for next week, will they? But they'll know it will be new. The old is buried! At the end of the funeral service, tell them to get ready for the resurrection, the revelation of the new dream, the vision of "where God is taking us." Leave them with a sense of anticipation—a whole new picture of how their future will look.

If this sounds like a fun idea to you, go to your CD-ROM and open the file titled "Change." The first page will help you get started as you plan for a "funeral service" for the old ways of doing youth group.

Tease the parents, too. Ask your senior pastor to include several announcements in the Sunday bulletin. Write little teasers that say, "God is taking our young people somewhere new. We are gearing up to do something incredible. It will be awesome, so get ready for the rollout." Prime the parents, so that when you're ready to unroll the vision to them, they'll more readily support it.

6. Preparing to make a BIG DEAL! You already know you're going to have a youth group name, logo, and room ready to unveil. Refer back to Chapter 5 for details here,

Make the vision so compelling that it fills in all the blanks between the dots of your plan.

but just remember that your kids really do need their own identity. That is why schools have mascots. Here are some things you can do with these identifiers to make a splash—

- Develop your own unique logo and get a banner made . . . BIG; have it ready and up on the wall, covered.
- Make T-shirts with your logo and Bible verse.
- Have business cards proclaiming what you are all about, so you and the teens can pass them out to all their friends. You could make them look like a ticket— "Free Admission to next Wednesday!" Be sure to include the new name of your youth group, your logo, and mission statement.
- Make a brochure showing "where we are now, and where we will be going over the next six months to a year."

With these small but effective actions, people begin to realize that they're not just coming to "a youth some-thing." They are heading into a vision. When you give them a big and broad vision, they'll want to be a part of it.

7. Paint the picture . . . for picture-perfect impact. Before the rollout, think about how you will use your words to paint a multicolored, multifaceted picture in their minds. Your youth room may not be the coolest yet, but there should be a clear difference between what it looked like *last week* and what it looks like *this week*. Don't just ask, "Here it is; who likes it?" Do an actual unveiling. Have the logo, mission statement, goals for the year, picture of the youth room, etc. all covered up, so when the kids walk in they know something is there but can't tell what it is. Then bring people all together for the big revelation. This is what you are doing with your vision, very slowly and deliberately getting ready to unveil it.

One thing you might want to do is prepare a video or a Power-Point presentation. Part of the unveiling is to say, "Here is the vision, and let me show you how we are going to get there." This is the time to connect the dots for everyone involved. Display the plan—three months, six months, nine months, one year. Show them what the flowchart looks like, and convey with passion how *each person* will be a part of this thing God is doing among you.

I can just hear you painting the picture, even now: "When people walk in these doors, they're going to feel so much love and acceptance. And we will have all kinds of kids here—some with tattoos and weird hair and piercings. They will all come. Be ready to open up your arms and hug them!"

How are we going to get 200 kids coming in the door? "We're going to have a happening service! So when they all get here, they'll enjoy an amazing band and riveting video clips. There's going to be drama, and comedy, and you will be putting those things together! Listen—you will reach your own generation for Jesus! *Can you think of any-thing more awesome than that?"*

Make the vision so compelling that it fills in all the blanks between the dots of your plan. Spell it out clearly to them. I would encourage you to have a couple of your leaders, adults and teens that you've pulled aside earlier, prepared to speak. (But make them promise secrecy until the unveiling night.) That night, call them up and have them offer testimonies. Let them share from their own hearts: "We can do this, I *know* we can . . ."

You have now laid it out. Now the rubber meets the road.

8. Ask people to commit to the Dream. After you've spent time painting the vision, you begin to ask the question, "Who is in this with me?" It's a simple question you can ask in many different ways, but at some point you'll need to say something like, "You guys can come here and attend, no problem. But, from this point on, *if you are going to be a member, then you need to get involved in the vision."*

Coaches do this when they plan for their championship seasons. It causes every player to make significant, sacrificial changes in lifestyle and priorities. They get up early, work hard in the weight room, eat right, and kiss that pavement every day. They know that they will endure pain. But, because of the vision, they *want* to do it.

You can do the same thing: "This is where we are going; are you with me? I need to know you are with me—and it means that you get enlisted in the plan in some way. You may be a greeter or you may help put things in the mail." Since you need all of your jobs lined up in advance, you begin asking the question at the strategic time. Follow through with those who are ready to get plugged into this vision by saying, "I need your time and I need your energy to see this happen." Tell them, "If we harness this energy together, then we can do this thing. But I need to know who will be with me."

Go ahead, draw a line in the sand; have an altar call. Who will be part of this vision that has come from God? "God is going to use you, not just me. All of us together!" Present such a compelling dream that it is worth the pain and sweat.

Have people come down to the front, and let them know, in great detail, the commitment you will ask of them—the hours in the office, for example. Lay it all out, because those who are grasped by the vision will be inspired to work harder than they've ever worked before. Because you have a detailed flowchart for your operational plan, you already know how many people you need, and where you need them. Enlist them that night.

Once you have prayed at the front of the auditorium or church, show them on the flowchart the different areas that will forward the vision. Have each of the different area leaders at the back of the room. Describe each area and who is in charge. Then dismiss your teens to go to the area that interests them. That's part of the package. Everyone gets involved that night in some part of the vision. Give them the business cards, T-shirts, etc., as a sign that you know they are committed. Once they're in their respective areas, make sure each leader is prepared to tell them what he needs for them to do, when the next meeting is, and then pray over that area.

CHURCH ON THE BIG SCREEN

We have rolled out the steps used in [*Revolution YM*]. We did the big reveal on a Sunday during our first youth-led worship service. A lot of people were amazed. I also used a lot of. . . stats and made a video to show the church on the big screen we installed in the youth center. Big hit!

—Duke, Youth Specialist

That night, all things change. Get them plugged in that night.

Finally, remember that this will be a big deal only if the parents are fully with you. Maybe in the past you've had to beg your parents to bring their kids to a youth meeting. No more! Now that you've told your youth, you can reveal the vision to their parents.

Go back to your computer and look at page two of the CD-ROM file titled "Change." Keep a running list of people who are supporting you in the vision.

To see revolution in this generation, we need a lot more than youth pastors caring about kids. We need every adult who calls himself a Christian to care about kids. When MTV wants to reach a generation, they don't just hire one person; they hire an army of people. Everybody at MTV cares about reaching teenagers with a corrupt message. We need an army of adults who care about church, and we need the whole church to care about your youth and to pray for the vision. You may want to sign up your parents, pastors, and deacons to go through the *Battle Cry for a Generation* book and study guide. You don't want to be alone in this effort to double your youth group every year for the next five years. We need our churches to be like hospitals to the broken-hearted teens of this generation!

This rollout is the night when all your planning begins to reap fruit. Your dream will start to become what you have seen in your heart for a long time.

Notes

CHAPTER SIXTEEN

The Ongoing Role of the Youth Specialist

If you've come this far in the book, you might be tempted to think, "Wow! Now I'm going to be really busy!" There are youth worker conferences you'll need to attend to help you discover a million things that you could try. The catalogs that fill your mailbox every day with new ideas and products will need immediate investigating. Right? Wrong!

Now that your plan is in place (and assuming you have unveiled it correctly), and your adult and teen leaders are leading the charge to accomplish the vision, you must decide where *you* should use *your* energy, based on *your* dream that the Lord has given you for youth ministry.

How is it that a CEO with 40,000 employees can run

It's important to remember that the reason you have leaders is so they can do the job, not you.

a company with time to spare, yet many youth leaders hardly have time to breathe? CEOs spend their time differently than you do. They invest their time and energy doing *only* the tasks no one else can do.

As Youth Specialists, we must keep asking ourselves, "What are the tasks *only I* can do?" Decide what tasks can be handled well by someone else, and let them go for it! After you have rolled out the vision for your youth ministry, you must focus your energy doing eight things that no one else can do:

1. Keep managing the plan. Take a close look at every one of your leaders' weekly reports and make sure they are "on plan." You know the old saying, "People don't do what you expect; they do what you inspect." It's true! As you look at their reports, which we described earlier, always respond with your comments. E-mail is a great way to communicate—it's fast and easy. I suggest you e-mail good comments only; if you need to correct, always do it in person. Your team needs to know that you are watching what they do, and whether or not they are moving in the right direction. You will spend time coaching them in any area where they are falling short.

It's important to remember that the reason you have leaders is so they can do the job, not you. Keep pushing them and developing them so they will be successful at their tasks. Just because you are inspecting what they are doing does not mean that you should start doing it yourself. Be careful to avoid this temptation.

2. Keep preparing a service each week. This includes all the elements of keeping teens' attention and helping them to really engage in their relationship with the Lord. Using media, PowerPoint, movie clips, object lessons, and discussion guides can all be a part of a creative, interactive service that really connects with their hearts. Obviously it means you must be prepared to speak and deliver great content.

If you have never taken any speaking courses, and you've never read anything that will help develop your speaking ability, begin now! If kids are bringing their friends to Wednesday nights, make sure what you do throughout the service is going to make those teens want to come back!

For the kids who already passionately love God, make sure you have a steak to put on the table for them. Too often I've seen kids get on fire at camp or at an *Acquire the Fire* weekend, or a mission trip, and they come back to sit in the front row and be fed. But the youth leader is talking to everyone else! "You guys need to get on fire," he says. And the kids in the front are saying "Amen!" Then the leader says, "You guys in the back need to be like these guys in the front." This goes on for two months, and all the kids start to think: "Haven't we heard all this before?" The fire goes out. They start thinking they've heard everything in the Bible, because the same single message is repeated over and over again. Don't let that happen!

Kids will starve to death spiritually if we do not feed them.

If you don't feed the kids spiritually, they'll get bored and distracted. The world will get their attention and the next thing you know you'll hear of them involved in some sin and lament, "I guess they were not as committed as I thought they were." Yes they were; they just starved to death spiritually even though they were coming to church! A Youth Specialist would never let this happen. We must specialize in making these on-fire converts into solid warriors and disciples!

Kids will starve to death spiritually if we do not feed them. At the most basic level, this means you can't be trying to think of something to say while driving to the meeting! It is our solemn responsibility to make sure each of our messages to the kids is awesome and amazing. When kids leave your Wednesday night service, they should walk away thinking, "This is the best ministry in the whole world!" They should be convinced in their hearts that nothing could possibly be more important than coming back next week because, "I love it here, I get fed, I feel loved here, and I feel God's presence here." Each week, make sure all the elements of an amazing meeting are in place and do it with excellence.

As you're planning your weekly meeting, make sure that your teaching themes are geared around your dream. For example, if a big part of your dream is to develop kids who love to worship God, then take three or four weeks to talk about "how to become a worship animal." That is what you want them to become. And if a big part of your vision also includes helping the kids become "ministry monsters," take a month and dwell on that. If part of your thing is about missions, spend weeks on it. As you teach, give awesome examples, make it funny, interactive, heart-felt, and inspiring. God may change your plan from time to time if something is really brewing in your heart, or some emergency comes up in your community. But you can keep coming back to the dream that drives the agenda of your meeting topics. *Your service topics ought to be driven by your vision.*

3. Keep rolling out the dream to the whole church body. Once you unveil the vision and plan to the pastor and the kids, you need to follow with the entire church body. Why? Because you need every member behind you.

Obviously, you need parents praying for you. You want them saying, "Amen! Amen!" to your inspiring decla-ration of the plan. "Folks, Pastor Jones bought into this thing, and I am telling you I need every adult to be pray-ing for us and considering becoming a volunteer. Pray, please pray!" You want them to take ownership of the vision.

Enlist their hearts by constantly giving them stories about real-life teens in your church and community. Show them the hurting teens, the successful teens, the failing

> You can keep coming back
> to the dream
> that drives the agenda of
> your meeting topics.

> # Our job is to give our adults a vision of what they could do because most do not know what they can do.

teens. Appeal to their compassion, because church people have good hearts, but they need to see and feel what you are talking about.

Then, when these folks see young people coming in with weird hair and piercings, they too are ready to hug them and love them and be the "parents" these kids don't have at home. Some of your church members, whose hearts have been melted for young people, will begin to take kids under their wings. Our job is to give our adults a vision of what they *could* do because most do not know what they *can* do. This is not a burden to us; this is part of our job!

The bottom line is, many adults are afraid of young people. So we can hug the "scary" kids in front of them. (Wouldn't it be great if every visitor who came into our meetings got hugged 10 times?) Suppose we gave church members such a vision that, when they're at the checkout counter with the kid who bags their groceries, they say, "You've gotta come to our youth meetings at church; they're terrific!" Wouldn't that be awesome?

Give the church a vision. Keep finding ways to keep it in front of them and keep every heart involved.

4. Keep looking at the forest. Keep the big picture before you at all times. Yes, it's easy to become sidetracked by problems, fires to extinguish, and conflicts to resolve.

Nevertheless, you must take your eyes off the individual trees and stand back to survey the whole forest. It's your job to keep a finger on the pulse of the whole living body of ministry, so you know if all the parts are working together to fulfill the plan—or not. You don't get down and micromanage each part. But you do poke your head in on different parts of the ministry you created and see if everyone is okay—encouraging, reminding, and lifting them up as needed: "Listen, I've got a Scripture for you guys," or, "Man, that looks great; good job!" Ask questions that refer the team back to the big plan:

- Are we on track?
- How is the worship team doing?
- Are you guys coming together in the media committee?
- How's it coming with transportation?
- What's happening these days with drama planning?
- Is everything that we prepared and planned happening, or not?

Maybe you're thinking, "Ron, if I have to keep my eyes on the big picture, does that mean I can never counsel kids one-on-one again?" No. What it means is that you're raising up other leaders who can do things like that.

You must take your eyes off the individual trees and stand back to survey the whole forest.

You have the whole dream to manage, a sacred stewardship from the Lord. You can't afford to get lost in the trees.

Sadly, some of us feel that we're called to be friends with every one of our kids. But if we have a hundred kids in our group, it's impossible for us to be friends with every one.

You say, "But that sounds so cold!" Keep this in mind: we're called to be *leaders* to them, all of them. More than our friendship, the kids need our God-given ability to teach them how to be strong men and women of God. That's what they need.

Yes, some kids may think that you preach really well on Wednesday nights and if they hung out with you as your friend, they would get more of that. And they probably *would* get more of that—but you can't do it with 100 teens! So you commission your leadership group of teen leaders and adult leaders to be friends to all the others. They can counsel. They can take calls from kids late at night, asking for prayer because parents are fighting. You take the higher-level emergency calls, because *you have to look over the whole forest.* You have the whole dream to manage, a sacred stewardship from the Lord. You can't afford to get lost in the trees.

5. Keep feeding your teen leaders and adult volunteers. You need an army of adults to work with you. You need an army of teenage young people to work with you. Therefore, part of your job is to know how to enlist them effectively. *Don't ask people to give you anything* (their time,

Keep feeding your team; don't let them go dry on you.

their labor, their love, etc.) *without giving them something in return.*

What do you give back? You give spiritual food, piled high with tons of encouragement. Your team meetings should be so much more than simply handing out assignments. Instead, ask yourself: "What am I going to do to plant a seed into their lives? What am I going to do to build my team up? What am going to do to make them stronger men and women of God?" Why? Part of your vision is to take this army of teens and make them into robust leaders. So you will do the research, read the books, and listen to the tapes to figure out what's going to make them into great leaders. As a result, you come into every meeting with that agenda.

Keep feeding your team; don't let them go dry on you. It is easy to overlook them because they are already strong, but make sure you keep feeding them, too!

6. Keep raising money. Sorry, but you can't quit doing this. And don't feel ripped off; it's part of life. That doesn't mean you should be taking M&Ms everywhere, selling them door-to-door all by yourself. But do realize that you simply must use some of your time for this.

If everything revolves around getting the thing started— rather than thinking the thing through and keeping the doors open—then failure looms.

Money. It's part of our job, not a curse.

Every nonprofit organization has to raise money. But take heart. If your ministry is really going to touch lives and change hearts, then it's worth it. On your agenda must be, "How, exactly, am I going to fund this thing?"

Yes, we now have a wonderful youth center. But a month later, will the doors be closed? Yes, if you're not bringing in the funds to support it. If everything revolves around getting the thing started—rather than thinking the thing through and keeping the doors open—then failure looms.

Some youth leaders are shortsighted and say, "God will supply somehow; let's just get the doors open!" But my experience is that *fulfilling our God-given responsibilities is a part of the blessing God graciously gives us.* Therefore, a big part of our job is to think long term. If you need proof, consider: How many empty youth buildings dot the country at the moment? How many coffee houses were started by a ministry, funded for a month or two, and then the doors slammed shut?

Money. It's part of our job, not a curse. The great thing is that if people can get money to fund stupid causes—to save the worms, to cool down the planet— surely we can get money for the greatest cause of all— reaching a young generation for Jesus before He returns.

7. Keep reiterating the vision. Make the vision fresh, real, and alive every day—every time you preach, or teach, or talk. The Lord of the universe is hardly boring! We can follow Him, constantly conveying the awesome adventure of involvement in His dreams for us. More stories, more new statistics about youth, more current events, more high-school stories in the news—all of this from you—help teens to continue on and press into the vision.

We tend to think that if we say it one time that they get it. They don't. Constantly look into how you can make the dream compelling and clear to them. Say it a hundred times, because they didn't get it completely or as clearly as you got it. You must sell the vision . . . and resell it.

8. Keep developing yourself. We must keep growing ourselves as leaders, as women and men of God. This means finding people who are beyond us in spiritual maturity and/or leadership skill to mentor us. It means asking, "What can I learn from them?" whether it's people that we meet one-on-one in our church, or our pastor, or leaders in our community, or authors of the books that we read. It's our job to learn from them and grow better, stronger, and more competent.

It is your responsibility to let God grow you as a leader of teens. If you don't keep growing, you won't be able to take anyone else with you. While you lay out your dream, introduce it, unveil it, and get the kids committed and

> While you lay out your dream, introduce it, unveil it, and get the kids committed and involved, you must keep taking in what you need—so you can keep giving out what you've received.

involved, you must keep taking in what you need—so you can keep giving out what you've received.

As you build your youth ministry from the ground up, you can't and shouldn't do everything yourself. But you must do these eight things to continue to watch the dream unfold in front of you. It does take focus. It does take work. But you can do it! In fact, you *must* do it. Your call is to rescue a generation of young people and speak truth into their lives.

Before you go on to the next chapter, take some time to think about the eight things youth leaders must focus their time on. Go to your computer now and open the CD-ROM file "Change" and look at pages three and four. Focus your energy on these things that no one else can do but *you!*

CHAPTER SEVENTEEN

Preempting Problems as You Grow

Problems. Conflicts. Messy messes!
We all have them in ministry, and we all want to move
through them as quickly as possible. The good news, of
course, is that most of our significant problems result from
growth. And growth is good, bringing much blessing to
everyone involved. We get to minister to more kids, we get
to touch more lives, and we get to see more people coming to Christ. We also face many more sticky difficulties.

But is it possible to prevent some of the problems in
the first place? Yes! In this chapter we'll look at some
growth-related problems you can expect, and I'll describe
a few proactive actions you can take.

Sadly, some folks who work with youth apply a

We must not settle for becoming a *wide* river; we want to be a *deep* river.

ministry-devastating logic: "Well, the more kids there are, the more problems there are. That means I must stay small and minister to fewer kids—see fewer kids come to Christ—because I don't want more problems."

No, we simply need to grow wiser so we can minister to more. Anticipate problems so you can resolve them. Nip potential problems in the bud by asking yourself a few pointed questions . . .

Is my heart deepening along with my ministry growth? As I mentioned in the previous chapter, your heart for God must grow right along with your ministry. It's also your responsibility to make sure that your leadership skills grow, that your family is stable, and that your personal life stays wholesome.

When our ministry expands, it's so exciting! As it grows wider and broader, so do we, until suddenly . . . we go shallow. We must not settle for becoming a *wide* river; we want to be a *deep* river. The danger for youth leaders is that as we seek to *expand* the ministry, we may sacrifice *depth* . . . our own! What good is it if we are full of one-line zingers that can really inspire an audience if we, ourselves, are shallow?

Let's be diligent about being in the Word and in prayer. Let's commit to challenging ourselves and letting our spouses and others speak truth into our lives. We must make every effort as the ministry expands, to continue on a deepening journey, growing along with our ministry. There is nothing worse than a shallow person, out of touch with God, trying to lead a growing ministry.

Am I remembering who I truly am? Monitor your ego! So you once had 30 kids, and now you have 60 kids. All of a sudden you have become an expert, and everybody in town is saying, "Wow! Did you hear they have their own bus, and their own youth building? This guy must know what he's doing!"

Naturally, you start thinking, "Hey, I'm doing pretty well." You didn't mean to develop this attitude, but it sneaks in. "I smell pretty good, I look pretty good, and, you know, I guess I *am* the coolest youth pastor in these parts." You may never consciously say it; you just start acting like it. Here's a good biblical corrective:

> *For by the grace given me I say to every one of you: Do not think of yourself more highly than you ought, but rather think of yourself with sober judgment, in accordance with the measure of faith God has given you.*
>
> —Romans 12:3

As your ministry begins to grow, God begins to bless. God does it. It is *His* work, *His* Kingdom, *His* glory.

And who are we? Well, we are sons and daughters of the Most High God. We are not God, though. We are sons and daughters of the Most High, joint heirs with Jesus Christ. But we are not Jesus Christ. We have to know this, deep inside, so we can lean on the One who is our life and

When your ministry expands, and you feel the subtle pull of an expanding ego, spend some time in quietness before God.

our strength and our reason for being. Everything flows from Him and works for His glory. Not our glory.

"But Ron," some say, "I have such a struggle staying humble!" Here's a great way to do it: have great quiet times. It is quite difficult to stay arrogant when you go face-to-face with God every day—when you bow your knee and your heart before Jesus regularly.

Can you worship the Lord of all with all of your heart, all by yourself? If so, can you feel proud in His presence? Or is it simply *gratitude* that wells up? (What else could there be?)

When your ministry expands, and you feel the subtle pull of an expanding ego, spend some time in quietness before God. Ask yourself: "Have I forgotten who God is, and who I am?" Then it's easy to keep yourself in perspective.

How proactive am I with my pastor? You've got your pastor "on board," of course, and he wants everything to work as you've planned. But here's what can happen: if your youth ministry really begins to grow, then people will start paying attention to . . . *you*. That's fine, but . . .

> . . . *you don't ever want the pastor to think that you are "doing your own thing."*

> . . . *you don't ever want the pastor to think that you believe, "This is my church."*

. . . you don't ever want the pastor to think that you have no need for spiritual authority in the church.

You want your pastor to know that you are in total submission to him and to the church. In fact, this is the spirit of a leader that Jesus held up as an example for the kingdom.

When Jesus had entered Capernaum, a centurion came to him, asking for help. "Lord," he said, "my servant lies at home paralyzed and in terrible suffering."
Jesus said to him, "I will go and heal him."
The centurion replied, "Lord, I do not deserve to have you come under my roof. But just say the word, and my servant will be healed. For I myself am a man under authority, with soldiers under me. I tell this one, 'Go,' and he goes; and that one, 'Come,' and he comes. I say to my servant, 'Do this,' and he does it."
When Jesus heard this, he was astonished and said to those following him, "I tell you the truth, I have not found anyone in Israel with such great faith."
—Matthew 8:5–10

This centurion held authority *over* scores of soldiers. Though he was a commander, he started by saying, "I am a man *under* authority." So it should be with us as we talk to our pastors. We can constantly remind him and ourselves that, "I am under your authority. I am under your leadership. Do you feel good about this plan . . . this event . . . this outreach, Pastor? What do you think about this

YM NOITULOVER

Never forget that ministry is about people.

idea?" We can submit things on a regular basis so that there is never a sense of "that youth guy taking over."

Instead, be proactive. Constantly, regularly, take the initiative to remind your senior pastor, "I am under your authority here. If this thing grows it is because you are blessing it, and you are allowing it to happen. It is all still under your leadership." Be the one to bring it up, so the pastor never has to say to you, "Remember, you are still under the authority of this church." No, you should be reminding him, "I am a part of your ministry here. This is awesome what God is doing. I am just a small part of it."

To what extent am I caring for individuals? Never forget that ministry is about people. It's not about how well we run a meeting, how well we preach, how well we administrate. It's about caring for people—talking to them, listening to them, encouraging them at every turn.

If there is no true caring, people start wondering, "Wait a minute; is this just a big show? Is this merely an organization or is this a *ministry?*" On the other hand, if teens and adults know that you care about them, that you really love them, then you don't have to remind them by saying, "We really care about people around here!" They already *know* you care about them because they see it and feel it.

When a king sits on his throne to judge, he winnows out all evil with his eyes.

—Proverbs 20:8

If you want to make sure your ministry is not "over-thrown," then make sure the people you lead know that you love them. Stay connected to them, talk to them, and listen to them. Before any big event, I'm usually out just walking through the auditorium, talking to kids, trying to stay connected, listening, caring, praying with some of them. Maybe you can't talk to everybody, but you can at least communicate care for those you do meet.

When they know that they are loved, you won't have to worry about people you serve in your authority. You pre-empt problems.

As my ministry grows, am I becoming more and more a statesman? This simply means that all the other youth groups in your area *will start looking to you* as your ministry grows. People from far and wide will call, "Hey, I heard your youth group has doubled in the last few months. How did you do that? Can I come visit sometime? Can you come and tell me about it or visit with our leaders?"

These folks are often really struggling and hurting. They'll ask you to pray for them and encourage them. They'll seek your guidance and even your companionship.

What can you do? Realize that an element of statesmanship must come with your success. As the Bible says: "A generous man will prosper; he who refreshes others will himself be refreshed" (Prov. 11:25). As God blesses

God will bless you as you refresh others.

us with success and growth, we're called to refresh others. Yes, give away the tips you have learned. Explain how to minister, how to grow a ministry, how to do this and that. Give it away and you bless others, helping them grow.

Youth groups aren't in competition! There are a lot more kids than all of us can handle right now. I know it's "not your job description," but give anyway. God will bless you as you refresh others.

This is a good time to think about preempting problems in more depth. Go to your computer and open your CD-ROM to the file titled "Problems." The first page will help you evaluate the steps you must take to remain a proactive leader. Be as specific as you possibly can.

Am I constantly grooming my leaders so they can lead autonomously? As a ministry grows, some leaders will be tempted to stay involved in the same way—doing everything. Instead, we need to work ourselves out of a lot of jobs. We do that with leadership training and delegation. It avoids all kinds of problems.

This is the sticky part: delegate even things that you *could* do (and that you could do very well). Groom other people to do those things. Then you can focus on those things that *only you can do,* the things you are *supposed* to do.

Take worship, for example. You help the leader understand: "This is the kind of worship I want, this is how many songs I want, this is how intense I want it to be, this is the kind of band or worship team I want you to have, and this is the way I want the kids to participate." You are shaping, molding, and defining. As you convey these principles to your leaders, soon they can proceed without you having to operate for them. You can back away, just as Jesus did.

Remember that Jesus had the disciples constantly watching Him work. In time His trainees were allowed to do some of it: "Hey, could you pray for that woman over there?" "Could you lay your hands on this one, or put some mud on that man?" Eventually He said, "Okay, I'm going to be in the background, but My Spirit will be with you. So now you go out and do all these things in My name. Be My eyes and hands and feet. Show the love and skill that I conveyed to you, and then come back to tell Me how it went."

He let them do it, and so must we.

With *Acquire the Fire*, I have a great team of staff and interns who operate things. I can show up at ten minutes before seven on a Friday night, walk on the stage, and everything is set. I know that, not only is all the technical stuff done, but people are prayed up, people are focused, and people are ready to minister. It just happens.

We need to understand what to delegate and what things not to delegate.

1. The ministry's quality. You are constantly involved in evaluating: "Is this good ministry, was that a good altar call, is this good worship?" You must monitor such things all the time. You don't have to do it all, but you set the standard.

2. The ministry's vision and direction. You can't say, "It's Brother Bob's job to lead the direction." No, if you are the leader, that is your job.

3. The ministry's finances. You have to be directly involved with funding. You can't say, "But I just want to think about the ministry." People will start to spend money in all kinds of foolish ways—or money won't come in at all. So many ministries cease to exist—or leaders get kicked out of ministry—because something bogus happened with the dollars. Don't let this happen to you.

It is the same with the mission trips we do in the summers. For a long time I used to travel to the countries to investigate them before we went. Then I would come back and do logistics and take care of all the details. Eventually, though, I worked myself out of this job. I took some people with me to those countries and taught them how to set things up. Now I'm involved in choosing some of the countries, but other qualified leaders set up all the logistics and handle every detail of a massive trip. I simply show up for the training when we all come together on our campus in Garden Valley. The point is, delegate or die young. (Or maybe you'll just be delirious your entire life!)

Look now at page two of the CD-ROM file "Problems." As you answer the questions on the page, think about how best to develop your leaders.

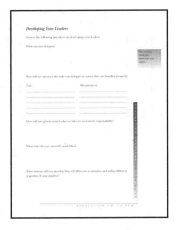

Having said all this about delegation, I must warn you: some things can't be delegated. There are still some areas of the ministry in which I am very much involved. You see, we need to understand what to delegate and what things not to delegate. At least three things should never be handled by others alone:

Am I refining ministry more than doing ministry? Once you have everything up and running, you'll spend your time going from one department to another, refining the picture. It's as if you are "tasting" the flavor of the whole ministry to see what needs to be added or taken away: "How does this part of the ministry taste?"

Let's say you find out that the evangelism team is going out every week, and they are only getting one person saved. So you go to that department to "taste" it— to see if that part of the ministry really agrees with your heart. You spend some time working with your evangelism leader, tweaking and refining how things work there.

Maybe you sense that the worship time was a little too long or boring or a little bit too much hype, not really intimate with God. You spend some time working on that with the worship leaders. When you are finished there, you move on to another area and spend some time with those

Staying connected to kids will help you develop a quality program that attracts young people and ministers to them where they are.

leaders. "Does this taste right? How does this line up with what is in my heart?"

You're not doing all the ministry work anymore. You can now rotate to different parts of the ministry, tasting here, tasting there. If anything doesn't taste right, you mix in new ingredients until it's right.

Go to your computer again, and refer back to the same file, "Problems." Answer the questions on the page about "Developing Your Leaders." Remember, your job is not to do everything. It's just to make sure all the jobs line up with what is in your heart, and to empower your leaders to lead.

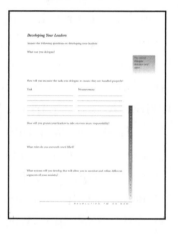

Am I staying spiritually connected to my kids? The Bible says in Proverbs 27:23: "Know the condition of your flocks." We are shepherds, and we do have precious sheep. Do we know their condition? Which of the kids are hurting; which are in spiritual trouble?

Here's one thing to know about teenagers: they are experts at being teenagers. They know what is cool. So if you keep asking them questions, you too will become more and more of an expert on teenagers.

One of the things we do to stay connected with kids is to work with them on our video scripts. We run them by the young people. Kids tweak them, tear them apart, chew them up, and spit them out. And then we *rewrite* the scripts. We run the rewrites by them, and then we do it again, and again, and again. We make sure we are not a bunch of old people saying, "This is really cool!"

I really have no idea what is cool. (How can any of us? It changes all the time.) Let's say you have an idea for a drama you want to do. Don't just say, "Oh, this is really awesome," when they are saying, "Oh great, I don't want to bring my friends to this." Why not run it by the young people?

Staying connected to kids will help you develop a quality program that attracts young people and ministers to them where they are. Teens are the experts on how they think and how their friends think.

I hope these questions will help you identify and prevent some of the common problems that occur in a growing ministry. As you grow and resolve each challenge, be ready to offer praise and thanks to the Lord. It is He who motivates you and creates every good thing that happens as you exercise your gifts for His glory.

Before we get ready to go on to Part 2 of this book, go to your CD-ROM again and find the file titled "10 Must

Haves." On this inventory, you can rate yourself on the 10 essential areas for success in youth ministry. As you build your ministry and implement the strategies outlined in this book, you will find that you make great improvements in each of these areas. Come back to the inventory in six months and see

the gains. Take it now and again to monitor your progress as you become a Youth Specialist!

Now, get ready to dig into Part 2 of this book! It's all about your personal life as a Youth Specialist. What could be more intriguing than that?

PART 2

The Personal Life of a General

CHAPTER EIGHTEEN

Keeping Your Spiritual Edge

Have you ever noticed that once in a while when you hear someone preach, you are so moved and so inspired that you want to jump up and shout amen! Or you want to fall on your knees and cry out to God with all your heart! You may have heard others preach on that same Scripture passage, but it never really came alive before—there was no bite, no thunder. How is it that it's easy to walk away from one speaker untouched, while someone else pours life into your soul and compels you to respond in repentance? The answer is the power of the edge.

You can tell when *the edge* is there and when it isn't. Some Christian musicians have it, and you can't help but

As Youth Specialists, we need to make sure that our ministry is potent.

weep when you hear their music. Others never have it; and some have it, but lose it. What exactly is *the edge* in ministry, and how do you make sure you have it and never lose it?

Many youth leaders demonstrate good teaching skills but have no real fire, and that disturbs me. It ought to disturb us all. As Youth Specialists, we need to make sure that our ministry is potent. If we are going to spend our energy in the trenches fighting for this generation and if we are to make a real impact in teens' lives we'd better fully understand this.

Let's begin by looking at what the edge is *not*. You know you've lost your edge when "pretty good" ministry is good enough, when you think you can do the work and programs of the ministry without the Lord, and when your involvement in ministry doesn't personally challenge you to press deeper into the things of God. In short, you know you've lost your edge:

- when you have **programs** without a **product**;
- when you have vast **resources** without **results**;
- when you have **preaching**, but you have no **passion**;
- when you go through **motions** but provide no real **ministry**;
- when you have many **services** but no **Spirit**;
- when you issue a **challenge**, but there's no **conviction**;
- when you display **emotion**, but it sounds **empty**.

Well then, what *is* the edge? For one thing, it's sheer *determination*.

Jacob had the edge. He had the edge when he wrestled with the "man" (God) in the desert: "Then the man said, 'Let me go, for it is daybreak.' But Jacob replied, 'I will not let you go unless you bless me'" (Gen. 32:26).

What determination! When you've got the edge, you have a *determination* to find God and to obtain His blessing. Jacob had that edge: "You're not going anywhere until I have your blessing and feel your presence transforming me way down deep in my being." Today's Youth Specialist might say it like this: "Lord, don't let me go through the motions of this quiet time (or this youth meeting, or this counseling session, or this fun night, or this sermon) without touching my life and touching others through me with Your fire. I *must* have the edge!" Do you have that Jacob-like determination?

Moses had the edge. He had the edge the very first time he looked Pharaoh in the eye and said, "Let my people go!" (You do NOT say that to Pharaoh unless you have some confidence in your God.) The edge also means having the *confidence* to make a demand on behalf of God. Moses had the audacity to make a demand because he knew the Almighty Lord would back him up. When you've got the edge, you can make a demand. It doesn't mean you go through life ordering everyone around. But you're confident enough to demand that the devil leave and to pray with more than hot air. Do you have Moses-like confidence?

If you have a word burning in your heart, you can't keep it to yourself. That's the edge.

Jeremiah had the edge. He had the edge when he realized: "But if I say, 'I will not mention him or speak any more in his name,' his word is in my heart like a fire, fire shut up in my bones. I am weary of holding it in; indeed, I cannot" (Jer. 20:9).

The edge means having a *fire* you can't keep down. The prophet proclaims, "I've got to say something about this. It's on fire inside of me. I cannot shut up!" When you've got the edge, you've got fire. If you have a word burning in your heart, you can't keep it to yourself. That's the edge: determination, confidence, fire. What else is it?

Elijah had the edge. He had the edge when he called fire down from heaven. He did not care about the trends of society—that so many others were worshiping Baal. He knew God would answer him and prove himself strong. When you have your edge you have a *backbone* like Elijah to stand against all the social norms that are ungodly.

John the Baptist had the edge. He had the edge when he said: "You are a brood of vipers. Show me the fruit of your repentance!" When you have your edge you can stand strong and not worry about what anyone thinks of you! You know you are clean, and are bold about pointing out compromises.

Peter had the edge. He had the edge when he looked at the crowd and said to the very people who had killed Christ, "But you crucified the Lord of Glory . . ." Their response was to ask, "What can we do to be saved?" When you have your edge you *compel people* with your heartfelt words and they come running to Christ! (In Peter's case, they didn't even wait for an altar call; they interrupted him before he was done!)

HOW DO I LOSE MY EDGE?

Here's the answer in a word: sin. Big sin. Small sin. Public sin. Secret sin. Compromises of all sizes will cost you your edge. If you have been convicted by God about an area of your life, and you persist in going against what you know is right, your edge starts to dull. You slip up in an area, slip up again, and then it becomes a regular part of your lifestyle. You keep "doing the work of the ministry," but it loses its potency.

HOW DO I GET MY EDGE BACK?

Here's another one-word answer: repent. Get rid of that sin. Turn your back on that small compromise that no one would really know about. God demands more of a leader. A leader cannot say, "Well, *others* do it!" If God has convicted you, then you need to do what HE is telling you to do. Go on a fast. Get away from the world. Return to your first love! Don't be content with "pretty good is good enough" ministry.

Sad to say, I have seen ministers who—after a massive moral failure—never got their original edge back. I know they are forgiven, and they know it, but somehow they "walk with a limp" the rest of their lives. So guard your edge, and don't take it lightly! It is the precious ministry of God to a dying world in all its full-blown potency.

HOW CAN I SHARPEN MY EDGE ONCE I'VE GOT IT?

This is the question every Youth Specialist ought to ask him or herself every day. I believe it initially involves making *three distinct changes* in your approach to ministry. You must move:

. . . from memories to present reality. It is natural for people to live from experience to experience. Who doesn't like to recall the "mountaintop" experiences with God and long to relive them again? But there's a better way.

Remember what Paul said to Timothy: "Fan into flame the gift of God, which is in you through the laying on of my hands" (2 Tim. 1:6).

Even Timothy had to be reminded to keep the fire burning. Our goal is not just an experience with God that we can remember and then try to repeat, over and over again. Our goal is not to simply sing about the day, 10 years ago, when God showed up and brought deep conviction so we can preach about it again, remembering, "Wasn't that an exciting day?"

Don't fall into the trap of building your theology and program around that one radical experience you had with God in the past. If reproducing a memory is your goal, you will pray this way: "Oh, God, rain your fire down again; give us another experience like the one burning in our memories." Instead, God calls us to consider *today.* He wants us to pray not just for an experience of revival, but for an entire lifestyle of glory. Do you see the difference? If we would stay "vived," we would not need to be "re-vived."

   . . . *from relightings to fanning.* Even after a real encounter with God, *it only takes about 24 hours for your relationship with God to go stale.* Here's how it happens: You have a wonderful meeting, filled with God's presence. You have some great music, you're on a spiritual high, and *it all happened after that one song.* So you say, "We are definitely going to sing that song again." You assume the answer is in the song.

But the song isn't what brings the fire—God alone brings the fire.

Another time you pray, and kids are convicted. Next time, you think: "I will pray just like that again." You hope to relight what was once on fire.

But the prayer isn't what brings the fire either—God brings it.

Rather than looking for a formula for fire, suppose we maintain a glowing inner fervor that will not die? You see, you are a man, a woman, from another world. People don't know what you know. They have not experienced what you have, because you have spent so much more time with God. You have a deep reservoir, a raging fire burning within you. God's glory shines in your eyes, glows through your entire lifestyle, and emerges for all to see. So when you stand to preach, you've got the edge.

God alone brings the fire.

Go for the glow. Fan the fire, day in and day out. It's about who you are in Christ, not what you do next.

Have you ever tried to light the coals for a barbecue using lighter fluid? I used to think that if I flooded the coals, the fire would burn; so I'd light it and leave. Ten minutes later I would return and it would be out. I would repeat the first step again. Then out it would go again. This looks like a lot of people in church today. Just "hoping one day it will stick." God wants to blow on us with His Spirit—like I learned to blow on those coals until they were bright orange. Rather than seeking to relight the fire, why ever let it go out? Go for the glow. Fan the fire, day in and day out. It's about who you *are* in Christ, not what you *do* next.

Fan it, fan it, until your normal walk is a bright glow of raging fire and passion for Him alone.

. . . from explosions to essence. On our very first mission trip in 1987, we went to a place where two volcanic mountain peaks sat side by side. One was an active volcano and one was inactive. I hiked with 60 teenagers to the top of the inactive peak, hoping that from there we could look down into the active volcano and see the fiery lava, bubbling and shooting up into the air.

Instead, we saw fog. The peak we stood upon was much higher, shrouded in the clouds. I just could not resist so I decided to hike over to the active peak, go up to the edge and look down. This was dangerous, but I took the risk. (I don't recommend doing this!)

I thought I would look down into the red-hot, boiling lava; instead, I saw some little glowing holes in a hard cap of stone. Every once in a while we'd hear the sound of explosions, so I decided to try to capture the moment on film. There was one picture left in my camera, and when I heard the next "pop," I snapped the shot. To my amazement, I captured little pieces of orange-glowing lava hanging in mid-air—an awesome display bursting out of dismal smog.

That is what we hope for in ministry, right? That little explosion. We just can't wait for the next pop. The real goal, though, is to have hearts of raging lava. The little bit that comes out of the top when you minister is nothing compared to all that lava, that stuff God is doing within you, forming you to be like Christ. That work is the fire raging deep in your soul. It is the very essence of your life, this relationship with the Almighty. This is what we're after—the glow of the deep fire of God. Not just hype, not just excitement, not just an experience. A lifestyle.

ENJOY CREATIVE TIMES WITH GOD

I'm sure you've realized by now that the changes above are really one movement described in three different ways. The crucial question is, have you made the switch? If so, you can keep fanning the coals of the fire. It's a matter of

> This is what we're after—the glow of the deep fire of God. Not just hype, not just excitement, not just an experience. A lifestyle.

Isn't prayer more than just asking for things? Perhaps it is a time to get to know God, time to let Him stir you up a bit as you spend silent moments listening to Him for a change.

spending time with God, and I believe He calls us to be very creative with Him in this relationship.

"But, Ron, how can I have creative times with God?" I'm glad you asked! Here are some ways:

Expand your prayer plan. Don't just pray for the same old thing by going down the same tired prayer list. For example, suppose you were to pray for some things that have no beneficial bearing on your own ministry? Could you intercede for someone else's ministry, someone else's youth group, someone else's church, or someone else's financial problems?

And isn't prayer more than just asking for things? Perhaps it is a time to get to know God, time to let Him stir you up a bit as you spend silent moments listening to Him for a change. Let Him stir up your heart for what He cares about—other people's ministries, missionaries you have never met before, other ministries you don't know much about (but you have a newsletter and see a need, so you pray).

Larry Lea came to speak to our staff and interns a year ago and said, "The most important thing in prayer is that you *connect with God.*" You don't have to remember all of the missionaries around the world . . . but at least connect.

Freshen up your worship. King David urged God's people: "Enter his gates with thanksgiving and his courts with praise; give thanks to him and praise his name" (Ps. 100:4). There is only one way to enter into the courts of the Lord, and that is with thanksgiving and praise. You can scream it, you can shout it, you can talk it, but there is only one way to get in.

Before Jesus came, the blood of sacrificial animals was payment for the high priest's entry into the Holy of Holies. But now . . .

> *It is impossible for the blood of bulls and goats to take away sins.*
>
> *Therefore, when Christ came into the world, he said: "Sacrifice and offering you did not desire, but a body you prepared for me; with burnt offerings and sin offerings you were not pleased. Then I said, 'Here I am—it is written about me in the scroll—I have come to do your will, O God.'" . . .*
>
> *And by that will, we have been made holy through the sacrifice of the body of Jesus Christ once for all.*
>
> *Day after day every priest stands and performs his religious duties; again and again he offers the same sacrifices, which can never take away sins. But when this priest had offered for all time one sacrifice for sins, he sat down at the right hand of God. . . .*
>
> *Therefore, brothers, since we have confidence to enter the Most Holy Place by the blood of Jesus, by a new and living way opened for us through the curtain, that is, his body, and since we have a great priest over the house of God, let us draw near to God with a sincere heart in full*

assurance of faith, having our hearts sprinkled to cleanse us from a guilty conscience and having our bodies washed with pure water.

—Hebrews 10:4–7, 10–12, 19–22

Don't kill anything; Jesus paid the price. The only thing left to give, then, is thanks and praise, the fruit of our lips. That opens doors.

Here's a creative approach I like to use: open your Bible and read one or two Psalms as if you had written them. Think about what David had in mind when he wrote, "As the deer pants for streams of water, so my soul pants for you, O God" (Ps. 42:1). Then say it over and over so that it becomes your own heart cry. "Yes, God, as the deer pants, so *my* soul longs for You!"

Thankfully, the Bible pictures the worship taking place in heaven. Let it move you into fresh and creative means of praise:

At once I was in the Spirit, and there before me was a throne in heaven with someone sitting on it. And the one who sat there had the appearance of jasper and carnelian. A rainbow, resembling an emerald, encircled the throne. Surrounding the throne were twenty-four other thrones, and seated on them were twenty-four elders. They were dressed in white and had crowns of gold on their heads. From the throne came flashes of lightning, rumblings and peals of thunder. Before the throne, seven lamps were blazing. These are the seven spirits of God. Also before the throne there was what looked like a sea of glass, clear as crystal.

In the center, around the throne, were four living creatures, and they were covered with eyes, in front and in back. The first living creature was like a lion, the second was like an ox, the third had a face like a man, the fourth was like a flying eagle. Each of the four living creatures had six wings and was covered with eyes all around, even under his wings. Day and night they never stop saying: "Holy, holy, holy is the Lord God Almighty, who was, and is, and is to come." Whenever the living creatures give glory, honor and thanks to him who sits on the throne and who lives for ever and ever, the twenty-four elders fall down before him who sits on the throne, and worship him who lives for ever and ever. They lay their crowns before the throne and say: "You are worthy, our Lord and God, to receive glory and honor and power, for you created all things, and by your will they were created and have their being."

—Revelation 4:2–11

The 24/7 elders are so stunned by God's presence that they cannot even stand up. They bow and say, "Holy, holy, holy," for the first million years and then the next million years. Can we be stunned by His presence for even a few moments? Creative worship means never singing a song just for the sake of singing a song, never letting it come off our lips without coming from a heart that is bowled over with God's majesty and goodness toward us. His grace truly is stunning—worthy of all praise for a billion years.

Read the Scripture creatively, always look for the character of God.

Color your readings with creativity. Bible reading is a primary means of spiritual growth, and it, too, can be done creatively to keep the fires burning. For example, try studying by theme, finding out all about forgiveness, or fellowship, or God's sovereignty, or church disciplines, etc.

Or approach Scripture through memorization for a while. As you memorize, you are meditating upon God's Word and His will—and that's a good thing! Now you have a little more revelation, a little more truth burning inside of you.

Or try biographical reading, studying Bible characters' lives. Find out everything you can about David, or Timothy, or Barnabas, or Paul. What can you learn from them about how to love and obey God? What warnings or cautions come through as you study their sins and mistakes? Such study fans the flames.

As you read the Scripture creatively, always look for the character of God. Do you know what He is like? For as you dive into the Scriptures, you enter a quest to know God. And as you explore, determine never to read a chapter in the Bible without thinking, "God, give me some of your character. Explain to me a little more of what You are like. Lord, feed me. I want to know You."

Getting to know Him means recognizing His matchless character all through the Scripture, Old Testament and New. "Why did you put that rule there,

Lord? What about that commandment? Why did you act that way?" Think about what He did, why He did it, what He said, when He said it, and to whom He said it. "What does this tell me about You? For You are the One I want to know better and better." He reveals Himself right here. His character is written all over the pages of your Bible. So read creatively, and look for God's character in every chapter.

Calendar-ize your seasons of solitude. I am not talking about moments with God in the morning; I am talking about getting creative with your time by planning whole seasons alone with Him. Why not enter those seasons on your calendar months in advance?

This doesn't mean you have to live up in the hills like a monk. You can be alone and still have your normal lifestyle. But I suggest you get rid of some things. Could you turn off the music? Unplug the television set? Stop the newspaper deliveries for a while? Just take the next season—one week, two weeks, or more—to be alone. You can be around people, but you don't have to be around the noise of the world.

It might well call for physical solitude, though. And for most of us it will feel awkward at first. We'll keep wondering, "What am I supposed to be *doing?*" Until we realize that God is calling us to stop doing for awhile; He is calling us just to BE. With Him.

We have this idea that "the anointing" is some magic thing that we ought to pray for right before we preach. But no, it is not this mystical little help that God gives us. The anointing forms, over time, by your time alone. Get alone *with* God and get the anointing *from* God.

For the man or woman who comes to know and love God as Father in such intimacy, the times of solitude are the most exquisite in all of life. They are "a rendezvous with the Beloved." They are anticipated eagerly; awaited with acute expectancy; relished with enthusiasm. In a word, these times are highlights of life.

From W. Phillip Keller, *Men's Devotional Bible* (Grand Rapids: Zondervan, 1993)

Your preaching will never be more anointed than your quiet times are. If you don't have an anointed quiet time, don't expect to have a good sermon. Don't expect to have a good counseling session. That is where the anointing comes from. It is raging inside you, stirring your heart up.

You can worry that your relationship with [God] has gone cold, that you've lost your spiritual edge. You can think it will take a lot of time, a month or so of spiritual discipline, to get going again with Him. Then you sit down and discover, in just minutes, that you don't have to do a thing—except take some time. Be alone with Him. In what feels like no time you are caught up again in your love.

From Tim Stafford, *A Scruffy Husband Is a Happy Husband* (Colorado Springs: Focus on the Family, 1981)

Forget your food (for a while). Jesus said in Matthew 6, "*When* you fast . . ." In other words, He expected us to be doing this as a part of our lifestyle.

When you fast, do not look somber as the hypocrites do, for they disfigure their faces to show men they are fasting. I tell you the truth, they have received their reward in full. But when you fast, put oil on your head and wash your face, so that it will not be obvious to men that you are fasting, but only to your Father, who is unseen; and your Father, who sees what is done in secret, will reward you.

—Matthew 6:16–18

Oh, God, give me that reward! It says, don't let anybody know you're fasting. That is hard. You begin a fast for three days, and you already have several lunch appointments set up. Or maybe you plan to block out your schedule and somebody else schedules an appointment for you to go eat lunch with another (usually someone "important").

If you want to fast for a week or even a day, it won't be easy. You have to maneuver around the obstacles. But there is a reward that only comes when you fast. You separate yourself and say, "Lord, I don't want bread from this world, I want the Bread that comes from heaven. That is what I am going to feast on. Lord God, stir me up. I don't have any more energy to live in this world. I need some manna. Lord, I need some manna."

Fasting sharpens you. It humbles you and gets you crying out to God. Revelation comes your way, and Scriptures come alive with meaning like never before. Fasting is much more than just going hungry. It is giving your hungry heart to God.

Fasting is much more than just going hungry. It is giving your hungry heart to God.

Your ministry is a direct reflection of what's going on inside of you.

THE BOTTOM LINE!

Everything we've been saying in this chapter boils down to one key point. So please listen closely, and take this to heart: *Your ministry is a direct reflection of what's going on inside of you.*

If you have your edge, and you are spiritually sharp, your ministry will cut deeply into human hearts and bring glory to God. If you have that raging fire in you, you'll be able to ignite other people. If you have the edge, it will show in your ministry.

Therefore, when you come to those times when you feel you just "can't seem to get through to the kids," look inside. You may conclude that the kids have hard hearts. But look inside. You've been preaching, you've been doing your meetings. You've been busy, but nothing's happening. Look inside.

Inside you are not living by your convictions and you have gotten dull. You have not really pressed through; you've forgotten how to *be* with God. Therefore the edge is dull, the fire has grown cold.

This is harsh, I know. But it is the truth. Groups take on the nature of their leader—or they leave. The people who stay have what you've got. If you have a raging fire, you make them hungry for it. You pass it on without even realizing it.

All the planning, organizing, and implementing we have talked about in the first half of this book are useless without your edge.

Now, stop everything and do whatever it takes to get your edge!

Notes

Watch Out for the Residue!

Time for a spin on the motorcycle! As I rolled it out of the garage into the sunlight, I noticed a little dust on the gas tank. No problem. I was soon zipping along the highway, expecting to leave any dust far behind in the wind. Not so. I looked down, and there it was—that thin, dusty coating defying a 60-mile-per-hour gale.

You can't find a much lighter substance on earth. You can barely touch it with your finger, yet it clings tenaciously to everything it encounters. That experience opened my eyes to something important about you and me: we easily lose our shine in the dust-laden atmosphere of our world.

And we can't just blow it off.

We easily lose our shine in the dust-laden atmosphere of our world.

The problem is, it's so easy to get along as a Christian and not have to deal with the layer of dust. After all, compared to somebody else (who's never been on a mission trip), we look pretty good. This dust that floats through our environment, however, the grime and residue of a fallen world, is the realm of "the ruler of the kingdom of the air" (Eph. 2:2). Satan himself is in charge of the dust. He's at home in it, and he'd like us to become quite comfortable with a little less spiritual sheen each day. Even if we are godly people, we live in an ungodly world; dust is flying everywhere.

It sticks to us with ease. Each of us could name hundreds of examples of how it happens. If you didn't see it live on TV a few years ago, then you probably saw a photo of that infamous kiss between Madonna and Britney. It's just one small example. You look at something like that and you are almost incredulous. You don't want to look . . . but then you do. And even though you don't want it to dust your mind, it immediately becomes a piece of lint landing ever-so-lightly in your consciousness. A piece of corruption from the world. You know it's not right, but those women look cool—and all of America just took a step down the staircase of what's "acceptable" in our society. As a result, some teenage boys now think it's cool to get their girlfriends to make out with one another. It really is okay, right? (Hey, we saw it on TV.) And why even mention the connection we now find between oral sex, junior-high girls, and Monica Lewinsky? It's not really sex, right? (Hey, we heard it on the radio.)

As Youth Specialists, we aren't in the ministry just so we can put on a few good programs. No, we want to rock the planet! Yet, if we look at past movements where God really "showed up," there was always a great cleansing revival filled with repentance, fasting, and seeking God with tearstained faces. How do we draw our kids into that kind of revolutionary, heart-wrenching longing for God? Instead of begging them to *please* come to church, what will it take to see them banging on the church doors because they *just can't stay away* from the Lord and His work among them?

I hate to say it. It's scary. But too many of us have gotten so used to having the residue of the world on us; we think it is normal. We walk around with a thin film of dust on us and don't even realize it, but then wonder why our ministry is not as potent as others. We must let the light of God shine on our souls so we can see the lint the world has deposited on us. Then we ask God to purify us from the accumulation of filth!

> We must let the light of God shine on our souls so we can see the lint the world has deposited on us. Then we ask God to purify us from the accumulation of filth!

NO MORE DUST—ON ME

Let's take our eyes off the kids for a moment. We, as youth leaders, must stay dust free. This is the bottom line of all our ministry efforts.

"But Ron," you say. "Isn't it true that we need to really know our current youth culture? How can we do that without immersing ourselves in it? We can't just stand outside and observe, right?"

Wrong. Go ahead, prayerfully observe. Then, prayerfully . . . *pray*. I'm tired of the excuse that says, "We need to relate to the world." So we go see all the movies, go visit all the bars, go dance at all the raves, and end up with a whole layer of dust on us. Soon we begin to think it's okay.

Have you ever sat in a room with the sunlight shining through in just the right way, so you could see every minute particle of dust in the air? At those moments you realize just how pervasive dust is. Even people who keep their houses "spotless" have to admit that a thin layer of dust covers everything. They can vacuum, but the vacuum cleaner won't catch it all; in fact, the vacuum blows much of it back into the air. That thin layer remains, in our homes and in our lives. Think about these two important things:

First, if we learn to tolerate a thin layer of dirt, in time we will gradually tolerate much, much more. Then, when we preach and teach and counsel, we won't have the fire at all; it will be a spark at best. Sadly, we'll think, "Well, the wind will blow it off, because I'm moving at a hectic pace, doing things for God. A little dust can't stand that kind of velocity." But it can. We live in a sinful world, and stuff is flying around us all the time. That's why, in my family, we hardly watch television any more—that's too much dust ready to settle into our minds.

Second, if we invite Jesus to invade our darkness, He will shine us up for effective ministry. We must constantly do this because we really won't see how the dust has affected us until we turn the lights up bright.

You were once darkness, but now you are light in the Lord. Live as children of light.

—Ephesians 5:8

I'm sure you've been to one of those car washes where the idea is to blow the dust off your car with a stream of water. I've found that I have to wipe the surfaces with a towel, though, if I really want it clean. It is the same way with our lives. As we start to feel the buildup of dust and corruption from the world—and the light comes in and we see it—then we have to let Jesus come right in and shine us up. How long has it been since you let Jesus shine you up?

The idea is to have nothing to do with the fruitless deeds of darkness. Jesus says, in effect, "I want to turn the light on and expose the dust particles in the culture and in your life."

As we start to feel the buildup of dust and corruption from the world—we have to let Jesus come right in and shine us up.

HOW TO STAY DUST FREE

We took our kids to see the movie *Cheaper by the Dozen*. This was not an off-the-cuff decision. We had read several reviews (even from Christian Web sites). "It's so funny!" they all said.

So we took the kids to see it. And yes, it certainly has some funny parts. It also has some blatantly sinful parts. The producers know that thousands of young children will see the film, so I have to ask: why did they insert morally damaging aspects into a film when they could just as easily have stuck with harmless, traditional values?

Yet we Christians march our kids in to see it all. The Christian Web sites screening such films weren't even tuned in enough to say, "Don't go see this; you'll get dust on you and your children. You'll encounter values you're trying to get them to oppose. Stay home and talk or play a board game together. It's not worth the damage." But none of them said that. My children got a big piece of dust on them.

> *Therefore do not be partners with them.*
> *For you were once darkness, but now you are light in the Lord. Live as children of light (for the fruit of the light consists in all goodness, righteousness and truth) and find out what pleases the Lord. Have nothing to do with the fruitless deeds of darkness, but rather expose them. For it is shameful even to mention what the disobedient do in secret. But everything exposed by the light becomes visible, for it is light that makes everything visible. This is why it is said: "Wake up, O sleeper, rise from the dead, and Christ will shine on you."*

Be very careful, then, how you live—not as unwise but as wise, making the most of every opportunity, because the days are evil.

—Ephesians 5:7–16

The light makes everything visible. If we are going to call our youth to be radical Christians, then we also have to ask Jesus to do some work on us. I suggest five clues to keeping the residue of the world from attaching itself to you:

1. In prayer, ask to see the dust in your life. This is difficult! Which of us really wants to see all that internal grime for what it really is? Yet we must start with an honest prayer, "Jesus, let me see the dust; turn on the light. Don't let me get comfortable in a dusty life." We are simply asking to live a life that is content to know God, to hear His voice, to be led by His hand. Do we really need more? Another Scripture that speaks to this—

> *"Your eye is the lamp of your body. When your eyes are good, your whole body also is full of light. But when they are bad, your body also is full of darkness. See to it, then, that the light within you is not darkness. Therefore, if your whole body is full of light, and no part of it dark, it will be completely lighted, as when the light of a lamp shines on you."*

—Luke 11:34–36

Jesus, let me see the dust; turn on the light.

The light makes everything visible. If we are going to call our youth to be radical Christians, then we also have to ask Jesus to do some work on us.

We get residue on our eyes—the lens into our soul—when we let dust settle on our conscience, our sensitivity to what is right and wrong. Then we're seeing through a glass that's much dimmer than it should be, and we can't see the things of God clearly. The Word of God doesn't make sense like it used to make sense. We can't hear His voice so well, and can't seem to discern His leading.

That's why we pray, "Lord, let me see that dust!"

Every once in a while, when I am praying, I get to see. It is humbling and humiliating. But it's also liberating when this happens, when that stroke of light comes from the Lord, and I have to admit: I can't *believe* I had that attitude. Now I see. I was so selfish. I am so embarrassed, because I see this big piece of lint that was invisible moments before.

I repent, and a little lint is wiped away.

Search me, O God, and know my heart; test me, and know my anxious thoughts. See if there is any offensive way in me, and lead me in the way everlasting.

—Psalm 139:23–24

Even though it is embarrassing, I would rather be humbled and deal with it. I get a raw glimpse of the flesh that still lives in me. I am me-centered, and I hate to remember that. But it is the first step toward something better. *Lord, turn up the lights and let me see.*

2. Once you see it, name it, and bring it to God. We're not just talking about dust "in general." It's not enough to know you're a sinner "in principle." No, Christ calls you to come to Him with full knowledge of your need, and a no-nonsense recognition of just exactly what's in your heart.

In many cases, you never sought the dust. It was in the air; you thought it was one thing—you read the reviews—you moved toward it, and then it betrayed you.

Maybe you walk by a magazine and catch a glimpse of something pornographic. You walk away, but now you have this piece of lint on you. It just sort of happens. Maybe it's a television commercial that violates you. You never saw it before, but it "dusts" you pretty good. Bring that to God in a humble way, and respond to Him. "Lord, I feel like I have been violated. I need to be washed in the blood of Jesus. I need You to cleanse me of the thing that I did not invite."

There is dust everywhere, and it's bound to land on us now and then. Thankfully, we can walk under the shower of forgiveness—the waterfall of grace. God can clean us off again.

> I am me-centered, and I hate
> to remember that. But it is
> the first step toward
> something better.

We are connected to one another in the Body of Christ. What we do is done in the body; what is done to me happens to all of us.

3. Expand the clean-up zone. If you're on a clean-up mission, you start with yourself but then you move out into a broader area. Do everything you can to protect your spouse and children, to create as much of a dust-free environment as possible.

You see, I don't think it's good enough to say, "We live in a dust-covered world, and we are going to get dust on us, and it's okay." No, I believe we must take preemptive action for ourselves *and on behalf of others.* The concept of Christian fellowship itself demands this. After all, we aren't Lone Ranger believers, even though we may be completely alone at any given moment. Here is what Dietrich Bonhoeffer, noted theologian and writer, had to say:

> *The individual must realize that his hours of aloneness react upon the community. In his solitude he can sunder and besmirch the fellowship, or he can strengthen and hallow it. Every act of self-control of the Christian is also a service to the fellowship.*
>
> *On the other hand, there is no sin in thought, word, or deed, no matter how personal or secret, that does not inflict injury upon the whole fellowship. An element of sickness gets into the body; perhaps nobody knows where it comes from or in what member it has lodged, but the body is infected. . . .*

We are members of a body, not only when we choose to be, but in our whole existence. Every member serves the whole body, either to its health or to its destruction. This is no mere theory; it is a spiritual reality. And the Christian community has often experienced its effects with disturbing clarity, sometimes destructively and sometimes fortunately.

From Dietrich Bonhoeffer, *Life Together* (San Francisco: Harper & Row Publishers, Inc., 1954), 88-89.

We are connected to one another in the Body of Christ. What we do is done in the body; what is done to me happens to all of us. My life in the Spirit is the life you live in the same Spirit. We must protect ourselves in order to protect one another.

We need to do things, then, that help insulate our "environment"—which includes all of our relationships in Christ. Therefore, again, ask Him to expose the dust that just landed on you, a member of Christ's body. It's for your good!

4. Stop inviting the dust to linger for "just a while." Just because there are dust particles in the air, and they are landing on me, doesn't mean it's okay for them to stay. That is why the Bible says, "Wake up, O sleeper, rise from the dead, and Christ will shine on you" (Eph. 5:14).

This is the embarrassing part, though, because what happens to us is so subtle. For example, you're enjoying a *Seinfeld* rerun, and it's genuinely funny. You can appreciate it, because God made you with a sense of humor. What you're watching is clearly innocent . . . until suddenly it moves into perverted sexual humor. Do you leave it on or shut it off? Do you invite the lint to stay and camp out?

Or maybe you put a rented movie into your VCR or DVD player at home and before long the words and innuendos start getting explicit. If I'm watching with my wife Katie, she'll say, "Ron, I don't like this."

I'll put her off saying, "Honey, it's going to get better . . ."

"But Ron, I don't like this . . ."

"This is a really good part right here," I usually say. "It's getting better."

You've been there, right? Most of the time, it doesn't get a bit better. And there I am, covered in dust.

We aren't watching blatantly bad mass-murder movies; we've got the ones with good recommendations from friends and reviewers. Can you join with me in asking the Lord to shine the Light on those things? We're in this together. I need you; you need me. The kids need us both. There is dust in our world, but that doesn't mean we have to invite it in and call it our own.

5. Remember you were designed to shine. Maybe the biggest challenge is forgetting what it was like to be shiny and thinking it's normal to be dusty. We aren't quite as dusty as the other guys, so it's okay. We're like the man who visited a psychiatrist complaining, "I've been misbehaving, Doc, and my conscience is troubling me."

The doctor asked, "And you want something that will strengthen your willpower?"

"Well, no," the man replied. "I was thinking of something that would weaken my conscience."

It all goes back to what we are hoping to reproduce in our ministries. If there is dust in our lives, we'll produce dusty disciples. Yet God is famous for cleaning us up and restoring us—making us new all over again. The scrubbing may sting for a moment, but the freedom and joy is well worth the trouble. It's what a life of intimacy with God is all about.

Notes

CHAPTER TWENTY

Living a Life of Honor: The Tough Questions

Several years ago, the new governor of Minnesota shocked me. I was watching him being interviewed on television—this big, outgoing former pro wrestler—right after he was elected. The interviewer asked: "Have you ever been with a prostitute?"

"Yes, I have," the governor answered. The response came without hesitation and seemingly not a shred of shame. "But that was before I got married," he added. At that, the interviewer moved on, completely satisfied, the implication being: *Ah! So you're a "regular kinda guy."*

It seems that society (including many Christians) constantly tries to find ways to maneuver around the question of right or wrong. Moral values that used to be universally

Moral values that used to be universally accepted are now open for negotiation.

accepted are now open for negotiation. In the case of the famous governor, he asserted that it was okay to be with a prostitute, since he was not married. If we were to debate whether this was right or wrong, we could take an eternity—even among ministers—to agree on what is acceptable. Instead of trying to weasel our way through justifying whatever we want to do, why not take the discussion to a higher plane? Instead of asking if it is merely right or wrong, let's ask, "Is it honorable?"

This generation seems to differ from past generations in its view of what it means to live honorably. These days, when the police ask gang members to tell about their bosses or to name their drug suppliers, they think they are living by a standard of honor by saying, "No, I won't rat out my friends." Yet these same people would not hesitate to kill someone they don't even know when told to. This is obviously a skewed sense of honor.

Who topped the charts as the biggest culprit (as far as the media was concerned) during the Clinton scandal several years ago? Linda Tripp. Why? She blew the whistle on the wrongdoing. She was considered a person without honor because she told on a friend.

As Christ-followers, we must have a high standard of honor. And it must rise above justifying the fleshly desires that keep convenient compromises in our lives. As successful Youth Specialists, we must live a step above what the "average" Christian feels okay doing. If we want deep spiritual results, we must be deep spiritual people and live a lifestyle that eradicates worldliness from our lives. So, how do we define honor?

ASK YOURSELF THE HONOR QUESTIONS

Clearly, our culture has a skewed understanding of what's honorable. In the midst of such an environment, how do we discern the honorable path? I believe we can get some help by facing the three tough questions that honor demands of us.

Question #1: Is your heart honorable? An honorable heart will dictate the kinds of relationships you pursue and how you treat people in those relationships. Do you value people as fully worthy human beings?

For example, let's say an associate pastor has been working for two or three years at a certain church. He preaches on occasion in the senior pastor's absence, does counseling, and leads several educational programs. Then one day certain influential people in the congregation say, "You know what, Mr. Associate, I really like it when you preach and teach. You have marvelous gifts; in fact, I like your sermons better than our senior pastor's. If you ever started a church, I would go to your church."

> If we want deep spiritual results, we must be deep spiritual people and live a lifestyle that eradicates worldliness from our lives.

Just because a program or plan looks successful doesn't mean it is honorable.

What soon happens to Mr. Associate? He suddenly senses God calling him to start a church! So he follows the call and launches a church half a mile down the road. "God called me; I can't help it," he says. He opens the doors and has 100 people in the pews, then 200 people, and it keeps growing. "See, it must be the Lord," he says. "Just look how many people are coming."

What has just happened? He has violated a primary principle of honor: *Mr. Associate used another person's "platform" to endear himself to people for his own personal gain.* With honor in our hearts, we cannot use people that way. We can't even say, "But look at all of the people here; it *must* be God!" Just because a program or plan looks successful doesn't mean it is honorable. If it started with divisiveness, the Holy Spirit is crying out, "Have you no honor?" The bottom line: we should never exploit another person's credibility for our own personal advancement and take something from them.

Consider this scenario. A guest speaker comes from out of town to preach at a church. The people love him and give him a big offering. He comes back into town to preach at *another* church, which loves him and gives him a big offering. This happens with two or three other churches in town. Then, after he's been to town several times, and he knows many people in town who love him, he feels God has called him to start a Bible study . . . in that town.

I'm sure you can see where this is going. He begins an advertising campaign, and all these loving people from the different churches say, "Oh, I am going to go to that Bible study. That's the guy who was such a good preacher!" And so he gets 200 people coming to the Friday night Bible study. Later, of course, God apparently "calls" him to start a church in this town. When he opens the doors, 500 people get sucked out of all the other churches—the same churches that offered him their platform, invited him to preach, and gave him offerings. He has endeared himself to these people and is taking advantage of that for his own benefit. Remember, just because crowds of people followed his lead does not mean he was honorable.

You can see how this same principle would apply to the role of youth pastor. Think again about our example from a previous chapter. You've accepted the role of youth minister and you tell your teens, "I will be here for at least three years." But after one year a "great opportunity from the Lord" comes along and you get a job offer to be a youth pastor on the other side of town and be paid "real money." So you violate your word and accept the job. Yes, you broke trust with all those teens you gave your word to, but they are "out of sight, out of mind." Your teens are now left with the impression that godly leaders lie. Worse still, half of your teens want to come across town to the new youth ministry you are starting. The old church is now divided; you have created a rift with the kids and the congregation.

Never exploit another person's credibility for our own personal advancement.

Living with honor compels us to commit and stay under the blessing of our spiritual leaders.

Living with honor compels us to commit and stay under the blessing of our spiritual leaders. Can you do any of the above and still have honor? Yes, if you have the blessing of your pastor. Yes, if you make it clear that: "We refuse to let anyone who attends the old church come to the new one we are starting." That's harder. But it's honorable.

Question #2: Is your mouth honorable? Having an honorable mouth means that when you say something, you mean it. You don't flippantly "sort of" give your word—"Oh yeah, I'll do that"—and then not follow through.

How many of us have done that? When it suddenly becomes inconvenient to keep a commitment, we look for a way to excuse ourselves from it. But shouldn't we keep our word?

When somebody asks me to pray for them, I say, "Let's pray right now." I don't want to say, "I'll pray for you," and then get busy and forget all about it. I recall a teen who came to me about a month ago at an *Acquire the Fire* convention. He asked me to pray for his ailing father. I prayed with him at that moment and then the teen asked whether I was going to continue to pray for his dad. "I want to, Tim, but I can't promise that for sure," I said. "So that's why I prayed with you right here." I didn't know if I would remember.

The teen asked, "Oh, so are you, like, too important or something?" His voice was full of attitude. I said, "No, I want to keep my word to you. I may pray for him, but truthfully, I may not because of all the things that I am doing and praying for." Remember that even the smallest promise that comes out of your mouth needs to be kept. Jesus said: "Simply let your 'Yes' be 'Yes,' and your 'No,' 'No'; anything beyond this comes from the evil one"(Matt. 5:37).

Look at this interesting story of deception from the Book of Joshua. The principle of being honorable with our speech goes all the way back to God's people in the Old Testament:

> When the people of Gibeon heard what Joshua had done to Jericho and Ai, they resorted to a ruse: They went as a delegation whose donkeys were loaded with worn-out sacks and old wineskins, cracked and mended. The men put worn and patched sandals on their feet and wore old clothes. All the bread of their food supply was dry and moldy. Then they went to Joshua in the camp at Gilgal and said to him and the men of Israel, "We have come from a distant country; make a treaty with us."
>
> The men of Israel said to the Hivites, "But perhaps you live near us. How then can we make a treaty with you?" . . .
>
> "This bread of ours was warm when we packed it at home on the day we left to come to you. But now see how dry and moldy it is. And these wineskins that we filled were new, but see how cracked they are. And our clothes and sandals are worn out by the very long journey."
>
> The men of Israel sampled their provisions but did not inquire of the Lord. Then Joshua made a treaty of peace with them to let them live, and the leaders of the assembly ratified it by oath.
>
> Three days after they made the treaty with the

Gibeonites, the Israelites heard that they were neighbors, living near them. So the Israelites set out and on the third day came to their cities: Gibeon, Kephirah, Beeroth and Kiriath Jearim. But the Israelites did not attack them, because the leaders of the assembly had sworn an oath to them by the Lord, the God of Israel.

The whole assembly grumbled against the leaders, but all the leaders answered, "We have given them our oath by the Lord, the God of Israel, and we cannot touch them now."

—Joshua 9:3–7, 12–19

These leaders suddenly discovered who their neighbors were! Nevertheless, since they had given their word they were compelled to keep it as an act of respect toward God Himself.

Our word means something. Yet how many of us excuse self-serving behavior with the "I heard God's voice anew" excuse. If we used that tactic in the business world, we would get sued—or go to jail!

Being honorable with your mouth is like enlisting in the army. It is your choice beforehand whether or not to join. But once you join, there is no turning back. You cannot get up the next day and say, "Oh, I don't want to go to boot camp," because it's a done deal. Once you give your word, you have no option but to keep it. You are a slave to the word you have given.

One further matter along these lines: don't make the mistake of thinking that it's permissible to go to the person you made the promise to and ask to be released. That unfairly puts the responsibility on the other person; that is, he becomes the bad guy if he *doesn't* release you. That isn't a choice he should have to make. This may soothe your conscience, and you may say that it's better than breaking your word. It isn't, however, the highest standard of honor.

Question #3: Is your mind honorable? Suppose all of your thoughts were splashed on an overhead projector for your church to see on Sunday morning. Are there hidden things you wouldn't want anybody to know? Hear the words of the apostle Paul:

> *Brothers, whatever is true, whatever is noble, whatever is right, whatever is pure, whatever is lovely, whatever is admirable—if anything is excellent or praiseworthy—think about such things.*
>
> —Philippians 4:8

Paul wrote these words because he knew that any of us can look like a saint on the outside and be pretty rotten inside. More serious than that, our thoughts will eventually shape us—one way or another.

To have honor in our thoughts means more than writing down our values on plaques for all to see. We have core values, and we have rules. We are an honorable ministry, but to be honorable people, we must also have pure hearts and minds.

In 2 Corinthians 13:5 we read, "Examine yourselves to see whether you are in the faith; test yourselves. Do you not realize that Christ Jesus is in you—unless, of course, you

Suppose all of your thoughts were splashed on an overhead projector for your church to see on Sunday morning.

How easy it is to do the convenient thing, rather than what is right!

fail the test?" We preach the Gospel of undiluted grace, yet we must judge ourselves in our progress toward sanctification. It is possible to see where we are in that journey. In fact, it's a moment-by-moment calling.

What, then, is the standard for each of these three levels of honor? I'll be honest with you. There are things that we have done as a ministry in the past that were not honorable. We can't ever be perfect. But as we discover things that are not honorable, we are obligated to make it right with people; we apologize, and we cleanse our hearts. We judge ourselves so that we need not be judged by others. When we discover little bits and pieces of dishonor in our heart, mouth, or head, we can bring these things to the cross and say, "God, I am so sorry. From now on, this is how I will keep my word. This is how I will live with honor."

DO THE RIGHT THING
(NOT JUST WHAT'S CONVENIENT)

How easy it is to do the convenient thing, rather than what is right! But honor demands that we will choose the long and narrow road that leads to life. Even if there is a quick win or success, and it might be easy, it may not be honorable. We need to grow to the point that we naturally say, "Yes, I could do that, but my honor just won't let me. I could seize that opportunity, or take advantage of that relationship—and no one would even know—but my honor would know, the honor that God has instilled in my heart."

The apostle Paul is our honorable exemplar here.

Am I not free? Am I not an apostle? Have I not seen Jesus our Lord? Are you not the result of my work in the Lord? Even though I may not be an apostle to others, surely I am to you! For you are the seal of my apostleship in the Lord.

This is my defense to those who sit in judgment on me. Don't we have the right to food and drink? Don't we have the right to take a believing wife along with us, as do the other apostles and the Lord's brothers and Cephas? Or is it only I and Barnabas who must work for a living? . . .

If others have this right of support from you, shouldn't we have it all the more?

But we did not use this right. On the contrary, we put up with anything rather than hinder the gospel of Christ.

—1 Corinthians 9:1–6, 12

Honor says: "I would rather support myself than cause any misinterpretation of my heart for you in the relationship." In other words, Paul is really saying, "I don't want your money because it might cost too much!" He could have demanded it as anyone else would have done; it was his right. "But I am not involved with you for my personal gain."

Honor demands that we will choose the long and narrow road that leads to life. . .

Now, as I close this chapter, I must admit that sometimes we do dishonorable things without even realizing it. Let's be on guard here, because we are human, and things can catch us unaware! When we do realize what's happened, we can determine to do something about it immediately.

One fall, while Teen Mania was still based in Tulsa, we had a big fundraising event. We invited teenagers who had been on mission trips to a dinner and encouraged them to bring their parents and supporters. We told everybody about our dream for the coming year and invited the adults to support the ministry of Teen Mania. Later, as that year unfolded, during the regular meetings I had with my senior pastor, I noticed a change in the atmosphere of our relationship. Something began to feel out of place between us, and I didn't know what it was. It just felt colder than it used to be.

"Pastor, is there anything I can do to warm up our relationship?" I finally asked. "It seems like something isn't quite right between us." My words opened the door for him to share with me what he was planning to share quite soon anyway. He related how, the summer before, he had really pushed his congregation of 5,000, saying, "You need to send your kids on missions trips." They took offerings and many kids went on trips.

But then came our fall fundraising event. The pastor had lent his credibility to the idea of kids going on missions, and there we were, saying, "Please come to this fundraising event, even though you've already supported missions, and start helping Teen Mania." To his way of thinking, we were "using" kids who'd been on mission trips in order to raise money for other Teen Mania programs. He said it didn't seem honorable.

I suddenly saw his point. It had seemed like a classic "bait and switch." I sure hadn't planned it that way; it never crossed my mind. But that's how it looked.

I hadn't even realized that what we did was wrong. But as I sat there with egg all over my face, he said, "You know, if I had known about your programming needs, I'd have been happy to help you raise funds. It felt as if you were pulling away something that I gave you for the ministry's sake, the ministry of missions."

I repented, and together we held another fundraiser with the clearest of purposes. He came and told everyone that they really needed to give to this ministry.

Honor means doing what's right even when something else is more convenient and could somehow be justified. It demands that we ask hard questions of ourselves, and it requires us to make restitution in any area where we fail to meet the highest standard. Choosing the honorable path may (and probably will) require more time, money, and effort, but will invite the favor of God on your life and ministry. This is the reward of living with honor.

Choosing the honorable path may (and probably will) require more time, money, and effort, but will invite the favor of God on your life and ministry.

Notes

CHAPTER TWENTY-ONE

Living a Life of Honor: How You Can Tell

As leaders, we are required to live with honor because we represent the Lord Himself. When most people consider the possible consequences for their sinful actions, their concern is for themselves. As leaders and Youth Specialists, we must consider the consequences to others if we violate our honor. Too many teens have turned their backs on God and walked away because of the horrible compromise they saw in a youth leader. It is our holy obligation to never cause one of these little ones to stumble, to go the extra mile to ensure that we live according to the highest standard of honor.

In this chapter, we'll explore more of the questions that can help us live up to those standards as we grow our ministries.

It is our holy obligation to never cause one of these little ones to stumble, to go the extra mile to ensure that we live according to the highest standard of honor.

CAN GOD TRUST YOU WITH HIS KIDS?

Let's think again about the great Moses as he was leading his "youth group" of weary, thirsty travelers in this recounting from Numbers:

> *The Lord said to Moses, "Take the staff, and you and your brother Aaron gather the assembly together. Speak to that rock before their eyes and it will pour out its water. You will bring water out of the rock for the community so they and their livestock can drink."*
>
> *So Moses took the staff from the Lord's presence, just as he commanded him. He and Aaron gathered the assembly together in front of the rock and Moses said to them, "Listen, you rebels, must we bring you water out of this rock?" Then Moses raised his arm and struck the rock twice with his staff. Water gushed out, and the community and their livestock drank.*
>
> *But the Lord said to Moses and Aaron, "Because you did not trust in me enough to honor me as holy in the sight of the Israelites, you will not bring this community into the land I give them."*
>
> —Numbers 20:7–12

Was God being too hard on Moses? We might think so, until we remember just how spiritually privileged Moses had been. After all, he'd stood before the burning bush, heard God's voice, participated in God's miraculous deliverances, and even received the Commandments directly from God's hands. Moses had been to the holy mountain and come back with his face aglow. Shouldn't someone this close to God share some of His patience and perspective?

You'd think so; but instead he threw a fit in front of everyone who looked to him for godly leadership. He let his flesh have its own way. And God basically said, "Moses, if you are going to lead my people, I can't be wondering when you'll fly off the handle and disrespect Me in front of them. I need to be able to trust you with those you lead."

Can God trust you that way? Does He know you won't let your bad mood destroy His credibility in one reckless action?

The reason we're Youth Specialists is that we want to help kids. The more your ministry is blessed, the more you can help. But the converse is also true: the more influence you have with kids, *the more you can hurt or disillusion them.* That's why living with honor is imperative and not an option. We must keep our flesh under control. Then God can trust us.

The more influence you have with kids, the more you can hurt or disillusion them. That's why living with honor is imperative and not an option.

How ironic that the world paints its lies so beautifully that if we dare reject them as false, our character is called into question: "Come on, why are you so intolerant?"

Are you holding to an enduring standard? Why is a solid standard so important? Influenced by society's massive confusion over right and wrong, postmodern teens say: "Well, it may be wrong for you, but it isn't really wrong for me. Different things are right for different people." This kind of muddy thinking has seeped into the church from the world's culture, and our young people are saturated with it. We must resist it!

I recently read something that both shocked and appalled me: Among American adults, only 46 percent think it's wrong to have a baby out of wedlock.[1] We are saturated by media messages in our country and, apparently, if you hear a lie long enough (in full color and with Dolby sound), you start to think it's the truth. How ironic that the world paints its lies so beautifully that if we dare reject them as false, *our* character is called into question: "Come on, why are you so intolerant?"

As leaders who hold to clear and objective moral absolutes, it is imperative that we not only live by those values, but also that we build them into the lives of the teens we influence. We must teach them where truth is found, and how to discern the presence or absence of it in the lives of others. Jesus said, "By their fruit you will recognize them" (Matt. 7:20). We need to see the "fruit" of people's lives and help our teens steer clear when that fruit is poisonous.

Do you avoid even the appearance of evil? We need to shout this Scripture from the mountaintops with our lips and our lives:

> *Each of you should learn to control his own body in a way that is holy and honorable, not in passionate lust like the heathen, who do not know God; and that in this matter no one should wrong his brother or take advantage of him. The Lord will punish men for all such sins, as we have already told you and warned you. For God did not call us to be impure, but to live a holy life. Therefore, he who rejects this instruction does not reject man but God, who gives you his Holy Spirit.*
> —1 Thessalonians 4:4–8

This passage speaks of controlling our bodies in holy and honorable ways. But the principle extends to our approach to morality in general—not just avoiding evil, but avoiding even the *appearance* of evil. "Abstain from all appearance of evil," says 1 Thessalonians 5:22 (KJV). If anything could even be *perceived* as evil, avoid it. If it *looks* wrong, it could scar your honor.

We need to see the "fruit" of people's lives and help our teens steer clear when that fruit is poisonous.

If something doesn't look good, don't do it. Don't give anyone an opportunity to make an assumption that is not true.

For men, this translates into a simple and unbreakable rule of thumb: *Don't ever be alone with a girl in your youth group.* Don't ever be alone with any female other than your wife. Don't be alone in the car with her, in a room with her—not anywhere. I don't even take our babysitter home. Katie does it, even though she doesn't like having to drive at 11 P.M. It is better than compromising my honor.

Remember this, men: if you're accused, you lose. Case closed. If something doesn't look good, don't do it. Don't give anyone an opportunity to make an assumption that is not true. Do not give any of the youth, their parents, or the church a reason to question your behavior, regardless of how innocent it may be. Living by this principle makes things a little bit harder, and a lot less convenient. But that's exactly how it must be in our day.

"But Ron, what about when I travel?" you ask. Here's what I do. When I arrive at the host church or convention site, I make sure I'm with a staff member and never alone. When I arrive at my hotel room, my hosts walk in, inspect it, make sure nobody is in there, then shut the door. If I order room service, I don't even answer the door. My hosts receive the food in their room and bring it over to me. I won't be alone with a woman. I won't enter an elevator with a woman. Guys, we just can't take any chances at all.

A matter of integrity. Benjamin Netanyahu became Israel's prime minister after Yitzhak Rabin was assassinated in 1995. During this crisis, I saw Netanyahu interviewed on television. Because he belonged to the opposing party, he would have run against Rabin in the next election. The news interviewer asked him about this national tragedy. "What do you think this does for you?" the reporter asked. "How will it affect your chances of winning?"

"I can't believe you would ask me that question," Netanyahu replied. "Don't you realize this is about our nation and our dignity? It is not about a party. I refuse to comment on that." I thought to myself, *Now, that is a big man.* Other politicians would have had a self-serving answer to such a question. Netanyahu, however, chose a higher standard of integrity.

Having integrity is a choice. Here are some rules of thumb that will keep you living with honor:

Make integrity an issue before it needs to be. I attended a Billy Graham crusade a few years ago and spoke with one of the staff people who'd been with the organization for 35 years, assisting Rev. Graham. I asked him, "Why does the Billy Graham Association have such an impeccable reputation for integrity?"

"We decided long ago to make integrity an issue when it wasn't an issue," he said. "We wanted to go the extra mile so no one could ever question us, either in the area of finances or morality. The result was that in the '80s, when so many other ministries were financially disintegrating, our organization didn't suffer that way."

Having integrity is a choice.

I encourage you to have ethics and morality in every area of your life. Build a solid foundation now, before the crashing waves hit. Then you will stand in God's strength through it all.

They took great pains to make integrity an issue long before they were faced with tough decisions. For years, they intentionally built an ethical foundation, strong enough to withstand any crisis that would come. I encourage you to have ethics and morality in every area of your life. Build a solid foundation now, before the crashing waves hit. Then you will stand in God's strength through it all.

Good intentions don't excuse bad choices. We humans tend to judge ourselves by our intentions and other people by their actions. We think, "Well, I didn't *intend* to do that, so it wasn't really that bad. I didn't *intend* to hurt that person when I broke my word. I didn't *intend* to break my promise, but things changed."

We have armies of politicians in Washington who want us to judge by intention rather than results, by motive rather than consequences. This is a subtle way of avoiding accountability, something that's crucial to Christian fellowship and effective Christian leadership. We can't sink to that level in youth ministry.

Always be "working on something" right now. The way to raise your standard of honor is to continuously work on developing your character. This doesn't mean that you can lift yourself up by your bootstraps or whip yourself into shape on your own. Rather, to "develop your character" means to open your heart for Christ's work in you. Consciously, daily, invite Him to transform your thoughts and deeds.

> *Do not conform any longer to the pattern of this world, but be transformed by the renewing of your mind. Then you will be able to test and approve what God's will is— his good, pleasing and perfect will.*
>
> —Romans 12:2

So, what are you working on right now? What part of your honor or your character are you asking Christ to renew? Here are some of the issues that developing Youth Specialists must work on:

How do you treat your senior pastor? It's easy to support him when you both agree. But when you disagree with an authority or pastor, how do you respond? What do you say and do? A run-of-the-mill youth leader might put down his senior pastor all the time (but a Youth Specialist would never find this acceptable). That is totally dishonorable. Work on it! Pray for him and never say one word—not even an innuendo or gesture—that would imply disrespect.

The way to raise your standard of honor is to continuously work on developing your character.

What kinds of comments do people hear you making about your spouse? What about your kids? How do you treat your kids?.

How quickly do you shut down improper communication? If somebody starts to tell a joke, and you can see that it's going south, what do you do? Do you say, "Don't tell me the punch line"? That would take some self-control, right? And suppose somebody starts telling you some "interesting information" about a brother in Christ? Can you say, "Stop, I don't want to hear it"? The problem is, people are much more willing to say dishonorable things than we are willing to stop them. We can work on it, though.

How do you treat your spouse and children in front of others? What kinds of comments do people hear you making about your spouse? What about your kids? How do you treat your kids? I was probably a pretty challenging kid, but I can remember a time when friends of the family came over to the house, and I overheard my mother telling them how bad we kids were. I was cut to the core and lived with low self-esteem for a long time afterward. After I began to grow in the Lord, I realized she wasn't really describing how bad we were as much as she was expressing her frustration at not being able to figure out how to get us to obey. There's a difference. It was her problem. Remember, when people speak negatively about somebody else, they are speaking negatively about themselves.

How well do you handle personal praise? You'll be tested in this area, because you will receive praise, and it will grow pretty quickly. I promise you this. You will be rocking the place and reaching kids. It will be exciting, and you will have to guard against pride because everyone will be telling you how great you are. Don't start believing this lie, because God is the great one, not you. Not me. We must take ourselves out of the picture and give God the glory.

So I leave you with this: the best way to stay humble is to stay real before God, realizing who He is and who you are. If you are having break-loose quiet times with God every day and really aggressively seeking Him, you will peel off flesh daily. It is impossible to have a prideful, haughty attitude if you are really in the presence of God every day. It reminds you that He is God, and you are not. This keeps us all humble and seeking to live with *honor*.

1. H.B. London, "Society's Moral Boundaries Sway," taken from Gallup's annual Values and Beliefs survey, May 20, 2005, http://216.109.125.130/search/cach?p=%22Christians%22baby+out+of+wed lock%22+Barna&prssweb=Search&ei=UTF-8&fl=www.family.org/pastor/pwbe/print/pwbe (accessed October 25, 2005).

Notes

CHAPTER TWENTY-TWO

Mandate for the Family Man in Ministry

I had come to a marital fork in the road. The road happened to be in India. It was hot, I was deathly tired, and my lips still burned from a less-than-satisfying meal of red-hot curry chicken. The worst part: Katie wanted to go home. *Day Two of a six-week preaching tour, and Katie wants to leave?*

We'd set up speaking engagements all over the country; Hindu people were waiting to hear the Gospel. I was pumped (even with my curry-burned lips). Our faces appeared on posters in a number of little villages, proclaiming in all the various dialects: "Come and see Ron and Katie Luce, evangelists from America!" (They thought we were big shots; they didn't know it was just us.) We had arrived in the country at 4 A.M.

after an all-night flight. The folks who picked us up at the airport had smiled and asked, "Are you feeling fresh?"

Are you kidding? Our heads were pounding!

After a few hours of sleep, we enjoyed a sweltering, four-hour train ride, standing shoulder to shoulder with people for much of the ride. We arrived at a missionary bungalow that was just a little more "elegant" than the excrement-daubed huts surrounding it . . . and don't even ask about the bugs!

By this time, my lips weren't hurting quite as much. But Katie was hurting. "Ron, this is just too hard," she said. "Why don't you go on without me? I can head back to Bombay and stay there with some missionaries until you're through."

That's where I hit the crossroads, one of those pivotal places in my life. Have you been there? *Am I going to choose ministry over my spouse?* That was the core of the decision.

I knew that whatever I did here, Katie would remember it for the rest of our lives. I felt the call of the hurting masses, and I felt the call of a yearning spouse, to whom I had committed my whole life. I knew that people were expecting us to appear all over the country for the next six weeks. This was a young preacher's dream; yet somehow, I knew I'd better make the right call here, or this would be the first of many "bad calls." I told Katie I would not go on without her. I would go back to Bombay with her. I told her whatever she wanted to do, I would do it, but . . .

"Before you tell me what you want to do, think about this. For centuries, the reason India has been so desperate for the Gospel is that the devil has used the primitive, difficult circumstances to chase missionaries away. It seems too hard. That is why there are over a billion without the

Gospel in India today. Are we going to let the devil chase us off too? I know it's hard, Katie," I said, "but I can't do it without you. I won't."

Something on the inside of Katie just rose up. "We won't let the devil run us off!" she said, with firm determination in her voice. We prayed. We covenanted together. And we went together, traveling all over that land, sweating in trains, living in huts, and yes, burning our mouths on foreign spices. And Katie saw even more miracles than I did.

YOUR MARRIAGE: THE FIRST PRIORITY

Do you realize that having a world-class family and having a world-class youth ministry are not mutually exclusive? You don't have to have one at the expense of the other. Yet I hear story after story of ministers' families falling apart, of pastors who threw themselves into ministry at the expense of their families. How can we make sure this doesn't happen to us? I believe the answer lies in keeping our marriages strong, healthy, and based upon biblical principles. A key passage is Ephesians 5:21–33. Look closely at Paul's words:

> *Submit to one another out of reverence for Christ.*
>
> *Wives, submit to your husbands as to the Lord. For the husband is the head of the wife as Christ is the head of the church, his body, of which he is the Savior. Now as the church submits to Christ, so also wives should submit to their husbands in everything.*
>
> *Husbands, love your wives, just as Christ loved the church and gave himself up for her to make her holy, cleansing her by the washing with water through the*

word, and to present her to himself as a radiant church, without stain or wrinkle or any other blemish, but holy and blameless. In this same way, husbands ought to love their wives as their own bodies. He who loves his wife loves himself. After all, no one ever hated his own body, but he feeds and cares for it, just as Christ does the church—for we are members of his body. "For this reason a man will leave his father and mother and be united to his wife, and the two will become one flesh." This is a profound mystery—but I am talking about Christ and the church. However, each one of you also must love his wife as he loves himself, and the wife must respect her husband.

—Ephesians 5:21–33

Many marriages in ministry don't *end up* being very wholesome because they weren't wholesome *to begin with.* Sure, these folks had a heart for kids, so they got involved in ministry; but when their marriages hit hard times, they blamed the ministry. The truth is, they really shouldn't have been in ministry until they had developed an enduring, healthy marriage. Wholesome marriage is all about our priorities, so let's dig into six principles for keeping our marriages a first-class priority.

Pray over your marriage with godly vision. I do this almost every day. I pray not just for my wife but for the kind of marriage we have—and will have in the future. *God, be in the midst of this relationship with us!*

Together, we've determined we'll have a marriage that's strong in the Lord. We won't settle for barely hanging on just because we have a marriage license. We'll deeply love one another—and love being with one another.

We actually put together a Marriage Mission Statement soon after our wedding. We put our ideas together, everything we'd learned about marriage by reading books and receiving the wise counsel of marriage veterans. We asked ourselves, over several weeks: "What do we want our marriage to be?" Then we composed a detailed statement, about three paragraphs long, which Katie wrote in calligraphy. We put some artwork around it and framed it.

Now there's no doubt in our minds what our marriage stands for. When we pray over our relationship, we include the kinds of things appearing in that beautiful vision on the wall. We had to take the time and effort, though, to soberly discern: "What, really, do we want as the fruit of this marriage?"

Together, read the best books about marriage. Over the years, we've read some great books about marriage. We discuss them, share what points made impact, and consider how we might apply the new information. The point is, in any marriage there are things we should be talking about with our spouses. But how do we know what those things are? And who will remind us?

Books can come to the rescue here. After all, any relationship can grow a bit dull if the persons involved always talk about the same old things: How was your day?

Wholesome marriage is all about our priorities, so let's . . . keep our marriages a first-class priority.

You are one flesh, not one spirit. You never become one spirit. You become *one in spirit . . .*

How are the kids? What's for dinner? (That last one is a favorite of mine . . . unless it's curry chicken.)

Reading together and talking about the qualities of a good marriage bring fresh insight to the relationship. I would encourage you to do this on a regular basis. And, gentlemen, did you know that when you bring the book home, your wife feels a deeper sense of security: *He cares about this marriage; he wants us to grow and develop together.* You can develop your ministry and build your marriage as well.

What books are good to read? Here are just a few we've enjoyed:

Fit to Be Tied, by Lynne and Bill Hybels
For Better or for Best, by Gary and Norma Smalley
The Five Love Languages, by Gary Chapman
Communication: Key to Your Marriage, by H. Norman Wright
Men and Women: The Giving of Self, by Larry Crabb

Submit to one another as brother and sister in Christ. This principle flows directly from Paul's words to the Ephesians above. Men typically go right to verse 22 and notice that wives are supposed to submit to their husbands as to the Lord. And, of course, it's an all-time favorite passage of

Scripture . . . for husbands. (Many husbands who aren't even Christians know this one.)

Some Christian husbands use this Scripture as permission to force their wives to bend to their will. Somehow they miss the statement in verse 21 where God calls the husband and wife to submit to one another.

You see, before you were married you were brother and sister in the Lord. And you still are, though you're now more than that. Your *unity* in the Spirit is the same as that existing between you and every other believer, but your *union* is of the flesh. Do you see the distinction? You are one flesh, not one spirit. You never become one spirit. You become *one in spirit* when you believe and receive the indwelling Holy Spirit. You don't *become* one spirit when you get married; you should *be* united by one Spirit before you are married, as two believers.

God expects brothers and sisters in the church to respect each other and listen to each other, to honor each other in every way. Here in Ephesians 5:21, we're called to mutually submit to one another, just as all believers must do among themselves. This means that I don't always have to be right. I may be the male, but that doesn't mean I am always right. I'm a human being and very fallible.

Then comes the specific application of this submission: wives are to submit to their husbands as they submit to the Lord, and men are to love their wives more than they love their own bodies. Which is the more "submissive" stance, then?

Clearly, if both partners are submitting to Christ and loving as He loves them, they will show the deepest regard for one another. No trampling. No refusing to listen. No plowing ahead without due consultation.

I've learned to trust
my spouse. I've also come
to realize that I'm not
the only one who can hear
from God.

Here's how it works for us. Katie and I promised from the beginning of our marriage that we would never do anything unless we were in full agreement. Sometimes she really wants to do one thing, and I really want to do another. What do we do? We just wait. We say, "We'll eventually get some insight about this, and we'll figure out the right thing to do." We wait before the Lord.

I've always thought it's best to be in full agreement on what we do, even if that means we do fewer things. That way, I know my wife is with me, heart and soul, and that every decision we make contributes to our togetherness. The result? I've learned to trust my spouse. I've also come to realize that I'm not the only one who can hear from God.

Gentlemen, do you know what headship means? Review again what Paul writes:

> *The husband is the head of the wife as Christ is the head of the church, his body, of which he is the Savior. Now as the church submits to Christ, so also wives should submit to their husbands in everything.*
>
> —Ephesians 5:23–24

Being the head does not mean that we get our way every time. Be the head, *not* the dictator, as Christ is the head of the church. Ephesians tells us that spouses are to mutually submit to each other, but sometimes a decision *must* be made and we just can't come to agreement. At those times, the husband must humbly submit to his headship calling and make the decision. Husbands, it's not a matter of wielding authority; it's more like sticking your neck out and saying, "I sure hope I'm hearing from God on this!"

Katie and I have been married for 21 years, and we haven't needed to take this path more than five times. With almost all of our decisions, we either agree or we wait. Those few times when I've exercised headship decision-making, I've sensed an anointing, a leading that comes from God. Many times a right decision can be made without us even understanding *why.* It is a matter of humble, reverent trust in God. It's far from a spiritualized "power play."

Men, we need to give our wives the confidence that, when necessary, their husbands will have the headship anointing to lead in a particular, tough decision-making circumstance. Then they can say, "Even if I don't understand the decision, I will trust God."

True headship is neither dominating nor dictating. It is trusting and listening. It's a "we thing," not a "me thing."

A wedding isn't a marriage. A wedding is just the beginning; then the work begins.

But husbands, I would caution not to take advantage of headship. True headship is neither dominating nor dictating. It is trusting and listening. It's a "we thing," not a "me thing."

Keep a healthy friendship intact. Someone once said, "Marriages are made in heaven, but people are responsible for the maintenance." I agree! A wedding isn't a marriage. A wedding is just the beginning; then the work begins.

But it can be joyful work. For one thing, our spouses aren't just marriage partners, they're our best friends too. Scripture gives us many principles related to healthy friendship that we can draw upon in our marital relationships.

Consider John 15:15, for example: *"I no longer call you servants, because a servant does not know his master's business. Instead, I have called you friends, for everything that I learned from my Father I have made known to you."* Wow! Jesus, Friend, shares His heart with us. Can you share your heart with your mate?

Ephesians 4:29 gives us more great relational help: *"Do not let any unwholesome talk come out of your mouths, but only what is helpful for building others up according to their needs, that it may benefit those who listen."* How many people speak unwholesomely about their spouses? If there's an issue, shouldn't we talk it out, "speaking the truth in love" (vs. 15)? Furthermore, according to 4:31–32, we must: *"Get rid of all bitterness, rage and anger, brawling and slander, along with every form of malice. Be kind and compassionate to one another, forgiving each other, just as in Christ God forgave you."* Wise counsel for any marriage.

But the most practical action, which can virtually guarantee our growth in all of these principles, comes in Ephesians 4 verse 26: *"Do not let the sun go down while you are still angry."* Any time humans interact, conflict may enter the relationship, but that doesn't mean we have to leave it there. We are intelligent beings; we can talk things out. As angry as we may legitimately be, we can refuse to let that anger draw us into sin. And we can make sure we go to bed with peace in our hearts about our love for one another, whether or not we've been able to resolve a particular problem.

As we approach our weddings, most of us consider the event as if it means entering into a settled state of life, as if we're joining a club. Once it's done, our membership is set. But suppose we changed the analogy a bit? Suppose we saw the wedding as embarking on a journey or entering a course of instruction that will last for a lifetime? We have the great privilege of spending life's years with our lover, learning to become the best of friends. What could be better?

Set up a 777 Plan—and stick to it! This is one of the things Katie and I do, no matter how busy we are. What is the 777 Plan? Every seven days we have family day, every seven weeks we have a three-day get away, and every seven months we have some kind of vacation or one-week excursion (either just Katie and me or with the kids).

Ministers are often the busiest people of all. Why? We hear the cries of others; we're moved to reach them, touch them, and help them with all the resources of God's goodness and grace. In the midst of this awesome motivation, we can leave our families in the dust. In fact, I think one of the biggest fears of wives is that their minister husbands will leave them lonely. "Will I even know you, once our kids are grown?" they wonder.

The 777 Plan can help protect us here. It's simple, and if you promise to stand by it, the whole family will know: regardless of your busy schedule, when those "sevens" come around, you are back together having family fun. Using the plan doesn't mean we don't talk and relate at other times. It simply means that we choose to focus on these times as the bare minimum, written in stone.

It's a matter of applying discipline to our personal schedules. Amazingly, in talking with others in ministry or business who never leave town, I find I'm spending more family time than they are! So, have a plan, and stick to the plan.

FAMILY AND MINISTRY: THEY GO TOGETHER

I began this chapter by stressing that you can have a great family and have a great ministry too. Then we moved on to explore the foundational principle underneath: put the love of your spouse above the love of your work. If this means shutting down and walking away from ministry for a while to make sure your marriage stays strong, then do it.

Moving on in Ephesians 5, we hear the apostle saying, "cleansing her by the washing with water through the word, and to present her to himself as a radiant church, without stain or wrinkle or any other blemish, but holy and blameless" (vss. 26–27). One of the ways to love your wife is to build her up. Washing her with the word means helping her to grow in the Lord. It's not that she can't do things for herself, but she knows that *you care about her spiritual nutrition.* She knows you're interested in that part of her and not that she's just fending for herself.

All of this involves the whole family, of course, including the kids. Remember our Marriage Mission Statement? We did something similar for our family relationships; we developed a written Family Covenant with the kids. We came up with four main points of character that we want our family to stand for. We talked with the kids about where (in the Scripture) those qualities came from, and then Katie wrote it up in calligraphy on parchment paper. Yes, another nice frame for the wall!

We made a big ceremony of this, announcing the event days in advance. I broke a brick in half and showed that the stuff inside the brick makes it strong. "Just like that," I told the kids, "the stuff inside our family makes us strong—or not." Then we talked about all four of the character traits we want inside our family. "Can we work really hard to make sure this is a part of our heart and the way our family lives?"

Each person had his or her comments about the covenant, and then we prayed over the document before each of us signed it. Finally, we made little laminated cards for each member, listing the four character traits of the

Put the love of your spouse above the love of your work.

Someone has said that the best thing you can do for your kids is to love your wife. It's true!

Luce family. A couple of the kids made necklaces out of them.

Covenants are good, but someone has said that the best thing you can do for your kids is to love your wife. It's true! And I would add: be a "governing unit" with her. Let your kids see your deep affection for her, and always be a solid front with her in disciplinary matters. Beyond this, I invite you to pay attention to a few practical DOs and DON'Ts.

DO really listen to your kids. I put this first, because everything else hinges on it. If kids know you're listening, they can overcome virtually any other problem that may arise between the two of you. Patient, active listening shows a caring, loving heart. And love conquers all.

There comes a point in a child's developmental process, too, when they begin listening for *you*. They want you to say something coherent back to them after you've listened. At that point I realized it wasn't enough for me to just go through the motions and physically be in the same room. *I had to tune into them.* I had to connect with them. How else could I know what was really going on within them?

These days we hear a lot about teens making bombs in their basements or going to school with machine guns. I can't explain it, but I'm quite sure the parents were disconnected from these kids. We can't let that happen! I encourage you to listen when the windows into their hearts are wide open. Be there; hear them; respond. The standard pattern is for a teen to say something like, "Sometimes I just feel really lonely"—and then they just kind of stop. They are waiting to see whether you are an open vessel for them. Are you ready to receive what's next? A window is opening, if you really begin to listen. Seize those moments. All you need to do is be quiet, or reflect back the feeling in the simplest way—"Lonely, huh?" Then the conversation continues.

DON'T let just "any old thing" into your house. "I will set before my eyes no vile thing," says Psalm 101:3. I would extend it like this: "I will let no vile thing come before the eyes of my family." We can frame all the family documents we want, but if the world is bombarding our kids at will every day, how can we fight back?

First, put a filter on your Internet. Don't rely on software filters, because teens can often find ways to "hack" them. Instead, sign up with an Internet service provider that filters content at the server level. There are scores of such companies to choose from, but you might start your search with Web sites like these . . .

- www.afafilter.com
- www.hedge.org
- www.cnonline.net
- christianbroadband.com

If kids know you're listening, they can overcome virtually any other problem that may arise between the two of you.

Why keep all the ministry to yourself? Involve your kids, even on mission trips.

Second, why not unplug the television set? We unplugged ours and just watch videos instead. Yes, we can hook the television back up for special things like a ball game, now and then, but we rarely do it. I trust my kids, but I don't trust that crazy Hollywood. (There are a lot of benefits; it's amazing how many toys my kids *don't* ask for anymore.)

DO involve them in the ministry. Why keep all the ministry to yourself? Involve your kids, even on mission trips. I'm getting ready to leave with them for Mexico in a couple of weeks. I'm taking the girls one week, and my son the next. I ask the kids to bring some of their toys that they'd like to give away to the children of the world. As they're giving, I arrange for a translator, so the kids can tell about Jesus at the same time.

See how it works? Whatever your ministry, get them involved. If God has called you, then He has called you as a family.

DON'T fear "touchy-feely" relating. Men, hug your kids and express emotion with them, whether they are boys or girls. My experiences at *Acquire the Fire* events give me this principle. Quite often I end up praying with and for kids who are deeply wounded by family situations. I have seen thousands of gallons of tears cried at altars all across America. *Most of these young people have not been hugged by their dads.*

A girl came to a concert last summer and then wrote me a note afterward, asking to go on a mission trip. She said, "The reason is because when I met you in that crowd, you hugged me. When I felt that hug, I felt like God was hugging me." But the effect of a hug from Dad goes far beyond that. Let's not be "too big a man" to hug. If your daughter doesn't get a hug from you, she will go to get a hug from a guy, maybe an ungodly kind of hug. One way or the other, she'll long for the manly affection that Dad never gave her.

I have learned a couple of things along the way, especially when it comes to daughters. My daughters and I have a secret handshake. We can be holding hands at any time and we don't have to say a thing to communicate our love. We will do four squeezes. I'll do four squeezes first, maybe, and it stands for "Do you love me?" Then she will do three, "Yes, I do." Then I do two, "How much?" And then she'll just squeeze and keep holding. Or maybe she will start it. It's our secret; we look at each other, and we know what's going on.

Do be ready to ask their forgiveness. I've had to do it myself, quite often. It works wonders.

REACHING HER CLASSMATES

It all started with my 13-year-old daughter and I praying about reaching her classmates and then her school. Within five months, every classmate was coming to our service, and some gave their lives to Christ!

—Glenn, Youth Specialist

When kids see a little bit of humility in their dads, it goes a long way.

Last night I was cooking dinner, and Hannah was helping me. She was grating some cheese next to a cup of garlic I had just sliced. She went to take a bite of the cheese and grabbed a piece of the garlic by mistake. Immediately, she began spitting it out all over the cheese!

"Hannah! What are you doing," I snapped at her. "Do you realize you have a cold? Leave the kitchen, now! . . . Well, you can stay; just don't *help* me."

I could tell I'd wounded her heart. I repented and apologized. I looked at her and said, "I don't care if I have to throw this all away and start over again. I should never treat you like that. I'm sorry." When kids see a little bit of humility in their dads, it goes a long way.

Don't just endure. Some men approach all of this thinking, "Okay, I have to add my family to my list." As if they just have to endure another added task! They figure, "Well, I do put food on the table and a roof over their heads, so I am a good father. Do I really owe more?"

But being a father *is* more. It's imparting life, character, love, and the love of God to our kids. Would you commit to being that kind of man?

It's time for us to prioritize, if we want to have a world-class family and ministry. You don't have to have a great ministry and a lame family. You can have both. However, you must count the cost and pay the price.

Having a great family takes concerted effort, it will not come automatically. Remember: nobody ever had a baby and hoped that it would get hooked on drugs one day. Nobody ever walked down the aisle and hoped they would end up with a nice divorce. They all had great intentions, but did not act on their desires. We all want great things, but we only get results by paying the price of heartfelt commitment, leaning on the grace of God for every accomplishment.

Having a family is a sacrifice. You either sacrifice up front, or you will sacrifice the rest of your life. If you don't sacrifice while they are young, then for the next 20, 30, 40 years (they are older a lot longer than they are younger) you may be paying the price of your kids having babies out of wedlock, going through divorces, and walking away from the Lord. If you sacrifice now, love them and pour your time into them, you will reap the benefit for the rest of your life.

I like what one famous preacher told me, "I promised God I am taking four people to heaven with me. My wife and three children are going with me for sure, and everyone else I bring is frosting on the cake." Let us all have the courage to keep our family and ministry in proper order.

If you sacrifice now, love them and pour your time into them, you will reap the benefit for the rest of your life.

Notes

CHAPTER TWENTY-THREE

God's Call for the Family Woman

[This chapter is a little different. Let me introduce Katie, my amazing wife. She'll be speaking to you here, directing her comments to our women readers, particularly the wives of men in ministry. But that doesn't mean you husbands can skip this chapter. It's absolutely crucial that you understand where the ladies are coming from as you work at having a great ministry and a wonderful family life together. So listen up!]

Ladies, I'd like you to imagine us talking together over coffee some afternoon. If I had a chance to sit down with you, and we had a long conversation, I'm sure we could learn a lot from one another. But since this is a book chapter, I'm going to have to do all the talking! Still, if we were to chat, what

Join in your husband's vision. It is a serious thing when the wife stands aloof in her heart from the vision of her husband.

would you remember from our conversation? I'm going to guess that a few statements like the following would stick in your mind . . .

"Watch out for the pearls!" I want you to hear how important this is: join in your husband's vision. It is a serious thing when the wife stands aloof in her heart from the vision of her husband. He may withdraw his own heart and ministry from you without even intending to do so. Jesus taught this principle:

> *Give not that which is holy unto the dogs, neither cast ye your pearls before swine, lest they trample them under their feet, and turn again and rend you.*
>
> —Matthew 7:6 (KJV)

There was a time when I was acting the part of the "swine" with my husband. Yet he graciously persisted in laying the pearls of his vision for ministry before me and inviting me to enter it with him.

When we first started Teen Mania, my heart wasn't in it at all; I was completely focused on foreign missions. You see, we had traveled overseas for six months, and we both had missions on our hearts. I felt sure that our life's calling would have something to do with missions. I knew that I was called to full-time ministry, but Ron and I weren't exactly sure what the Lord had planned for us. During this time we traveled to 25 different countries and saw God move in powerful, mind-blowing ways.

We prepared our hearts before we went, praying that we would lay hands on the sick for healing and that people would come to know the Lord in droves. And it happened. In India, we saw two ladies healed of blindness; as I prayed I watched their eyes turn from cloudy white back to beautiful brown. I also saw a lady get up and walk—someone who hadn't walked in years and years! Best of all, over 20 thousand people came to know the Lord as a result of just the two of us preaching the Gospel. We saw Hindus wiping the dots off their foreheads, pulling off the bracelets symbolizing their worship of a myriad of other gods.

Now, if you were me—if you'd seen all these things happen before your eyes—would you be excited about missions? I was overwhelmed; I was sure this was our calling. However, while we were in Indonesia, we fasted for three days, laying our lives before the Lord and asking Him specifically what we were to do. I was praying, with missions on my heart; Ron was praying, with missions on his heart.

But the Lord had put teenagers on his heart too.

American teenagers.

So he shared that with me—cast his pearls before me. And I said, "You have got to be crazy!"

"But Katie . . ."

"Ron, think about all we've seen. Then think about those American teenagers—they have a church on every street corner. Where is the need here?"

"But Katie . . ."

"Those kids can turn on the radio and get saved—but

look at these people. They've never heard the name of Jesus before. Are you *crazy?*"

Ron was gracious. "Let's just pray about it," he said.

So we went home, and I began to pray about it like this: "Lord, if You have really put this on his heart, then stir up my heart too, because I don't have one ounce of burden for teenagers. I am intimidated by them, and I don't know how to relate to them anymore."

That's when the Lord opened up my eyes and showed me the big picture. (I need to see the big picture to know *why* we're doing what were doing. Are you like that?) I began to *see* teenagers in a new and fearful light—how the evil one had ravaged them with gangs and drugs, suicide and sex. I saw a whole generation with broken hearts, and then I saw God and *His* heart for these young people. It seemed the Lord Himself was ready to raise up the standard of youth ministry.

I also saw that, in those days, there were barely any youth pastors being paid a salary. Youth ministry wasn't a priority to very many pastors or to the church body at large. But I saw what God wanted to do and I became so excited about it. I began to see the vision, how we could take teenagers—this broken generation—and help them know God's plan for their lives. God could be glorified through their changed lives. Then I thought about this: how many of these thousands and thousands of teens calling out for help *might someday travel to the mission field and far outstrip anything Ron and I had ever done there?*

Of course, that is exactly what God has been doing over the years since my own heart was broken for teens. Through Teen Mania, countless young people have gone overseas to pray for the sick, minister in the name of Jesus, and witness the victory of the cross over illness and death. Year after year God has multiplied our efforts beyond our greatest imagination, and He is glorified.

All of this to say, *share the ministry vision with your husband.* God knew what He was doing when He put the two of you together. You are one with him; you are called together with him. He put that vision in your husband, and He will put it in you. But also pay attention to the pearls of God's vision, the priceless treasure of doing His will as a family.

"You're either building or destroying the ministry." You may have a Mr. Gung-Ho Preacher husband filled with awesome vision, and sometimes it feels like you're being carried along by his momentum. But it matters just as much where *your* heart is in the ministry. I remember the days when I had real little ones at home, two- and three-year olds, and I just rode along on Ron's coattails. I figured, "Why do I need to get up early and pray? I'm changing diapers all the time, and who needs to be anointed for that? Ron is the one out there speaking and counseling, so why do I need to be anointed?" That is a lie from the pit. *You have the power to make or break your ministry as a couple.*

> *The wise woman builds her house, but with her own hands the foolish one tears hers down.*
> —Proverbs 14:1

Share the ministry vision with your husband. God knew what He was doing when He put the two of you together.

You have the power to make or break your ministry as a couple.

God must think we are pretty important to give us that kind of power in our homes. And be assured, this has everything to do with ministry, for a ministry rests on the pillars of family unity. It flows from the wholeness of the couple together, from the quality of their walk with God together. That is, the health of your family unit determines the health of your ministry. And the enemy has taken the offensive (if you haven't already noticed!) to destroy homes because of this truth. He knows that if he can tear down families, he can devastate the effectiveness of the church. So let us be wise to his schemes!

Ron and I were driving to the airport one day, along with two church leaders who were shepherding a church in trouble. In fact, their church was falling apart before their eyes. As we talked, my heart grieved for these men. The senior pastor's wife had left him to pursue her own career. You see, her husband was very zealous for the Lord—so zealous that he had neglected his home life. The associate pastor seemed to be in the same boat. They were hard workers, but their families were in shambles, and their church was no better.

As we talked with these two men, we realized that they were broken, confused, and deeply wounded. This was the leadership of the church! They weren't wimpy little guys—they were strong in the Lord—yet because of their two messed-up families, a whole body of believers suffered and withered on the vine. How important it is to manage our homes wisely and well! It's a two-person job.

He must manage his own family well and see that his children obey him with proper respect.

—1 Timothy 3:4

Even in laying out the requirements for church leadership, God put the priority on family and its management. He cares so much that we are strong and united in Him and His work. In youth ministry this has special importance because, day in and day out, you minister to teenagers who face serious family dysfunction—or no family structure at all. So when you come to them with a strong marriage and family, you speak powerfully into their lives before you even open your mouth.

You and your husband are like the head and the heart of your family. If the head and the heart break down, then the whole body dies. Similarly, together you are the head and the heart of your youth ministry.

Make your husband your priority, and don't get sidetracked by placing your children at the center of everything. Love your children with all your heart, more than your own life, but never let them run the home. Sadly, it is all too easy to make your home an exclusively child-centered environment. This is especially true when you have new babies with all their legitimate demands, day and night. You give them every ounce of your being, all your

A ministry rests on the pillars of family unity. It flows from the wholeness of the couple together, from the quality of their walk with God together.

Make your husband your priority, and don't get sidetracked by placing your children at the center of everything.

energy and love. What a challenge, then, to keep that priority of loving your husband first!

But this is your calling. This is the path to loving your child in the deepest way—to stay "one" with your husband. Only then will the family be all that your child needs it to be. You are to make your husband the priority because your children are counting on that from the bottom of their hearts. Whether they can express it verbally or not, it is exactly what they need. Your rock-solid relationship with your husband is their refuge, their whole security in life.

"If you don't let him go, you'll lose him." Here is a Scripture I love to pray over my husband:

> *The king's heart is in the hand of the Lord; he directs it like a watercourse wherever he pleases.*
>
> —Proverbs 21:1

I believe with all my heart that God is directing Ron's heart. He is the "king" in our family, so I pray this verse over him. Clearly, there is, for me, an aspect of letting go in this verse: letting go of my own husband and trusting his heart into the hand of the Lord.

I am a living testimony to the power of holding on. I was terrified of letting my husband go. Why? Because my husband is such a "go-getter." He's a visionary; as God directs, he will follow.

When we got married, Ron would say things like, "I have to go. I have to travel. We can't influence the kind of people that God wants us to influence if we just stay right here in peace and comfort." Every time he would say those things, I'd feel a big lump form in my throat. I'd grit my teeth and fight to hold back the fear. Where was my security? I wanted to scream, "No! Just stay here with me!"

A certain Scripture helped me at this point, though:

> David, wearing a linen ephod, danced before the LORD with all his might, while he and the entire house of Israel brought up the ark of the LORD with shouts and the sound of trumpets.
>
> As the ark of the LORD was entering the City of David, Michal daughter of Saul watched from a window. And when she saw King David leaping and dancing before the LORD, she despised him in her heart.
>
> They brought the ark of the LORD and set it in its place inside the tent that David had pitched for it, and David sacrificed burnt offerings and fellowship offerings before the LORD. After he had finished sacrificing the burnt offerings and fellowship offerings, he blessed the people in the name of the LORD Almighty. Then he gave a loaf of bread, a cake of dates and a cake of raisins to each person in the whole crowd of Israelites, both men and women. And all the people went to their homes.
>
> When David returned home to bless his household, Michal daughter of Saul came out to meet him and said, "How the king of Israel has distinguished himself today, disrobing in the sight of the slave girls of his servants as any vulgar fellow would!"

> *David said to Michal, "It was before the LORD, who*
> *chose me rather than your father or anyone from his*
> *house when he appointed me ruler over the LORD's peo-*
> *ple Israel—I will celebrate before the LORD. I will become*
> *even more undignified than this, and I will be hum-*
> *iliated in my own eyes. But by these slave girls you*
> *spoke of, I will be held in honor."*
>
> *And Michal daughter of Saul had no children to the*
> *day of her death.*
>
> *—2 Samuel 6:14–23*

Apparently King David was a go-getter too. He danced so enthusiastically before the Lord that his clothes fell off! And his wife despised him for it.

She wasn't blessed for that attitude, but she instructs me. I have always prayed, "Lord, don't ever let me get between Ron and You, what You want to do in his life and in our life together. Don't ever let me despise Your work in him!"

During the first year of my marriage, I called home to Mom, thoroughly frustrated. Ron's heart was "out there with God," as usual. He happened to be away from home, and I felt as if his heart was so involved with the ministry that nothing was left for me. I told my Mom these things. But did she encourage my complaints? No. She simply raised the question: "Katie, can you thank God that Ron is out doing God's work?" God began to deal with me, and I began to let Ron go.

Then the message was reinforced when I received a letter from a good friend who lives in Panama. She's a missionary there with her husband, raising their children in the jungle. She is an incredible woman with great wisdom, whom I deeply respect. "I had to let my husband go," she said. "I had to die to that grasping, that longing for a security based in my husband. How else could I learn to rest in the security of God?"

Sometimes her husband would need to go deep into the jungle to find new tribes who'd never heard of Jesus. He couldn't know in advance what he'd find, whether the people would be friendly or deadly hostile. He would be gone for days, sometimes weeks at a time, with no ability to communicate back with her. She had to let him go because God was directing him and her in the work. "If you do not let your husband go like that, Katie," she wrote, "then you will lose him. It's a scary, blessed paradox, isn't it?"

She told me that God put the "go" in our husbands' hearts, and so we must let them do all that God has called them to do. So with the fear of God in my heart, I did let Ron go. And God has been faithful to me in all of the things that I desire for our marriage and for our relationship.

Here is the great blessing: Ron now preaches all over the country and *I have total veto power* over his travel plans for *Acquire the Fire* events. That means I can say, "Honey, I don't want you to go that many times this year," or "I don't want you to go this weekend, because important things will be happening here at home." Ron has given me the authority to do that, and I am blown away by God's graciousness and His favor on my life because of this. My husband has given me the respect to trust me with that power. But it is only because I let him go, only because I laid it down before the Lord and adopted the vision God gave him.

We need to give him more encouragement than anyone else, be his Number One Fan.

"If you're his Number One Critic, it won't help you at all." Really, can we make things better by complaining? Have you ever known it to work?

Let's suppose he's got the vision, and he calls home to report on all the marvelous things God is doing in the ministry. You're angry, though, because he's not home. You're angry because he didn't call earlier, or didn't call more, or didn't . . . whatever. Will it help you to complain and criticize? If God is building him up, and teenagers are thanking him for his ministry to them, and you pull him down over the phone, will he want to call again just as soon as he can? Will he be itching to report to you as soon as possible, to share and relate and be mutually encouraged?

Or will he avoid his Number One Critic?

We have to bite our tongues during those challenging times when he is more involved in the ministry than we are. We need to give him more encouragement than anyone else, be his Number One Fan. That way, our presence becomes a haven for him, our voice becomes the music of encouragement in his ears, the foretaste of loving arms that he looks forward to feeling ASAP!

I can hear you say, "Well, Katie, what if he is indeed neglecting me and my feelings? What do I do then?" The answer is, pray. And when he is home, you lighten up and adore him. It's not easy, but if you go to God with your needs, He will give you the unconditional love that no person on earth could ever provide. Yes, God will answer your prayer because He wants you both to work as a team.

I have prayed that our home would be full of peace, a haven for my husband. I make it clean and orderly and beautiful and . . . fun. I push back the all-too-natural chaos with pretty music and candles and cleanliness. I am the manager of my home, as a sacrifice of praise and thanksgiving to the Lord. Amazingly, all of this melts Ron's heart in his love for me.

I want Ron out there and going, because God has called him to do it. (I even told him this year, "I can't imagine you being gone *less* than you are now. How could the work get done?") Yes, I want him out there, but I want him home with me, too. This is the key: when he's home, *I want him home with me in his heart.*

"You might have to hem and haw for a while." Many of us with ministry husbands will need to learn how to speak and teach too. For example, I speak to our intern girls and sometimes speak at *Acquire the Fire* conferences. I love it because it's a time when I can pour into other people what God has been pouring into me.

Speaking is so vital because through your words you establish God's kingdom in people's hearts. When God gave your husband the vision, He gave it to you as well, because you are one. It is likely that you will be expected to teach. Now that puts fear and trembling in

I am the manager of my home, as a sacrifice of praise and thanksgiving to the Lord.

some of us. But if you will take hold of Scripture and speak it over yourself, God can change your heart about that fear. You can speak with confidence and authority.

If you aren't used to it, you'll shake a little bit, your mouth will go dry, and your palms will get wet. You'll hem and haw. But your heart will shine through. Your love for God will be evident, and that is what will be conveyed. So just keep doing it and know by faith that you are really establishing the kingdom of God in hungry hearts. Here are some Scriptures to help you:

> *God did not give us a spirit of timidity, but a spirit of power, of love and of self-discipline.*
>
> —2 Timothy 1:7

> *The LORD said to me, "Do not say, 'I am only a child.' You must go to everyone I send you to and say whatever I command you. Do not be afraid of them, for I am with you and will rescue you," declares the LORD.*
>
> *Then the LORD reached out his hand and touched my mouth and said to me, "Now, I have put my words in your mouth."*
>
> —Jeremiah 1:7–9

> *The Sovereign LORD has given me an instructed tongue, to know the word that sustains the weary. He wakens me morning by morning, wakens my ear to listen like one being taught. The Sovereign LORD has opened my ears, and I have not been rebellious; I have not drawn back.*
>
> —Isaiah 50:4–5

> *"I have put my words in your mouth and covered you with the shadow of my hand—I who set the heavens in*

place, who laid the foundations of the earth, and who say to Zion, 'You are my people.'"

—Isaiah 51:16

Feel better? I'm sure you can find many more encouraging Scriptures as you edge toward those fearful waters of speaking and teaching in public. And I know you will be amazed at how God uses you. You will be amazed because, with your humble heart, God will show Himself strong on your behalf. (And if you think you're hot and have it all together, the Lord will help with that, too.) Just humble yourself before Him; He'll lift you up and use you in love and service. Thanks be to God!

I know you will be amazed at how God uses you. You will be amazed because, with your humble heart, God will show Himself strong on your behalf.

Notes

CHAPTER TWENTY-FOUR

Avoiding the Ragged Edge

I came across a startling quotation the other day: "The world is run by tired people." Is that true, I wondered? Then I realized how I could definitely make it into a true statement: "The *church* is run by tired *ministers.*"

Sad, but true. People who want to change the world don't get very much sleep. Yet the Scriptures paint a different vision.

> *God is not a God of disorder but of peace. As in all the congregations of the saints . . . everything should be done in a fitting and orderly way.*
>
> —1 Corinthians 14:33, 40

If we're walking around fried, frazzled, and fatigued, is God pleased?

Paul is speaking of worship practices in this passage, but the principle holds true in general: God does things in peaceful, orderly ways. We can look at the stars and the planets, how things perfectly circle and rotate, and we see an orderly Creator. In fact, in any area of creation we see the orderly hand of our God at work. In His commands to the church, too, God calls us to be people of peace and order.

If we're walking around fried, frazzled, and fatigued, is God pleased? If we're constantly ragged and barely limping along, will we be an encouraging presence in the ministry? And if we constantly stretch ourselves too thin, how can we claim to offer people "life, and life more abundantly"? The dark circles under our eyes belie our message every time.

I can't tell you how many times I've had youth pastors come to me after an event and ask, "Ron, how do I keep from running myself into the ground? How do I organize my personal life so I'm not so ragged in the ministry?"

The initial response is to think. Think carefully. *Why is it* that we live such frazzled lives?

TIME WASTERS ARE WASTING US!

For one thing, we fill our lives with time wasters. But we don't call them time wasters; we call them "letting down"—indulging in things like television, movies, and ball games. These are things that are making noise in our lives, and they suck our lives away. Yes, I feel as if, when I sit in front of the tube, there's a giant vacuum cleaner sucking the life out of me. It's sucking my brains, my time, my potential, all the things I could be dreaming of and praying for.

These are indeed time wasters, because I'm letting somebody else have an adventure for me, letting *them* enjoy the adventure that I never get around to experiencing for myself.

"Come on, Ron!" you say. "We need to chill sometimes."

I know that. But wouldn't it be much better to have some fun with your kids, for instance? One of the things I love to do is wrestle with my kids. Sometimes I just tickle them, close my eyes, and listen to them laugh. Have you listened to the innocence of a child laughing his heart out lately? That's not a waste of time; it's standing under a waterfall of peace.

But we say, "After this movie then I'll work," or "After this next thing," or "After this ball game and then . . ." I'm all for watching a good game now and then. But could we be a little more alert to that sucking sound?

WE JUST CAN'T SAY "NO!"

You hear, "Oh, can you help with this?" Then what do you answer? Have you learned yet that somebody else's sudden little crisis is not necessarily your immediate emergency? We need to learn to say "no" to off-the-cuff requests. We need to learn the difference between the important and the merely urgent.

Of course, we don't want to hurt anyone's feelings.

Saying "no" means not letting others control your time.

But assertiveness can be carried out with all due respect and appropriate tact. It just takes some practice. Try standing in front of the mirror for a few minutes each day and practice saying:

> *Hmm, sorry, but I'm already booked for that time slot.*
> *No, I've already blocked out that time for family.*
> *I'm afraid I can't; I've scheduled that time for*
>   *another matter.*
> *No, my policy is never to . . .*
> *No, that wouldn't be the best use of my time right now.*
> *No.*

You get the idea. The more you practice, the less fearful these kinds of phrases will become. You need to learn them well to stay sharp in ministry.

Just the other day one of our interns e-mailed me, "This lady called and is thinking about coming to *Acquire the Fire*. She wants to talk to you about it." I e-mailed him back and told him to have her talk to his supervisor. Why? As much as I'd like to, I can't talk to every person who wants to talk to me. I'm guessing that you're in a similar situation. So set those boundaries. It's an essential form of "no" for all of us. It requires having competent people around you, of course, who can screen your calls and stand in for you when needed. Then say "no" and delegate. Otherwise, instead of effectiveness we end up with busyness.

The problem is, we think we have a full life because we're doing this and we're doing that. But being busy is not a sign of being effective. Engaging in more and more activities usually means we know less and less of our families, of ourselves, of our God. This isn't good.

Saying no means not letting others control your time. You set your time and your agenda based on what you know is your vision for your family, vision for your ministry, and vision for your own spiritual growth. This doesn't mean you don't allow for diversions from time to time. But that's why you raise up other people around you to be able to handle things. Then you can say, as the leader, "No, if there are other people who can do that, let them do it."

VISIONLESS, WE'RE FRAZZLED

If you have no vision for your own personal development, that's a prime ragged-edge producer!

"I want to grow in the Lord and be a better leader," you say. "And I want to change the world." Good. But here's the point: only if you're driven by a vision will you be able to prioritize the steps and stick to the things you need to accomplish for overall effectiveness. *I need to read this much Bible; I need to spend this much time reading other relevant material; I need to spend this time going to these seminars, seeing these people, doing these things.* When you don't have a vision driving you, you tend to do things—perhaps many things—without purpose. You get involved in activity for activity's sake. And so you get totally frazzled.

If you have no vision for your own personal development, that's a prime ragged-edge producer!

You also need a real vision for your family and for your marriage. We've explored this in the previous two chapters, but I'd like to add an important point here: agree with your spouse about the amount of time you will spend at work versus the time you spend with your family. You can't say, "Honey, I've got a job, and I'm a volunteer youth pastor, and I have to do both those things. So I'll come home and eat and stuff, from time to time . . ."

No, family comes first. When we first started the Teen Mania ministry, I said, "Katie, I want you to know that I don't really believe in a 40-hour work week, but according to this Western mind-set, 40 hours is what people are supposed to work. So the only time that I feel belongs to me, that I feel I could fully give to the ministry, is 40 hours a week. Anything outside of 40, I am going to ask you for permission to work." We have agreement about this, because I'm not going to do whatever I want to do and drag her through life with the occasional guilt-inducing, "But God cares about all those people, don't *you*?"

Don't get me wrong, I definitely work more than 40 hours per week, but Katie and I agree on it in advance. We plan out our family times. Any time outside the 40 hours does not come out of our family times, but out of my discretionary time. What do I mean by that? Well, the time hanging out with other guys, TV, movies, sleep . . . all that is discretionary. I can cut into that all I want to work for the ministry. I will not cut into the family time.

It's not our right to drag our spouses through life saying, "But God told me." We are a team in this thing. We are one unit, one family, and if God told you, He can tell your spouse, too. It's more important to have unity than to have your own way when it comes to time.

I also refuse to do things that infringe on our trust. For example, sometimes opportunities come our way that are outside the bounds of our time agreement. Usually, I don't even tell Katie about those; I just pass them up. However, occasionally I might say, "Honey, do you think we could do this? Do you think I could travel here? I'm only going to do this if you agree." Since I don't ask this very often, she knows that if I do it must be something we should really pray about and consider.

NOT HEARING FROM GOD, WE GET CONFUSED

Once you have an agreement with your spouse about time demands of ministry and home, then you need to think about your time with God. Organizing your personal life has to start with that. Are you really connected with God as you carry out your ministry? Are you hearing from Him every day? If not, what's the point?

Your relationship with God is what fuels your ministry, so time with Him has to be the highlight of your day. "Man, I can't wait until tomorrow morning and my quiet time with God!" It's the thing that keeps you kicking, keeps you excited for life itself.

Make it a profitable time. Include some diligent study, and always be learning. A story is told about John Wesley, the great 17th-century revivalist, field preacher, and

Your relationship with God is what fuels your ministry, so time with Him has to be the highlight of your day.

scholar. He once received a note that said: "The Lord told me to tell you that He doesn't need your book-learning, your Greek and your Hebrew."

Wesley answered, "Thank you, sir. Your letter was superfluous, however, as I already knew the Lord has no need for my 'book-learning,' as you put it. However, although the Lord has not directed me to say so, on my own responsibility I would like to say to you that the Lord does not need your ignorance, either."

We need not be frazzled in ministry. But to avoid becoming one of those "tired ministers" who run the church, we've got to slow down, learn to draw our energy from the rest that God gives us. I leave you with how Pastor Mike Breen puts it in his *LifeShapes* seminars:

> *If we're to understand how we're to continue, we need to know how we are started. How did we get this thing going? Or, more to the point, how did God get this thing going?*
>
> *Well, He made us on the sixth day, and after a busy day being created, we spend the next day resting. We're made for work. We're made for fruitfulness. We're made for productive activity. But our very first whole day experience is what? Rest. So, here's the first little piece of revelation about the rhythm of life that God wants us to invest in.*
>
> *We work from rest, not rest from work. Human beings are designed to work. But they're designed to work from a place of rest. Not to crash into rest from too much work.*[1]

1. Mike Breen, *Living in Rhythm with Life Teaching DVD* (Colorado Springs, CO:Cook Communications Ministries, 2006).

CHAPTER TWENTY-FIVE

Stay Saturated!

After a pouring rain, I noticed a water leak in my office, a little one, just over the windowsill. I couldn't tell where it originated, because of the ceiling tiles, so I set a garbage can on the sill to catch the tiny drops. It was an annoyance, but it wasn't enough to flood me or wreck the furniture. It was a drip; I certainly wasn't saturated.

However, during the Christmas break last year we experienced a different kind of leak in one of our dormitories. I think it occurred right on Christmas Day over that weekend. A two-inch pipe froze and broke, and no one was there to notice it for two days.

The leak sprung on the second floor, and it flooded the floor below—all the walls, all the desks and beds, all the carpets. It dripped down everywhere. What a mess!

We hired professionals to dry everything out, and it was an amazing thing to observe. They drilled holes at the

Think about "the greatest possible amount"—so full that there is no way to hold any more. What would it be like to know God that way?

bottom of all the walls, inserted hoses attached to big air blowers, and blew air into the walls for many days. They also set up a huge dehumidifier to pull out 25 gallons of moisture a day!

That's more than a drip. The place was saturated. But what does *saturation* really mean?

> *to soak;*
> *to fill;*
> *to load to capacity;*
> *to cause a substance to unite with the greatest possible amount of another substance;*
> *to cause to combine until there is no further tendency to combine.*

Think about "the greatest possible amount"—so full that there is no way to hold any more. What would it be like to know God that way? To be saturated with Him?

Actually, we're saturated with lots of things these days, aren't we? Some of us are saturated with sports; we know all the teams and statistics, and we can't wait for the next game to begin. Others are saturated with movies, or music, the Internet, or television sitcoms. Some are saturated with news, so they're glued to CNN or Fox every minute of the day. "Suppose I missed the latest headline!" they think. It sends chills up their spines. (I have to be careful here; I, too, love to know what's going on in the world.)

There's nothing inherently wrong with most of the things that grab our interest. Many of them can be enjoyed as gifts from God. But saturation? It's too easy to be a servant of God and still saturate ourselves with things *other than* God. In fact, whatever completely permeates our lives—isn't that really our God?

How then, with such busy lives, can we be saturated with God? Let me suggest this: *We could start by making our personal space a God-friendly environment.*

CREATE A GOD-FRIENDLY LIFE

We talk a lot about user-friendliness. What about a God-friendly environment in our own personal lives? It would be an environment where God finds it easy to hang out, where He would smile and say, "I like that. I'm going to show up here some more." Imagine! The kind of life space where God says, "That's where I want to be."

We have seeker-sensitive services, but what about God-friendly services? And how about a God-friendly life?

In the same way that we can choose the nature of our "personal space" whether we're driving in a car or sitting in a restaurant, we can create a space in our lives that will delight God's heart and invite His presence. How can we do that?

Start your saturation first thing in the morning. Jump in the tub. Don't stand under a thin trickle where you have to

Start by making
our personal space
a God-friendly environment.

Jump in the tub. Don't stand under a thin trickle where you have to bounce around to get wet.

bounce around to get wet. Isn't that what some of our quiet times are like? Here's a little Scripture, a little prayer. *Whoa, I got a drop, so I'm good to go.* No; dive in!

Psalm 63 speaks of "following hard after" God, seeking Him with all our heart. Psalm 5 tells us to come early in the morning and seek Him. Even Jesus, the Son of God, rose very early in the morning, while it was still dark, to go and hang out with His Father. If Jesus felt it necessary to "dive in" like that, how much more should we feel the need?

Some people say, "But I'm not a morning person!" No problem. You can saturate in the evening. Jesus worked ministry late into the night, too, then He got up early and had time with His father. Why? Because He wanted to be saturated.

This is a life pattern that says, "God, I really want to connect with You! Feed me, feed me! I don't want to just read a little verse and a poem; I have to get some food." We must get on our faces and say, "I love You, Lord. You are God." We have to really submerge ourselves in worship.

Invite the tsunami of God's presence to hit you. The great tsunami of December 2004 was 60 feet high when it hit Sri Lanka, Sumatra, and so many other nations. Entire villages were washed away. Some people who lived in concrete houses survived, while their neighbors, living in huts, perished. Things that were stable and built solidly gave refuge.

When you invite the God-tsunami to hit, realize that all of the things not built on a firm foundation are going to be washed away. Sometimes we become very comfortable with our huts and habits, the ways of our comfortable lifestyle. There are things we like to do and things we like to see. When God "hits," it's as if He says, "If you really want my presence, then all of the things built with straw and stubble will need to be washed away."

Invite the tsunami to hit, but realize that God is constantly inviting us to come up to the mountain with Him. We will definitely need to leave some things behind for our own good. *Drop the weight and baggage to get where I am.*

Without a doubt, if we choose to walk with the Lord, there will be a demand on our lives. We will have less of the world, less of our own ego. If we want more of His presence, His tangible saturation, then more of the flesh must go.

It is so easy, after you have been with God a while, to think, "I am a pretty decent person, and God must be pleased with me compared to my neighbor over there." But this isn't a competition. God works with each of us wherever we are. He starts there and grows us as we open ourselves to His sanctifying Spirit. Are we closer to Him than the next guy? That's not the question; the real question is: am I closer to God at the moment than I was a moment ago? It's a matter of keeping an open heart.

Are we satisfied with being just a little damp? Or shall we get drenched? God sets higher standards for us the longer we are Christians. We are supposed to go from glory to glory.

God sets higher standards for us the longer we are Christians. We are supposed to go from glory to glory.

I want to know Christ and the power of his resurrection and the fellowship of sharing in his sufferings, becoming like him in his death, and so, somehow, to attain to the resurrection from the dead.

Not that I have already obtained all this, or have already been made perfect, but I press on to take hold of that for which Christ Jesus took hold of me. Brothers, I do not consider myself yet to have taken hold of it. But one thing I do: Forgetting what is behind and straining toward what is ahead, I press on toward the goal to win the prize for which God has called me heavenward in Christ Jesus.

All of us who are mature should take such a view of things. And if on some point you think differently, that too God will make clear to you. Only let us live up to what we have already attained.

—Philippians 3:10–16

Press on! Invite the tsunami to hit, but realize some of the cherished huts will be washed away.

Realize it's bigger than you. That is, realize this thing called the presence of God is an amazing experience worthy of all reverence and awe. The psalmist says, "The LORD confides in those who fear him; he makes his covenant known to them" (Ps. 25:14). God will show us secrets; He'll show us what He's really like. He will whisper and give us insight into the deep things of His nature—if we respect Him enough to listen.

> *If there is any focus that the Christian leader of the future will need, it is the discipline of dwelling in the presence of the One who keeps asking us, "Do you love me? Do you love me? Do you love me?" It is the discipline of contemplative prayer. Through contemplative prayer we can keep ourselves from being pulled from one urgent issue to another and from becoming stranger to our own and God's heart. Contemplative prayer keeps us home, rooted and safe, even when we are on the road, moving from place to place, and often surrounded by sounds of violence and war. Contemplative prayer deepens in us the knowledge that we . . . already belong to God, even though everything and everyone around us keeps suggesting the opposite.*
>
> From Henri J. M. Nouwen, *In the Name of Jesus* (New York: Crossroad, 1989)

This kind of prayer is a listening attitude that waits in the presence of the awesomeness of the sovereign Lord. Some haven't heard from this Lord in so long, yet if we aren't sensing His presence, then we might ask whether we truly honor and fear Him as we ought.

He will whisper and give us insight into the deep things of His nature—if we respect Him enough to listen.

We marinate in God until we taste like Him. Meditate upon God's Word until all the flavor sinks in.

My son Cameron was reading through the Bible, and he came to me about one particular story. In that passage, the fire of the Lord came and filled the temple after Solomon prayed and dedicated it to God. Cameron said, "Think about how much they must have honored the Lord for Him to show up like that!" I thought, *Lord, I want to honor You like that.*

Marinate until you're flavored. I could speak of "meditating," but I would rather call it marinating. That is, we marinate in God until we taste like Him. It's a marvelous analogy, isn't it? Meditate upon God's Word until all the flavor sinks in.

What a contrast to checking off the Scriptures we're memorizing! Could we marinate in those words, too, until we begin to take on their godly characteristics? I have enjoyed a whole new season of meditating on Scripture over the last several months, and I'm amazed at what's happening to my mind. The thoughts of God are becoming my thoughts . . . naturally, like second nature. Is there a greater blessing in life?

Scripture abounds with invitations to marinate . . .

This book of the law shall not depart out of thy mouth; but thou shalt meditate therein day and night, that thou mayest observe to do according to all that is written therein: for then thou shalt make thy way prosperous, and then thou shalt have good success.

—Joshua 1:8 (KJV)

Blessed is the man that walketh not in the counsel of the ungodly, nor standeth in the way of sinners, nor sitteth in the seat of the scornful. But his delight is in the law of the LORD; and in his law doth he meditate day and night.

—Psalm 1:1–2 (KJV)

I will meditate in thy precepts, and have respect unto thy ways.

—Psalm 119:15 (KJV)

My hands also will I lift up unto thy commandments, which I have loved; and I will meditate in thy statutes.

—Psalm 119:48 (KJV)

I remember the days of old; I meditate on all thy works; I muse on the work of thy hands.

—Psalm 143:5 (KJV)

Meditate upon these things; give thyself wholly to them; that thy profiting may appear to all.

—1 Timothy 4:15 (KJV)

What would a little marinating do for the rest of your day? How would it change what happens between your praise sessions? Ephesians 6 talks about prayer without ceasing. It really is walking in communion with a very personal God.

He is worthy of every morsel of my mind, my being, and my lifestyle.

CONSIDER YOUR MOTIVE

But why? Why should we do all of this? It would be easy just to say, "Do this, and you will have more peace, more joy, a much better life." That would be true, but the fact is that most things we hear preached today are self-centered. It's about us, what we want and what we'll get.

No! It's all about God. What He wants and what He gets. Otherwise, we are no different from the local humanists. Humanism says the goal of life is for humans to be happy. When that penetrates our Gospel, when we are following the rules just to keep from going to hell, then we have actually moved far away from the Gospel.

Why should we saturate ourselves in God's presence or live a lifestyle that will invite His friendship? Because *He is worthy of every morsel of my mind, my being, and my lifestyle.* He is worth the price that Jesus paid on the cross for me. And He deserves all that was bought there. He is worth all that I am, 24/7, until the day I die.

I could never repay Him, of course, but He is worth it all. If I never received one blessing, if I had no more joy and no more peace than anyone else, God would still be worth every amount of mental, spiritual, and physical energy that I have. He deserves nothing less. Clearly, then, the reason for staying saturated in Him is that it's an act of worship that He deserves in every way.

It is also the reason for all our outreach, at home and abroad. Jesus paid on the cross for the sins of the world—even if we preach, and no one ever says yes. All people we try to reach are sinners just like us, and, like us, they don't deserve salvation. But when Jesus gave His life, He offered Himself, the perfect sacrifice, for all mankind. A God-centered life and motive says, "You paid for them all; You deserve them all." Doesn't He deserve everything that He paid for? Therefore, our motive for outreach is: Christ deserves the reward of His sacrifice.

Let our motives be pure, in saturating ourselves and in reaching out to others. As a Youth Specialist, you will often face people you don't have a heart for. But do you have a heart for God? Whether or not you have a heart for those particular people or not, He paid the price for them. It is about pleasing Him and proclaiming His message. He is worth our all.

Our job is to go and tell a world of people about Who really owns them. So many teens you'll invite to your youth group will have rough edges and tons of character flaws. You might not like them very much. No matter. God sent His Son to die for them; He is worthy of all their hearts, all their souls for the rest of their lives. Our job is to help them see that. And really, is there a better job in the whole world?

A God-centered life and motive says, "You paid for them all; You deserve them all."

Notes

CHAPTER TWENTY-SIX

The Message of the Youth Specialist

This may be the most important chapter of the book. Thus far, we've discussed how to build a thriving youth ministry from the ground up with tried-and-true principles using lots of stories to illustrate the effectiveness of this paradigm. We've talked about the personal life of the Youth Specialist and the demands God puts on us.

But once we've built the ministry, and we've got our lifestyle in order, what is it that we are actually here to preach? The core of our message is critically important for a number of reasons. Despite all that has been done in the name of Christ for youth ministry, and all that's been done for the sake of ministry in general in America, we still have a morally bankrupt society.

Despite all that has been done in the name of Christ for youth ministry, and all that's been done for the sake of ministry in general in America, we still have a morally bankrupt society.

Considering the number of megachurches, TV ministries, radio ministries, printed matter, different translations of the Bible (to say nothing of the multiple Bibles most Christians have stored in their closets), as well as some 5,600 new Christian books published each year, why is it that we live in a culture where there is more divorce; more pornography; more demonstrative, arrogant, bold sinning than ever before? How could those two trends co-exist *unless the message proclaimed is either the wrong message or it is not penetrating deeply enough to change convictions in the heart of the hearer?*

If we work to rescue a generation, we'd better make sure the message we are proclaiming is the message that produces radical life-change in the hearts of every person that hears it.

What follows is a summary of what I believe are the absolutely non-negotiable imperatives (no matter which branch of Christianity you might come from) for producing the change the Bible refers to. To see a generation won to Christ and be swept off its feet, and to see our teens become a real, vibrant witness to this world, we'd better make sure we include the following:

TOTAL AND COMPLETE COMMITMENT

Do not soft-sell what the Gospel asks of us. Phrases like, "All you have to do is pray this little prayer," mislead people and misrepresent Christ. We use so many words, phrases, and concepts that are actually unbiblical in our asking people to come to Christ. We say, "Do you want to accept Christ?" Someone please show me where that is said in the Bible. There is only one place in one translation that I have ever found that even alluded to "accepting Christ."

In normal English vernacular, we don't even use the word "accept" that way, yet in ministry we use it to say, "Do you want to somehow get connected to God?" in the same way we'd say, "Do you *accept* Visa?" or, "Do you *accept* MasterCard?" Is this what we're talking about?

The word "accept" also has weak overtones. We'll ask, "Will someone accept John, because we all know no one really loves him?" Is that what Jesus is? Someone with no self-esteem who needs our acceptance? *Please accept Him into your heart.* When we ask people to come to Jesus in this way we end up with a mentality that produces *passive Christians at best.*

People in church also say, "Have you *received* the Lord?" It's true that in John 1 you'll find the word "receive": "To those who receive Him, He gave power to become the sons of God." But the word "receive" in the Greek means, "to embrace or hold on to." The way we communicate it, it sounds more like a passive word. *If you bring people to Christ in a passive way, they will remain passive Christians their whole lives.*

Do not soft-sell what the Gospel asks of us.

If you bring people to Christ in a passive way, they will remain passive Christians their whole lives.

Have you heard someone say, "Do you want to have a personal relationship with Jesus Christ?" Nowhere in the Bible do I see Jesus asking us to enter a personal relationship with Him. Obviously when we make Jesus the center of our lives, we embrace Him as our Master and our King. We get a very personal, very close relationship because He lives inside us. You can't get any closer than that.

All of these phrases substitute watered-down rhetoric for the reality of what being a Christian really is: total and complete surrender to Jesus Christ. Here in America, we embrace a kind of "cultural Christianity" that looks at total surrender as "radical" or "untamed." People think, "Well, I'm not a Muslim; I'm not a Jew; I guess I'm a Christian." Those raised in church end up inoculated against a totally-sold-out message of the Gospel.

I've stopped asking people if they want to become a Christian. Jesus never asked anybody if they wanted to be a Christian. People were called Christians because they followed Christ and imitated Him. It was actually the secular world that first came up with the idea, "Hey, let's call them Christians." Now I ask people if they would like to become a "follower of Christ." Thirty-two different times, Jesus mentioned the phrase, "Follow me." We are not called to be Christians but to follow Him in our hearts, with our lifestyles, with our actions, and with our motives. One day we'll follow Him to heaven as devoted followers.

In Matthew 16, Jesus said, "If anyone would come after me, he must deny himself and take up his cross and follow me." Denying ourselves means to give up our selfish ambitions, our selfish drives, our selfish desires, and our selfish lifestyles.

Compare this to *enlisting* in the army. Enlisting is a lot different than joining. Following Jesus is a lot different from "just pray this simple prayer with me." When you enlist, you sign on the dotted line. You sign over the ownership of your life and you are no longer in charge. This is the kind of challenge that Jesus laid out in the Gospel. This is the kind of challenge we must lay out if we are to become real followers of Him.

In addition to totally enlisting, we need to make sure that we are not simply providing "fire insurance"—offering people an escape from hell. We can scare them out of hell. But they end up making a foxhole decision just to avoid pain or punishment, rather than to run to Christ with their whole hearts. There is a big difference between running from hell and running to Christ.

We don't want bare-minimum Christians, yet our altar call says, "If you want to come to Christ, *all you have to do* . . ." How dare we cheapen grace that way? All you have to do is turn your back on the world, take up your cross, and follow Him. All you have to do is change your lifestyle, change your heart, and change the direction of everything you are.

I ask people if they would like to become a "follower of Christ."

As we call people to Christ, we need to make sure they become God-seekers, God-lovers, and God-followers.

The Bible says He rewards those who diligently seek Him. As we call people to Christ, we need to make sure they become God-seekers, God-lovers, and God-followers. The psalmist says, "As the deer pants for streams of water, so my soul pants for you, O God" (Ps. 42:1). We want to produce a world of young people who turn to Christ, follow Him, and yearn for the deep things of God all the days of their lives.

As Youth Specialists, I would recommend we NEVER, EVER, EVER use these overused, inaccurate, unbiblical, and misunderstood phrases when asking people to come to Christ:

- Do you want to accept Christ?
- Do you want to receive Him as your Lord and Savior?
- Do you want a personal relationship with Christ?
- Do you want Him to save you?
- All you have to do is pray this simple prayer with me . . .

Instead, once you have painted a picture that Jesus is really worth giving your all to, invite young people to become followers of Christ with phrases like:

- Are you ready to turn away from the world and its lies and come running to Jesus?

- Will you enlist in His army today, signing away your life to do whatever He wants?
- Would you like to have the miracle of a new heart? Jesus called it being born again, and only He can give it. But to get it you must turn away from the world.

With this kind of appeal, there may be fewer people coming to the front to pray, but at least they will become real followers of Christ. Who cares how many are crying their eyes out at every altar call we give if it is only emotion and not true conversion?

WHAT KIND OF CHRISTIAN ARE WE PRODUCING?

Once we have asked young people to enlist, asked them to give their all, now we need to think deeply about who they are to become. I'll use the metaphor of the military once again. When people enlist in the military, the boot camp process is a total stripping down of their civilian identity. The military changes their hair, clothes, and puts them through pain to strip away their old habits. They receive a whole new set of clothes, habits, and a new lifestyle. So it must be with us, as we begin to help young people form their new identity as followers of Christ.

Who cares how many are crying their eyes out at every altar call we give if it is only emotion, and not true conversion?

God is looking for people who are marked by devotion.

Just like in the military, Christ-followers, too, have a code of conduct: the Bible. It doesn't guarantee that we'll be perfect, but it does tell us what things a Christian *should* be marked by.

Devotion. God is looking for people who are marked by devotion. They don't just shout that they love Jesus; they are so devoted to Him they'll follow Him to the death. It doesn't matter if the circumstances are hard or easy. They will follow Him until the end. Even if He doesn't answer another prayer, they will stay devoted because they love Him so much, and He has already done so much for them.

Defiance. We need to produce young people that live in defiance of the enemy's tactics. That love what is true and hate what is sinful. Too many people that call themselves Christians still love the world. The Bible clearly tells us that "friendship with the world is hatred toward God" (Jas. 4:4). The mere fact that we have to beg them not to listen to secular music or watch these programs shows that in their heart of hearts they still love the world and are attracted to it. They are letting the world entertain and coddle them. We need to teach teens to see through the lies no matter how cool the music or movies might be. We must teach them that they are being brainwashed with lies and must turn away from anything that contradicts the truth of the Bible.

Courage. Most people who call themselves Christians look more like cowards than courageous followers of Christ. They give in whenever they are confronted about their faith. They give in whenever temptations are presented to them. They are not like the men and women of old who stood for their faith even though it could cost them their lives or limbs. Martyrs like Polycarp were burned at the stake and yet kept praising God despite their persecution. We need to produce young people with backbone. We must show them that because of what Jesus did for us, and the courage He demonstrated on the cross, we can do the same. Jesus showed us how to be courageous.

Endurance. This is one of the lost evidences of our faith. People don't endure a workout program, a diet, or even marriages. The most supposedly sacred commitment in our society is not endured very long. In fact, today many couples have changed their wedding vows from "till death do us part" to "for as long as our love shall last." (At least they're being honest.)

People say, "Lord, I will die for You. I will do anything for You." But when it rains on Sunday, they don't go to church because they might get their hair messed up. We need to produce young people who are fit to endure. Who are battle-tested and have put on the armor of God, and are ready to fight the good fight of faith.

Jesus taught us how to endure as He went to His death with silent dignity. In six hours of hanging on the cross (after being whipped and tortured and spit on and

We must teach them that they are being brainwashed with lies and must turn away from anything that contradicts the truth of the Bible.

We need to produce young
people with backbone. We must
show them that because of
what Jesus did for us, and the
courage He demonstrated on
the cross, we can do the same.

beat up, with a crown of thorns shoved into His head),
Jesus was utterly silent with the exception of about one
minute's worth of speech. In the silence, He screams a
message to us, *"This is what it looks like to endure."* He saw the
joy set before Him. This is the kind of Christ-follower we as
Youth Specialists are called to produce.

CHRIST-FOLLOWERS ARE GROWTH-ORIENTED

When someone joins the army or the navy, it's natural
to anticipate progressing up through the ranks. What soldier would want to enlist as a private, and 20 years later still
be a private? Yet we have churches full of privates who
haven't progressed a step in 20 or 30 years. Perhaps they
think they have made a decision and since they're going to
heaven they have no obligation to do anything else. Let's
be sure we give our young people the paradigm that *once
enlisted, there are a lot of ranks to grow into:* There's basic training. There's advanced training. There are special ops.
There are covert ops. There are all kinds of places you can
advance in the Kingdom and grow in your faith.

I recently talked to a young man in the army. He said
that when you enlist as an E-1, after two or three years you

can get promoted to E-4 without doing much of anything. All you have to do is *be there,* do your time, and you automatically advance. After E-4, if you want to move on to sergeant level, you have to study. You have to go through special training and prove yourself.

We often see people slip into church as an E-1 and then slide into E-4 without any effort, but there they remain. They never do more than just show up on Sunday and then wonder *why* they are going nowhere in their faith. We need to help young people see that growth and training is a natural part of being a follower of Christ. To have an "illustrious" career in the things of God, you must increase in rank and continue to grow.

WE ARE DISCIPLES SO THAT THEY CAN DISCIPLE OTHERS

In Western Christianity, we have built the kingdom of God one person at a time rather than multiplying the growth *exponentially.* Jesus taught exponential growth: all the disciples made other disciples who made other disciples and so on.

There is an example of this level of discipleship in Bogotá, Colombia, where a church of 120,000 people and a youth group of 40,000 trains their members to make disciples. This is a natural part of Christianity.

We need to think in terms of multiplying, not just adding, and so do our teens. So often, we treat discipleship

Jesus taught us how to endure as He went to his death with silent dignity.

Jesus taught exponential growth: all the disciples made other disciples who made other disciples and so on.

as if it were optional. Instead, we should train our young people to think that they too need to win people and disciple them. They need to pass on what they have learned.

If everyone in your youth group reached four or ten people this year, how big would that be? Think exponentially. Train your kids to multiply themselves. When you do, you will give them a priceless jewel that they will treasure the rest of their lives. Your teens will continue to perpetuate the kingdom of God long after they have grown up and moved away and gotten married.

WORLD CONQUEST IS IN OUR DNA

People join an army because they know that there is a war to win. Part of our drawing people to Christ is helping them understand they have left the army of darkness and have joined the army of Light. Jesus said in Matthew 11:12: "From the days of John the Baptist until now, the kingdom of heaven has been forcefully advancing, and forceful men lay hold of it." Part of the natural course as a soldier in the army of Light is to help forcefully advance the Kingdom. This message that has changed us so deeply and so profoundly cannot be kept to ourselves. The One who died on the cross is worthy of proclaiming to the ends of the earth.

Understand it's not an extracurricular activity to share your faith with your friends; it's a fundamental part of the job description, part of your life. It's not an extracurricular activity to go on a mission trip in the summertime. It's part of your DNA, what you're made of. It's what you're going to do for the rest of your life.

Why? Because *that is what a soldier does.* A soldier goes to win the war, to win the battle at hand. Right now in North America we are entrenched in the battle for this generation. We have to train our young people that they are marching into battle. They are marching into war. What is the strategy they need to use each day, each week? We've got to train our teens that there is a war for souls all around the world with the Hindu, Muslims, tribal people, atheists, and Buddhists. People are lost, and it's our job as soldiers of the King to get this message to the ends of the earth.

Jesus said, "This gospel of the kingdom will be preached in the whole world as a testimony to all nations, and then the end will come" (Matt. 24:14). It's our job to make soldiers who will fulfill this commission. Jesus fully intends and expects for us as His representatives to accomplish this goal. It is not optional. It's not just for the radicals. It's for the normal follower of Christ.

After all the work is said and done, let's make sure our message is potent and produces a life change. We are helping our teens go somewhere in their faith so they can share it with others. We can get the job done—reach this generation, reach the world, and bring a smile to our Father's face. That is the job of every Youth Specialist.

Part of our drawing people to Christ is helping them understand they have left the army of darkness and have joined the army of Light.

Great Commission Competition

By Jeanne Mayo

I. THE PURPOSE

Every youth ministry needs seasons of strong, fresh growth. A format like the "Great Commission Competition" can do incredible things to jump-start growth and fresh energy in your youth ministry.

II. THE OVERALL PLAN

Competition is a part of every teenager's life. Thus, the Great Commission Competition takes the motivation of competition and places it within a positive and Christ-honoring framework. Teams are formulated among the youth group, and they compete against each other for three months (12 youth services). Points are given for three things only: (1) bringing guests, (2) getting guests to return for four weeks, and (3) keeping the "regulars" attending.

The first prize needs to be a trip of some sort that will excite the members of the group. We have done everything from taking trips to Disney World to winter ski trips. Trips are not nearly as expensive as you might think; you can cut down on costs by driving wherever you go. I get adults from the church to underwrite the cost of the trip before the competition even launches. (Approximate the cost of the trip and divide it into 5–10 parts. Then approach 5–10 individuals in the church and present your vision for reaching more youth in your community. Explain The Great Commission Competition and ask them to underwrite it for a specific amount. In this manner, money should never be a problem.)

III. THE POINT STRUCTURE

Since the goal is fresh growth, the point structure is weighted in that direction. We give 1,000 points for every first-time visitor. Then give 2,000 points for every one of those visitors that the team gets to return to youth group the second time. (It does not need to be necessarily the very next week.) We give 3,000 points for every one who returns a third time, and 5,000 points for everyone who returns a fourth time. The reason we do this is to create a habit. Thus, if a guest returns to your group on a repeated basis, you have a very good chance of having this person become a regular part of your group.

In order to reward the faithfulness of your individuals who are already attending, we give 1,000 points each week for every *regular* present. (*Regulars* are all attendees who are not in the visitor category. After a visitor completes their four-week attendance, they count as a regular and the group begins to get 1,000 points each week for them if they return.) Also, you cannot allow points to be given for a million things. Keep the point system simple so you reach your goal.

IV. THE LEADERSHIP STRUCTURE

Each team needs to have a core group of leaders. We use a key male and key female to run the group (college-and-career age or adult). Then we match them with key teenagers from the group to serve as assistant leaders.

Two key principles are important as you put together your leadership teams:

1) Divide up your sharper kids so one group does not begin with an obvious advantage. Explain to your teams as you formulate them that you appreciate that they are mature enough to handle not always being with their close friends. Explain that it is vital that we all understand the mission and purpose for The Great Commission Competition. The real purpose is not to win a trip (though we all want to be energized and enthusiastic about that). The real purpose is to build the kingdom of God. Thus, we cannot just leave best friends and buddies together. We want this to be more than "Christian clique time." We want to divide and conquer!

2) Try to keep most of the kids you place on a team within a two-year span of each other (like seniors and juniors, etc.).

To place teams together with too wide of an age span will create tougher motivation needs. Obviously, your core leadership team may or may not be within that two-year span.

The ideal leadership team for each of your group would be one key male leader and one key female. However, realizing that you may not have enough sharp guys to run all your teams, sometimes when you have a really sharp woman, she is all right to "fly alone" without a male counterpart. You also need between two and five "assistants." Create your own titles for them.

V. HOW DO YOU LAUNCH THE GREAT COMMISSION COMPETITION?

Step #1: Determine the number of teams you will have.

Determine the number of teams you will have. This may rise and fall on the number of leaders you have available. It will also be controlled by the number of students you have. The ideal numbers would be one team for approximately every 8–15 students that you have attending the group. (If your group is smaller, make teams of five.)

Step #2: Choose key leaders.

Choose key leaders (captains) and talk to them alone first. Sell them on the importance of just loving teenagers, and tell them this only lasts for three months. Explain that you would love to have them stay on in the ministry with you after the three months, but they are not obligated. Ask them to give it a try for these three months and leave an eternal dent on hell by helping to see kids come to Christ.

Step #3: Choose key assistants.

The "assistants" you choose to go with each team are usually quality students. They may not necessarily be tremendous Christians at this point, but they are students who are looked to as leaders and who are needed to help the momentum go in a positive fashion. (Though they may not be "tremendous Christians," my personal feeling is that they do need to be Christians.)

Step #4: Divide your group into teams.

Mentally begin to divide up the remaining students in your youth group onto teams. Start your lists and work with them for quite a while, making sure that you have enough quality people in each group for it to go well. It is fine to ask your leaders for written preference of some people they would love to have in their group (if they know any). Prepare them for the fact that if there is too much duplication of requests, they may not get their requests fulfilled.

Privately, let your leadership teams look at the team lists once they have been compiled to see if any changes need to be made. (Be sure to do this step before you go public with the team listings.)

Leadership teams need to determine a name for their teams so a sense of identity can be created pretty early in this process. (You as the leader may want to have them clear the names through you to make sure the names are sharp.)

When formulating the team lists, be sure you put names and correct phone numbers. Phone contacts become key. Work with your team leaders on what to say when they call people.

You may consider giving each team a "prospect list" with the names of other possible candidates for the youth group that do not attend. These names can be former attendees, teenagers who come on Sunday morning but not to the youth services, etc. This should be divided and given with phone numbers.

A key note: tell leaders that everyone has to stay away from each other's prospect list for one month. After that time, the names on the entire prospect list are published and open game for all leadership teams. Obviously, these become great leads and help to jump-start the competition. Some of your greatest additions, however, will come from the friends your teenagers will invite who have never darkened the door of a church facility.

Step #5: Prepare your team leaders.

Prioritize motivation with your leaders before you introduce this to the total youth group. Tell them that their excitement will make or break this whole thing. Encourage them to remember that we are all doing this to see fresh people come to Christ. Thus, we want motivational competition which remains positive, not negative.

Talk through with your leadership team any possible negatives or complaints that people will have so they know how to answer them. (For example, "I don't think we should do this because Christians shouldn't get a prize for asking people to church!" Please remind them that there will even be a reward system in heaven.)

Also, tell everyone that the points will be kept a guarded secret (even from the leaders). But if, in the first month, one team gets so obviously ahead that everyone else loses motivation, ask to be able to divide that team in the first few weeks so the overall goals of the competition do not die due to loss of motivation in the other teams.

Step #6: Determine how you will collect points.

I suggest a simple group time each week for about 10 minutes and a simple form that everyone in the group fills out at this time. (Group time is usually in the middle of the youth service because it gives the leaders time to greet visitors warmly and motivate the group to keep going.) Create a simple sheet that everyone can fill out during that group time; each group must have a specific secretary who collects the sheets and tallies the weekly results onto another pre-prepared form. Each secretary turns everything in that night to a preselected "keeper of the points" before leaving.

Again, it is vital that this information remains absolutely private, or motivation is lost very quickly.

These forms will also provide great follow-up for you because you can request visitor names and addresses. Obviously, a letter, call, or card from the leader's office is great. The main follow-up, though, is done over the phone by various members of the group making calls to the visitors. Anyone in the group can help with the follow-up. However, I suggest that you place the main "follow-up ball" in the camp of your leadership teams. Obviously, you must motivate them toward genuine friendship evangelism. Keep calling!

VI. HOW DO YOU PRESENT THIS TO THE GROUP?

Remember that the way in which you and your leadership team positively present this to the group will be very crucial. Thus, plan a night when you can launch this evangelism effort. Make the whole night around the idea of reaching out to others. Explain the Great Commission Competition (or anything you choose to name it), and do something fun like a skit or slide show (or both) to announce the prize trip. Stress that we are going to have fun, Christian competition, but that our obvious motive is to bring people to the youth group, so they can eventually come to know Christ.

End with a great time of prayer and commitment. You may want to announce the teams that night and let them gather together for a few minutes in the middle of the service so the leaders can motivate their group (i.e. "We are so glad we are together"; "We are going to have the best group").

When you announce the teams, be sure to preface it with comments like, *"Thank you for being mature enough not to whine if you are not placed with all your best friends. We are trying for the next three months to reach out and build the kingdom of God, so we do not want to be a bunch of Christian cliques. When we announce your group, please act excited! Your team leaders are in a pretty scary position because if you act like you don't want to be with them, it will make them feel pretty rotten. So please be mature enough to be positive when I announce your teams."*

Make sure you announce that you have a special outreach night planned for the first week of the competition. Do not expect to have your kids bring people to the service if they are going to be ashamed of it. Work with your leadership teams to make this first night really special. Plan the entire three months of services realizing that you want them to be something that your kids will not be ashamed to ask their friends to attend.

As far as your trip, please also realize that you do not have to plan something for the exact end of the three months. You do need to be able to fulfill your promise within six weeks of the conclusion of the competition. Pre-think what you are going to do about students who join the winning group as the competition goes along. We usually told them that they were welcome to come on the trip, but we prorated the cost to them. (For example, if they became a part of the winning group in the last month, we paid for one-third of their trip but asked them to pay for two-thirds since the competition lasts for three months.)

VII. CLOSING COMMENTS AND PAST RESULTS

As the leader, realize that negative, superspiritual people will always have a reason why what you are doing will not work. Just kindly keep your motivation high and realize that people are people. Do not fall into the trap of allowing negative people to mess things up for everyone else.

In previous ministry groups, this simple activity usually increased our attendance (even after the conclusion of the competition) by about 33 percent. Most youth ministries that have tried something similar to this, after my suggestion, report that they have had huge, sustained growth. This approach is especially effective in sustaining growth because you create a habit for people to invite their friends to youth group. Another good thing about this approach is that it works with a very small group and with a large one.

This competition gives your kids an easy excuse to invite their friends without sounding all spiritual: "Could you come to youth group with me this week? We have a great thing going on called the Great Commission Competition. You could even come with us on our trip if our group wins. Besides, I think you'll like my youth group. Would you come with me this week?"

The other joy of this effort is that it can easily become a launching pad for small group ministry in your youth group if you desire it to be. People will become addicted to the work of the ministry, and you will find some incredible leaders coming out of the process. I wish you God's best!

May these months together be a fun-filled catalyst that sparks growth, excitement, and spiritual revival among your youth group. Indeed, new faces have a way of getting everyone and everything pretty charged up!

Scripture Index

Genesis 1:27	86	Proverbs 21:1	404
Genesis 12:1-4	99	Proverbs 27:23	312
Genesis 32:26	319	Proverbs 29:18	78, 239
Exodus 3:7	97	Isaiah 50:4-5	410
Exodus 18:15-18	89	Isaiah 51:16	411
Numbers 20:7-12	366	Jeremiah 1:5	49, 154
		Jeremiah 1:7-9	410
Deuteronomy 7:1-2	147	Jeremiah 20:9	320
Deuteronomy 7:22-23	148		
		Ezekiel 33:8-9	88
Joshua 1:3-7, 9	142		
Joshua 1:8	428	Daniel 10:12-13	140
Joshua 1:13-15	145		
Joshua 9:3-7, 12-19	358	Malachi 1:6-9	25
		Malachi 1:13	26
2 Samuel 6:14-23	406		
2 Samuel 15:2	242	Matthew 5:37	357
		Matthew 6:16-18	333
1 Kings 3:5-13	88	Matthew 7:6	398
		Matthew 7:20	369
Psalm 1:1-2	429	Matthew 8:5-10	305
Psalm 5	424	Matthew ll:12	444
Psalm 25:14	426	Matthew 16	437
Psalm 42:1	328, 438	Matthew 24:14	94, 445
Psalm 63	424	Matthew 25:14-30	210
Psalm 100:4	327	Matthew 28:18-20	94
Psalm 101:3	391		
Psalm 119:15, 48	429	Luke 2:19	135
Psalm 139:23-24	344	Luke 11:34-36	343
Psalm 143:5	429	Luke 16:8	218
Proverbs 11:25	308	John 3:22	200
Proverbs 14:1	401	John 3:22-30	182
Proverbs 20:8	307	John 15:15	386

Acts 6:2   90

Romans 12:2   71, 373
Romans 12:3   303

1 Corinthians 1:25   23
1 Corinthians 9:1-6, 12   361
1 Corinthians 14:33, 40   413

2 Corinthians 12:9-10   91
2 Corinthians 13:5   359

Ephesians 2:2   338
Ephesians 2:10   88
Ephesians 3:20   80, 170
Ephesians 4:1   40
Ephesians 4:15   386
Ephesians 4:26   387
Ephesians 4:29   386
Ephesians 4:31-32   386
Ephesians 5:7-16   342
Ephesians 5:8   341
Ephesians 5:14   347
Ephesians 5:21   383
Ephesians 5:21-33   379, 380
Ephesians 5:22   382
Ephesians 5:23-24   384
Ephesians 5:26-27   388

Philippians 3:10-16   426
Philippians 4:8   359
Philippians 4:19   218

1 Thessalonians 4:4-8   369
1 Thessalonians 5:22   369

1 Timothy 3   245, 247
1 Timothy 3:2, 4-5   43
1 Timothy 3:4   403
1 Timothy 4:12   22

1 Timothy 4:15   429

2 Timothy 1:3-6   39
2 Timothy 1:6   322
2 Timothy 1:7   410
2 Timothy 2:2   244

Hebrews 10:4-7,   10-12, 19-22
                             328

James 4:4   440

Revelation 4:2-11   329
Revelation 7:9   95
Revelation 13:8   154

Subject Index

3M, 160

777 Plan, 387

A
Abraham, 77, 99, 100

Absalom, 242

Armstrong, Neil, 169

B
BHAGs, 168ff

Barnabas, 31, 100, 330

barriers, 178

Bonhoeffer, Dietrich, 347

Breen, Mike, 420

Bright, Dr. Bill, 52

C
centurion, 305

CD-ROM, 86, 91, 103, 136, 161, 165, 177, 179, 187, 188, 189, 190, 191, 192, 193, 195, 248, 277, 278, 281, 283, 300, 308, 313

Cho, Dr. Paul Yonggi, 26

church members, 132, 229

Coca-Cola, 160

commitment, 102, 436

core values, 162ff

credibility, 46

Critical Stress Factors, 187

D
Daniel, 141

David, 31, 100, 242, 327, 328, 330, 406

discipling, 30, 31, 443

Disney, 26, 160

drama ministry, 192, 254, 284, 295, 313

dream, (see "vision")

E
Elijah, 320

evangelism, 15, 18, 64, 161, 311, 447ff

events, 27, 28, 273ff, 307, 447ff

excellence
    God is worthy of, 24, 25
    Makes people feel important, 28
    Makes victory plausible, 28
    Persuasive, 27
    Shows love and caring, 27, 27, 28, 273ff, 307, 447ff

explosion of teen population, 29

F
facility/youth room, 126, 127, 282, 283

family/marriage, (see "marriage")

Family Covenant, 389

fasting, 332, 339

Financial Plan, 212

flowchart, 193

Ford, 160

funding, 215ff

G
General Motors, 45

goals, global, 30

Graham, Billy, 371

Great Commission, 94, 101, 108, 123

Great Commission Competition, 447ff

Grove, Andy, 170

growth, spiritual, 121, 122, 242

H
honor, 351ff

I
identity, group, 124ff

identity, personal, 99, 124

Intel Corporation, 170
Internet, 118, 129, 130, 391
Invent the Future, 186, 199ff

J
Jacob, 133, 319
Jeremiah, 49, 154, 320
Jesus, 57, 58, 94, 95, 97, 109, 113, 129, 146, 182, 183, 200, 201, 210, 211, 218, 238, 305, 309, 357, 430, 436, 441
John Mark, 31, 100
John the Baptist, 182, 183, 320
Joseph, 47, 77, 81, 83
Joshua, 141, 142, 143, 144, 178, 240

K
Keller, W. Phillip, 332
Kennedy, John F., 169, 173
King, Martin Luther, 77

L
Landry, Tom, 67
leadership
   cup, 52, 59
   foundation of, 58
   growth, 57, 68ff
   need for, 57ff
   philosophy of, 66
   reasons for not growing, 60ff
   teen, 128
logo, 125

M
Malachi, 25
Mark, (see "John Mark")
marketing, 29, 114, 127
marriage/family, 237, 253, 379ff, 397ff
Marriage Mission Statement, 381
Mary, 135, 217
media (in ministry), 129, 130, 131, 174, 225, 291, 295
Mission Statement, 156ff
missions, 99, 100, 101, 107, 108, 123, 133, 134

Moses, 77, 89, 96, 97, 141, 147, 240, 247, 319, 366, 367
Motorola, 220
Mullins, Rich, 134
music ministry, (see "worship")

N
NASA, 169
needs of teens, 118
needs vs wants, 219
Netanyahu, Benjamin, 370, 371
Nouwen, Henri J. M., 427
Now Plan, 186ff

O
Operational Plan, 211

P
parable of the sower, 50
parents, 131, 223
pastor, 132, 229, 230, 275, 304, 306, 373
Paul, 22, 31, 32, 38, 39, 40, 42, 100, 111, 322, 330, 359, 360, 361, 414
Peter, 31, 100, 321
planning, 153ff, 277
Polycarp, 440
prayer, 248, 326, 343
Proctor & Gamble, 220

Q
quiet time, 325ff

R
radio, 129, 130
recruitment, 193, 248
relationship with spouse, 374, 379ff
repentance, 321, 339, 363

S
service, 127, 128, 188, 192, 194, 225, 280, 284, 291, 292, 318, 423, 447ff
sin , 321, 337ff, 434

solitude, 331

Solomon, 88, 428

Stafford, Tim, 332

Strategic Plan, 205

T
team building, 237ff

team meetings, 259ff

teenagers
   explosion of, 29
   marketing to, 29, 114, 127
   needs of, 118

television, 129, 130, 131

Timothy, 22, 31, 32, 38, 39, 42,
322, 330

V
vision/dream, 77ff, 101, 102, 103, 133
   Why we don't dream, 80ff
   Why we should dream, 86ff

volunteers, 129, 193, 276

W
Wal-Mart, 160

Wesley, John, 419

worship/music ministry, 128, 161, 170,
192, 206, 245, 254, 295, 309, 310, 311

Y
youth culture, global, 30, 127

"youth guy," 33, 60

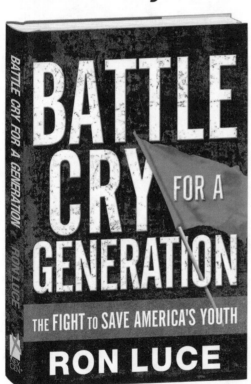

today is d-day

The Allied invasion of Normandy became the turning point of World War II. Against formidable odds, nations came together to fight off evil—to win a war that once seemed un-winnable and to secure freedom for future generations.

Today we face our own D-Day. Now is the time for us to come together to win a war for this generation of young people. We have the chance of a lifetime to preserve for the children of America a future of freedom and promise. In this book, I will sound the alarm and the call to battle. I will share with you information and challenge you to action. This is a war for the heart and soul of a generation that we can win, if we *all* take action.

WHEN INACTION HURTS

The Nazis had stormed across Europe, pillaging and destroying the people and the land. They were determined to impose their ideology and values on the world and they had conquered virtually every nation they desired. Even as they threatened England with total domination, they seemed indestructible. Yet plans were being laid for a strategic counteroffensive.

The best minds in the free world had put nearly two years into the planning of the D-Day invasion. Still, everyone knew it could easily fail. None of the leaders felt secure or lived without worry. They knew the conflict would leave many children fatherless. They also knew that, even after losing many lives, the whole plan could still prove futile. It might only stir up a more ruthless Hitler.

Europe's volatile weather played an important role. If it rained just a little longer or harder, the whole thing would have to be called off. If the counterintelligence was unreliable, thousands of soldiers could walk right into a trap. Allied commanders had leaked false information to the Nazis to make them think the invasion would come from another region. But did they take the bait?

Yes, the generals knew there was great risk to their plan, but they knew there was *greater risk if they did nothing.*

The sad truth is that for several years England had been pleading with the United States to join the war effort. We had watched Hitler and his throngs of uniformed butchers annihilate nation after nation. Yet we remained inactive, a nation isolated and satisfyingly self-sustaining. For a long time, the horrifying pictures and stories from the war failed to provoke a response that could have saved many lives.

England continued to implore us to get involved. After all, they said, this war would eventually come right to our own homes, if we didn't soon wake up to the danger. They asked for money and troops. When Britain's Prime Minister Winston Churchill addressed a joint session of Congress in his famous speech—when everyone knew he was going to ask for money—he opened his remarks unexpectedly. He said to the senators and congressmen: "I did not come to ask for money ... (a long pause here and sustained applause from the joint session) ...*for myself.*" Another pause. And then those final two words were answered with sustained applause that indicated he had succeeded in getting Americans to think about the terrible predicament confronting the people of Europe.

Churchill had called America to admit to its self-centeredness. He helped us realize there is something more important then self-interest. Americans began to understand that our future fate was tied to the current fate of others. We got involved but we still did not send troops. It would take the enemy blowing down our own back door at Pearl Harbor to summon forth our warriors.

ACTION SAVES LIVES

It's been said that the parents of the Baby Boomers are "the greatest generation." Having endured the Dust Bowl, the Great Depression, and World War II—and pressing through all the other hardships to preserve our nation—they deserve the title. We are enjoying quality life in America today won by their sacrifice.

One thing that made them so great was how they rallied together as a nation to meet a deadly foe. It seemed *everyone* took ownership during World War II. The men went to war, and the women went to work! People lived on rations and paid whatever price necessary to win that war. "We can do it" was their motto.

I hope that you'll see the great need for a similar kind of rallying as you learn about the ravages of the war being waged upon our teens. Today our adults must also arise. Though the weaponry is different, our war is just as fierce. It will require the same level of sacrifice, the same grim resolve. And no one is exempt of involvement if we mean to have victory. Every father, mother, businessman, grandparent, pastor, and youth pastor must hear the call.

Why do I begin by speaking of war? Because I have seen the enemies of our children march across the land, leaving ravished young hearts and minds in their wake. I have seen the wounding effects. I've listened to the stories of teens hurting, broken, and bleeding (some by their own hands). I've seen the signs of war, and you have too. Yet to no avail. Too few of us have taken action. Too few seem to realize that the enemy really is at our own back door.

It is time for us to wake up and acknowledge that this is our war for the hearts of today's teens and for the future of America. It is time now for us to get involved, not only as supporters but as warriors.

THE FACE OF THE ENEMY

Most of us had never heard the name "Al-Qaeda" before President Bush described the terrorist group in his post 9/11 address to Congress. He told us of its founder, Osama Bin Laden, who has since become a household name. We learned the group was well-funded and had established "sleeper cells" all over the world. It dawned on us that this newly revealed enemy was very smart and quite sophisticated. These certainly weren't simple-minded people living in the desert with a few machine guns.

Clearly, we would need to get to the center of the power structure, because the future of our nation depended on it.

That is also the case with the enemy who plots against our young ones—the techno-terrorists, the virtue-terrorists. They are terrorists of a different kind, but they are terrorists just the same. Here's why:

They are deeply funded and thoroughly organized. Like Al-Qaeda, they have money and they have plans. These enemies don't just promote violence on the silver screen; they are various entities with various motives. They use their technology and marketing arsenal to create and/or allow the culture of destruction to thrive happily among our teens. Certainly the entertainment media is the dominant form of influence and thus a huge culprit.

Consider MTV, whose parent company, Viacom, recorded revenues of $6.84 billion in 2004[1]. While MTV would never say its chief aim is to "destroy a generation," it is in fact doing that by seeking to make money off young people, no matter what it takes. The company has organized a "cradle to grave" program for your kids. It starts with Nickelodeon, then Nick Jr., both of which are owned by Viacom. These networks begin to train small children as to what is cool and what they should want to look like. They introduce them to pop icons and get them wanting their music and action figures. By the time the kids are interested in music videos, MTV presents a whole new world for them to "enjoy."

They are subversive and effective in promoting their agenda. These enemies of decency are already in our "nicest" families, as you'll soon see. Yes, even in the best of Christian homes. They've crashed through the gates, pushed down the door, and landed on the living room couch. Psalm 1:1 says "Blessed is the [person] who does not walk in the counsel of the wicked." We have a generation that isn't "blessed" because it has allowed the wicked to shape its values for life.

Many Christian parents are shell-shocked:

"How could my little girl end up pregnant?"

"Why are our kids using such language?"

"I thought I taught my son better than that. Why is he getting drunk all the time?"

"How could she wear something so skimpy to a party? That's not how I raised her!"

Maybe *you* did not raise her after all. Maybe the kids are exact replicas of the terrorists who actually raised them. Considering the proportion of time your kids spend "under the influence" of the virtue-terrorists, why are you surprised? The world has kidnapped our kids right under our noses. We have invited the terrorists into our homes and paid them to corrupt our kids. And considering the fact that 88 percent of kids raised in Christian homes do not continue to follow the Lord after they graduate from high school, it looks like the terrorists are winning.

A CALL TO ACTION

As you read through this book, you'll see a battle plan unfolding, a strategy that calls for your personal, dedicated involvement. I want you to see its basic outlines up front so that, as you read each chapter, you can constantly think about finding your personal assignment, or mission. This is not a casual suggestion. This is a serious call to arms. As the dire plight of our young people hits you in the pages to come, I believe you'll truly want to become heavily involved in this war. You'll want to find an assignment that demands your all and pushes you to reach out to young people who are being destroyed in the fray. So here is a summary of how you can enter the battle. There are two parts to the battle plan:

1. The National Campaign

☐ Go online at **www.battlecry.com** and enlist today in the Battle Cry Coalition to receive regular e-mail updates on exactly how to pray and stay involved in practical ways of reaching out to this generation.

☐ Voice your opinion now about how this generation is being bombarded with sexual images, telling stories that have happened in your family or community that demonstrate how this infection is hurting our teens.

2. The Front Lines

☐ Find a group of people (Sunday school class, Bible study, home group, or group of Christians at work) to go through this book with you. There's power in numbers: inspire others to get committed to this generation with you.

- ☐ Give a copy of this book to your pastor and youth pastor. Follow up with them once they have read it. Brainstorm together: What steps can you all take as a church to reach out to teens in your community?
- ☐ Talk to your local youth pastor/leader to find out how your gifts can be used to expand the youth ministry.
- ☐ If you have no youth leader in your church, make an appointment with your pastor right away—and volunteer for the job! Feel free to contact us at **www.teenmania.org** for all kinds of practical tools on what to do with the teens in your group to build them into an army for God.
- ☐ Find ways to invest financially into youth ministry, either locally or nationally. Research youth ministries that are making an impact on teens. Then give!

Finding your assignment is crucial. As you read this book, keep asking yourself: What is touching my heart right now? What need can I meet? What interests do I have? What gift can I use? Remember: Real lives are waiting on the other side of your obedience.

Stop right now and look over the above lists. Check which actions intrigue you even now. Everyone can do something. Plan time into your schedule now so you'll be ready for action as you become motivated by the things you'll learn in the coming pages. Come back to these lists frequently as you read each chapter.

For all the practical ideas mentioned in this book, there are a thousand more ways to enlist your energies in this cause. If you cannot find someone to join up with in the battle for a generation, start a brand-new movement in your area. Rally other parents and leaders in your town. Don't accept no for an answer. If you have never been involved in youth ministry before, start now. Then go get all your friends. It will take *all* of us.

Everyone is invited; everyone is required. "We must do better than our best. We must do whatever is required to win." These were Winston Churchill's words as he faced a determined enemy head-on. It is also the battle cry for a generation today.

Ron Luce

the car's on fire

Chances are you didn't wake up this morning and decide, "Today, I'll be a hero." Opportunities for acts of heroism rarely show up on weekly planners or "To Do" lists. Instead, they intrude into everyday life, demanding split-second choices at great personal risk. At least that's the way it happened for my brother Ralph. One Sunday morning in the summer of 1998, Ralph steered his car out of the congested, post-service church parking lot. In the car ahead of him were two teenage girls. About a mile down the road, the girls halted their vehicle at a four-way stop, then proceeded carefully into the intersection as Ralph, his own car packed full with his wife and five small children, waited his turn to follow.

Without warning, a pickup truck sped through the intersection and slammed broadside into the car containing the two teenage girls. Ralph watched in disbelief as the driver, 17-year-old Ashley, was thrown from the car and killed instantly. His disbelief turned to horror as the car burst into flames, trapping the unconscious 14-year-old

I NEED PRAYER. I am really struggling a LOT right now. Since I was about six my dad has verbally abused me, and on occasion physically. When I was twelve, my great-grandfather started molesting me. And then seventeen days ago . . . this hurts me the most, I was raped when I was leaving work. I feel so dirty and used and abused and ashamed and I don't know what else. I feel like I'll never be clean. I have so much hatred in my heart right now. I hate my life. I want to kill myself to get away from the pain! It hurts! I can't handle it anymore! PLEASE HELP! — *Anonymous*

Amy inside. Ralph was suddenly out of his car and racing toward the burning vehicle. Somehow he managed to pry open the car door and, grabbing the belt loops of the limp and helpless teenager, free Amy from the inferno. Soon after Ralph pulled Amy to safety, paramedics whisked her away to the hospital where she fully recovered.

Suddenly Ralph was the town hero. He had saved a girl's life! Congratulations began pouring in from all over town, including the mayor's office. The local paper featured an article about Ralph's selfless act. When I discovered what had happened, I called Ralph to express my amazement at his courage. I tried to imagine what had inspired this father of five to risk everything—his personal safety, his family, his life—for a girl he barely knew.

Finally I asked him the question that was eating at me: "What were you thinking? I mean, what was going through your mind as you approached that burning car?"

"You know, Ron," Ralph replied, "I didn't do anything that anyone else in my position wouldn't have done. I don't know how I did it. All

I know is that *when the car is on fire, you do whatever you have to do to get the girl out!*"

People, the car is on fire and the youth of America are trapped inside. Suicide, abortion, alcohol, drug abuse, and violence are fiery flames licking at the wreckage of many young lives. The stakes are staggering—we have in America today 33 million teenagers, the largest group of teens since World War II.[1] This generation of youth has the potential to impact our nation—economically, politically, spiritually—with every bit as much force as the Baby Boomers have. These young people are our sons and daughters, brothers and sisters, grandsons and granddaughters, nieces and nephews. They are the future of America. We've got to get them out—whatever it takes— we've got to get them out.

NATION AT A CROSSROADS

Our nation has the proud heritage of being founded on Christian principles; many of our founding fathers were godly men. For two centuries we have enjoyed a society that—while not thoroughly Christian—is based on many of the moral imperatives from Scripture. But as our population has fallen from core evangelical, Bible-based beliefs, so has our society in our desire to be a tolerant, inclusive society. There is no longer a potent majority that speaks out when traditional biblical values are violated. This fact alone bears serious reflection, but I fear our present reality is much worse.

It is well documented that the percentage of Bible-based believers has steadily decreased since the Builder generation, as reflected

whatever direction this new generation takes, so it will take the nation.

in the following table from the book *The Bridger Generation* by Thom S. Rainer:[2]

- *Builders (born 1927-1945): 65% Bible-based believers*
- *Boomers (born 1946-1964): 35% Bible-based believers*
- *Busters (born 1965-1983): 16% Bible-based believers*
- *Bridgers (or Millennials, born 1984 or later): 4% Bible-based believers*

Think about what this means. While many Americans today may call themselves "Christians," only four percent of Millennials affirm themselves as church-attending, Bible-believing Christians. If that statistic doesn't alarm you, it should. It should alarm us all. Why? For the answer, we can look at the legacy left by previous generations in today's culture.

DECLINE OF CHRISTIAN CULTURE

For as long as many of us can remember, we have known that when the Boomers hit a certain age, their sheer numbers would affect all of American society more than any other generation in modern times. Today's corporate, political, and religious leaders are the Baby Boomers. With only 35 percent firmly believing in Scripture, they have shaped our culture with the following results:

- *Morally corrupt films and television programs*
- *An increasingly perverted music industry*
- *The pornographic invasion of the Internet*
- *Civil initiatives promoting gay marriage*
- *Battles to remove the Ten Commandments from public buildings, and fights to take "under God" out of our Pledge of Allegiance*

If these are the struggles we face now, with 35 percent of the largest generation of Americans affirming a belief in Scripture, can you imagine what America will be like when today's teens become the next generation to dominate the population, with only 4 percent currently claiming to be Bible-believing Christians?

Seventy-one million Millennials (33 million now in their teens) hold our future in their hands. Our national destiny is linked to this new generation. Try to imagine a society that mocks the fact that "under God" was *ever even in* our Pledge of Allegiance. Try to imagine the motto "In God we trust" taken off our money. Imagine all references to Christ and His cross removed from all emblems and city logos. Try to imagine a world where a pastor can go to jail for saying homosexuality is wrong. Current news stories confirm that these unfortunate events are already happening here and in other nations around the world. If we think Christians are persecuted and marginalized now in the U.S., imagine being the laughingstock of society! Is this the price we must pay for neglecting to build a solid biblical framework into the hearts of our children and our children's children?

WHO WILL SAVE AMERICA'S YOUTH?

History is rich with examples of first-generation believers who paid a high price for their faith. That price was paid so future generations could thrive in a society with religious freedom. To those early believers, America was a "city on a hill," a nation set aside for God's purposes—a country established for good and fruitfully blessed so that we might take God's message to the ends of the earth.

I'M DROWNING
in my sea of blood, hate, and deception. I'm drowning ... dying. Does anybody care? — *Beth*

The Word at Work . . .
Around the World

What would you do if you wanted to share God's love with children on the streets of your city? That's the dilemma David C. Cook faced in 1870s Chicago. His answer was to create literature that would capture children's hearts.

Out of those humble beginnings grew a worldwide ministry that has used literature to proclaim God's love and disciple generation after generation. Cook Communications Ministries is committed to personal discipleship—to helping people of all ages learn God's Word, embrace his salvation, walk in his ways, and minister in his name.

Opportunities—and Crisis

We live in a land of plenty—including plenty of Christian literature! But what about the rest of the world? Jesus commanded, "Go and make disciples of all nations" (Matt. 28:19) and we want to obey this commandment. But how does a publishing organization "go" into all the world?

There are five times as many Christians around the world as there are in North America. Christian workers in many of these countries have no more than a New Testament, or perhaps a single shared copy of the Bible, from which to learn and teach.

We are committed to sharing what God has given us with such Christians.

A vital part of Cook Communications Ministries is our international outreach, Cook Communications Ministries International (CCMI). Your purchase of this book, and of other books and Christian-growth products from Cook, enables CCMI to provide Bibles and Christian literature to people in more than 150 languages in 65 countries.

Cook Communications Ministries is a not-for-profit, self-supporting organization. Revenues from sales of our books, Bible curriculum, and other church and home products not only fund our U.S. ministry, but also fund our CCMI ministry around the world. One hundred percent of donations to CCMI go to our international literature programs.

CCMI reaches out internationally in three ways:

· Our premier International Christian Publishing Institute (ICPI) trains leaders from nationally led publishing houses around the world to develop evangelism and discipleship materials to transform lives in their countries.

· We provide literature for pastors, evangelists, and Christian workers in their national language. We provide study helps for pastors and lay leaders in many parts of the world, such as China, India, Cuba, Iran, and Vietnam.

· We reach people at risk—refugees, AIDS victims, street children, and famine victims—with God's Word. CCMI puts literature that shares the Good News into the hands of people at spiritual risk—people who might die before they hear the name of Jesus and are transformed by his love.

Word Power—God's Power

Faith Kidz, RiverOak, Honor, Life Journey, Victor, NexGen — every time you purchase a book produced by Cook Communications Ministries, you not only meet a vital personal need in your life or in the life of someone you love, but you're also a part of ministering to José in Colombia, Humberto in Chile, Gousa in India, or Lidiane in Brazil. You help make it possible for a pastor in China, a child in Peru, or a mother in West Africa to enjoy a life-changing book. And because you helped, children and adults around the world are learning God's Word and walking in his ways.

Thank you for your partnership in helping to disciple the world. May God bless you with the power of his Word in your life.

For more information about our international ministries, visit www.ccmi.org.